THE ART OF JOHN GARDNER

SUNY Series in American Literature

David R. Sewell, Editor

THE ART OF JOHN GARDNER

INSTRUCTION AND EXPLORATION

PER WINTHER

STATE UNIVERSITY OF NEW YORK PRESS

Published by
State University of New York Press, Albany

For information, address State University of New York
Press, State University Plaza, Albany, N.Y. 12246

Production by M. R. Mulholland
Marketing by Theresa A. Swierzowski

Library of Congress Cataloging-in-Publication Data

Winther, Per, 1947–
      The art of John Gardner : instruction and exploration / Per
Winther.
            p.   cm. — (SUNY series in American literature)
      Revision of thesis (Ph.D.)—University of Oslo, 1985.
      Includes bibliographical references and index.
      ISBN 0-7914-1113-3 (CH acid-free). — ISBN 0-7914-1114-1 (PB acid
-free)
      1. Gardner, John, 1933– —Philosophy. 2. Gardner, John. 1933–
—Technique. I. Title. II. Series.
PS3557.A712Z95   1992
813'.54—dc20
                                                                91-25001
                                                                CIP

10 9 8 7 6 5 4 3 2 1

FOR GISKEN

CONTENTS

ACKNOWLEDGMENTS

The Art of John Gardner: Instruction and Exploration origi-nated as a doctoral dissertation presented to the University of Oslo in 1985. The present book is a revised version of that dissertation.

I wish to express my deeply felt gratitude to Professor Brita Seyersted, who served as my dissertation director. Trying to meet her high professional standards was a constant challenge and source of inspiration. I remain greatly indebted to her for her wise and astute criticism of the dissertation in progress, and for her kind encouragement throughout.

I also owe a debt of gratitude to Professors Orm Øverland and Paul Levine for their very helpful comments during the *disputas.* Professor Øverland has since read the revised manuscript and offered a number of welcome suggestions for improvement.

I further wish to thank Dr. William Murray, the University of Iowa, and Dr. Gerald Wood, Carson-Newman College, for their interest and stimulating discussion in the early stages of my research. The whole manuscript was written at the University of Oslo, and thoughts of appreciation go to those friends and col-leagues at the American and British institutes who have encour-aged me in my work. Professor Stein Haugom Olsen kindly read Chapters 1–6 of the dissertation in manuscript; I greatly benefitted from his incisive comments in matters of literary theory and methodology. Dr. Chester P. Sadowy and Dr. Olav Lausund deserve special mention for their expert help with specific points.

The initial research for this study was undertaken during a year's stay at the University of Iowa. That stay was made possible by the University of Oslo and the Norwegian Ministry of Educa-tion, which granted me a year's leave of absence, and by a generous grant from the United States Educational Foundation in Norway, which provided me with the necessary extra funds for the year. The Norwegian Council of Research for Science and the Humani-ties provided the additional funding needed to complete the disser-tation.

I am indebted to the American Institute of the University of Oslo for giving me office space and access to its many facilities. I have made liberal use of the institute's excellent library, as well as the libraries of the British Institute, the University of Oslo, and the University of Iowa.

Grateful acknowledgment is made to the following publishers for permission to quote from their works:

Georges Borchardt, Inc., for quotations from these books, all by John Gardner: *Jason and Medeia*, Copyright © 1972, 1973, 1974 by John Gardner; *October Light*, Copyright © 1976 by Boskydell Artists Ltd.; *The King's Indian*, Copyright © 1972, 1973, 1974 by John Gardner; *Freddy's Book*, Copyright © 1980 by John Gardner; *The Art of Living and Other Stories*, Copyright © 1974, 1976, 1979, 1981 by John Gardner.

Alfred A. Knopf for quotations from *Grendel*, *The Sunlight Dialogues*, *Nickel Mountain*, and *Mickelsson's Ghosts*, all by John Gardner.

Richard Scott Simon Limited for quotations from John Gardner, *Grendel*, Copyright © 1971 by John Gardner.

Lord John Press for quotations from John Gardner, *Poems*.

Basic Books, Inc., Publishers, New York, for quotations from John Gardner, *On Moral Fiction*, Copyright © 1971.

Allen & Unwin, part of Harper Collins Publishers, for quotations from Brand Blanshard, *Reason and Goodness*.

INTRODUCTION

John Gardner's untimely death in a motorcycle accident in September 1982—he was then only forty-nine years old—stopped short a remarkably versatile and prolific literary career. Gardner is no doubt best known as a writer of fiction, but he also tried his hand at poetry, children's books, and plays for the stage and the radio, as well as opera libretti and film and television scripts. He was a literary critic, a book reviewer, and a medieval scholar.[1] Gardner's first novel, *The Resurrection*, was published in 1966, but it received little attention from reviewers and critics. However, during the first three years of the following decade one new novel came out every year, and now the literary establishment began to take notice. The year 1973 also saw the publication of *Jason and Medeia*, an epic, and over the next ten-year period Gardner treated his audience to three more novels and two collections of short stories. All the controversy surrounding the publication of two non-fictional books—his Chaucer biography (1977), which gave rise to accusations of plagiarism, and *On Moral Fiction* (1978), which created a stir because of rampantly iconoclastic views on the role of fiction—turned Gardner into something of a literary celebrity, and by the end of the 1970s he had himself become part of the literary establishment.

Wide-ranging critical attention to Gardner's fiction was scant during his lifetime. The first book of Gardner criticism appeared the year he died (Morace and VanSpanckeren 1982).[2] In 1983 came David Cowart's *Arches & Light: The Fiction of John Gardner*. This was the first book-length study by one author. The year after Gregory L. Morris followed suit with a book entitled *A World of Order and Light: The Fiction of John Gardner*. Since then there has been a steady interest in Gardner's fiction, as witnessed by the publication of Robert Morace's extensive bibliographical study of 1984 to supplement John M. Howell's *Bibliographical Profile* of 1980. Two more collections of essays, in 1983 (Mendez-Egle, ed., *John Gardner: True Art, Moral Art*) and in 1985 (Henderson, ed., *Thor's*

Hammer: Essays on John Gardner), and the many articles on his novels and other works that have been published throughout the 1980s further attest to the attention given to Gardner's works. One more book-length study appeared toward the end of the decade, Leonard Butts's *The Novels of John Gardner: Making Life Art as a Moral Process* (1988).[3]

The emphasis of in-depth analyses so far has been primarily thematical. Cowart, Morris, and Butts give very lucid accounts of Gardner's key ideas on philosophy and life as these find expression in his works. They are less concerned, however, with the technical aspects of his writings. In this study I, too, touch upon Gardner's themes, but above all I focus upon aspects of Gardner's artistic technique. Gardner is a highly *literary* artist in the sense that his fiction is controlled by an elaborate set of theoretical considerations. For a fully developed assessment of his art, we need to establish some sort of causal relationship between this theoretical superstructure and the kind of fiction it begets. In seeking to establish such a relationship, I begin by focussing upon the *philosophical and theoretical* foundations of his approach to literature before moving on to describing the practical ramifications of the underlying theory, that is, the *artistic techniques* that Gardner's theoretical orientation has led him to develop.

It would seem that this is an approach which Gardner himself might have approved of. In an essay written not long before his death ("Learning from Disney and Dickens"), Gardner revealingly reflected on the role of meaning in art. It is a confessional essay, published posthumously, in which he outlines the contours of his literary education. This education involved, among many other things, learning the analytical concepts of New Criticism, and, more importantly, it also brought him into close and lasting contact with medieval literature. Much as Gardner appreciates these formative influences, he cannot help but acknowledge that they "betrayed [him]...into an excessive concern with significance." "It's probably the case," he goes on to say, "that novels and stories are more interesting if, in some sense or another, they mean something. But it has begun to dawn on me that—in fiction, as in all the arts—a little meaning goes a long way." When, therefore, one has analyzed

> every symbolically neat detail in a story like "Death in Venice" or "Disorder and Early Sorrow"—when one has accounted for every verbal repetition, every pattern and rela-

tionship, and set down in alphabetical order every thought to be lifted or wrenched from the story—one discovers that, when you come right down to it, Mann has told us nothing we didn't know already.

In short, what Gardner's life in letters has taught him is that "fiction simply dramatizes."

Examining closely the thematic import of Gardner's novels and stories, one finds that what he observes about Thomas Mann holds true also for his own fiction. In other words, it is not as a writer of ideas that Gardner most insistently commands our attention. One does not say this, obviously, out of a wish to berate this author's literary powers. Taking issue with John Barth's famous essay, "The Literature of Exhaustion," Gardner remarks in *On Moral Fiction:* "Insofar as literature is a telling of new stories, literature has been 'exhausted' for centuries; but insofar as literature tells archetypal stories in an attempt to understand once more their truth—translate their wisdom for another generation—literature will be exhausted only when we all, in our foolish arrogance, abandon it" (66). In his art Gardner deals with age-old and universal issues: the balance between order and disorder, freedom versus necessity, the necessary relations between the individual and the larger community, man's struggle with the forces of "wreckage" and mutability, and the inescapable limitations of human understanding: in brief, the question of how man is to deal with what William James called, with a phrase that became one of Gardner's favorite quotations, "the buzzing, blooming confusion." Gardner's works make no claims to startlingly new insights into these issues; his chief contribution to literature is his ability to *renew* old truths for his readers, to imbue these truths with new vitality.

This is not to say that Gardner's themes lack significance. However, when the ideational thrust of his works is restated in nonfictional terms, we find that they, to use Gardner's own phrase, tell us "nothing we didn't know already." Needless to say, no study of Gardner's fiction can, or should, disregard his ideas; for instance, it can be a matter of considerable significance to discover and explain the circumstances that make a writer choose to work with one set of ideas rather than with another set. The present study addresses this and other related questions repeatedly, and it will be shown in the following that the nature of Gardner's themes is an important factor in determining his profile as an artist. However, his *manner of developing* his themes, his *way of dramatizing* his ideas, ought to be an even greater concern for anyone who wants to get a firm grip on Gardner's true artistic identity. Gardner managed to cultivate that one gift a writer must have if he is to maintain his spell on readers: a voice which is distinctly his own. The main focus of my study, therefore, will be on some important defining characteristics of that voice.

My emphasis on Gardner's voice, the actual manifestations of his compositional method in his works, has directed my choice of which texts to concentrate on. This is not a chronological book-by-book study; instead I have allowed the logic of my presentation to dictate the order in which I present my textual documentation. For instance, I spend a good deal of time discussing the ideas of *On Moral Fiction*, not because this is in itself an important theoretical work, but because it provides many clues to Gardner's own artistic practices. Those texts that receive my most detailed attention are *Grendel, The King's Indian, The Sunlight Dialogues,* and *Jason and Medeia,* simply because in my opinion they give us Gardner at his best, revealing the impressive powers of his many-faceted talent. It is in these texts that we see demonstrated most clearly the considerable potential of the artistic techniques which he developed and polished to suit the needs of his particular imagination.

In these books, too, Gardner reveals that he is less the "reactionary," nonexperimental writer than *On Moral Fiction* and the reading of his more traditionally crafted novels might lead one to believe, novels like *The Resurrection, Nickel Mountain, October Light,* and *Mickelsson's Ghosts.* This is indeed a point worth noticing. Not least because of his strident denunciation of the artistic experimentation of contemporary writers like Barth and Coover in *On Moral Fiction* the postmodernist aspects of Gardner's own art have often been overlooked. But Gardner is every bit as conscious of "epistemological uncertainty" as the so-called new fictionists; he, too, engages extensively in metafictional strategies and fabulation, as I try to make clear, for instance, in my discussion of the aesthetic foundations for his collage technique (Chapters 5 and 6). It is simply wrong, therefore, to assume that Gardner's call for "moral fiction" is synonymous with an invitation to write traditionally realist and didactic novels and short stories.

In my study I address at some length *Freddy's Book* and *The Art of Living,* the first a less than successful novel, the other an uneven collection of short stories. I do this, then, not because of their artistic agility, but because they offer fictionalized explorations of the tenets of rational morality, a school of thought which greatly influenced the thematic thrust of Gardner's art, as well as the compositional methods which he came to prefer. I give very scanty attention to *The Resurrection* and *The Wreckage of Agathon*. The former is the work of an apprentice, excessively weighted down by rather schematic philosophical speculation; it fails to excite because it is imperfectly crafted, giving us ideas rather than living characters who might engage our imaginations. *The Wreckage of Agathon* is a livelier and more interesting novel, but I discovered that there was very little I could say about this book which I had not already said, or was going to say, about those texts that intrigued me the most.

My study is organized in keeping with a clearly definable line of reasoning which I have found to influence the conception of Gardner's works, a line of reasoning which explains why his books come to us in the shape and form that they do. Chapter 1 discusses how Gardner develops his ideas on art as instruction and exploration in various fictional and nonfictional contexts. To Gardner the proper function of art is to *instruct*. But art can only provide truly profitable instruction if it instructs by *exploring*, by submitting whatever "truths" it wants to tell to the severe test of the medium through which it works. In Gardner's opinion art affords man the best instrument there is for probing the depths of human understanding.

In asserting such a crucial epistemological function for art, Gardner relies heavily on the concepts of *rational morality* and *the theory of expression*, concepts which are explained in Chapters 2 and 3. In these chapters the main issue of the present study—Gardner's art—will from time to time be thrown slightly out of focus. However, in my opinion there are some very good reasons why we should take a close look at the theoretical underpinnings of Gardner's artistic method. John Gardner will forever be associated with the terms *moral fiction* and *moral art*. Because he stated his case so clumsily in his book on that topic, readers are likely to respond superficially to his views and, possibly, his art. They will then fail to discover that Gardner's theoretical platform is a far less ramshackle construction than the rambunctious *On Moral Fiction* may at first suggest, that behind his bombastically stated critical opinions there is a coherent and wide-reaching system of carefully reasoned convictions.

In his review of *On Moral Fiction*, Alfred Kazin takes Gardner to task for his failure to be explicit on this point. When Gardner hastily says, "I need not take space here for a full defense of

the idea of the moral: a shortcut will be sufficient," Kazin reso-
lutely shoots back: "No, sir" (36). The present study tries to
amend Gardner's omission by covering some of the philosophical
territory that Gardner so breathlessly cuts across in *On Moral Fiction*. In Chapters 2 and 3 it will be argued that Gardner's dual call
for art as instruction *and* exploration *is* logically sound and that it
is motivated by the findings of the so-called rational moralists.

The teachings of rational moralists like R. G. Collingwood
and Brand Blanshard deal with this apparent paradox. Exploration
and instruction are here seen to be walking hand in hand. Because
man in his best moments is always governed by the principles of
rational morality (serving the common good because in so doing
one also ultimately serves the individual good), man will, provided
he confronts his problems seriously and listens to the best advice,
inevitably secure the steady evolution of the race. But man is not
always governed by rational morality; therefore artists who can
instruct through exploring are necessary. Through careful and
repeated scrutiny of human dilemmas with a view to finding what
conduct, attitudes, and emotions are most likely to further the
development of civilization, the artist instructs through a truthful
examination of the alternatives before us: the absurdist and absolutist ravings of a Grendel or a Sunlight Man, however understandable in psychological terms, *are* likely to bring pain and destruction, and Jonathan Upchurch and Jason's settling for acceptance of
human limitation and love *is* salutary to themselves as well as
others.

Hence my subtitle, which to some may sound like a contradiction in terms. *Instruction* in art is generally seen as synonymous with *didacticism:* literature communicating preconceived
messages to readers. *Exploration,* a much more palatable concept
to twentieth-century students of literature, generally presupposes
absence of preconceived opinion, and it may seem odd that the
twain should be thus joined through the conjunction *and* rather
than, say, *or*.

It is indeed possible to see Gardner's artistic technique, determined by his commitment to exploration in art, as a *corollary* to
some of his deepest psychological and philosophical convictions.
There is a very close correlation between Gardner's philosophical
beliefs and his artistic practices. In Gardner's opinion man receives
the best instruction possible in honest art; on the findings of rational morality, therefore, he postulates both the *possibility* of and
the *need* for an art which explores.

Chapters 2 and 3 are thus meant to serve as theoretical underpinnings for Chapters 4–7, in which I study *how* Gardner's theoretical views translate into practice, that is, *the artistic methods he employs* in order to fulfill the artist's mission of instruction and exploration. One conscious method of exploration for Gardner is to *engage the literary tradition*, to draw on the vast store of wisdom and technical skills demonstrated by writers that have come before him; most notably this strategy has given rise to his experimentation with *genre* (Chapter 4) and, even more important, his *collage technique*, that is, his conscious use of literary allusions and the integration of borrowed literary material into his own texts to explore and communicate whatever "truths" he arrives at in his writing (Chapter 5).

This "echoic method" is the most tangible result of his deep involvement with literary tradition, and it has shaped the direction of his art in a number of ways. If one were to determine Gardner's "voice" as a writer, his allusive method would certainly be a defining characteristic of prime importance. Chapter 6 is a case study of how Gardner puts his collage technique to use. The text under scrutiny is "The King's Indian," one of Gardner's most successful creations, in which he fully explores the rich possibilities of this technique; in this novella he has integrated a number of borrowed scenes and lines from Poe's "Pym," Melville's *Moby-Dick*, and Coleridge's "The Rime of the Ancient Mariner" into his own narrative. The reason why one text has been chosen for extended and careful scrutiny is that Gardner's allusive method operates on many levels and some of its effects have ramifications that affect the whole design of the text; therefore, in order to analyze and assess his collage technique adequately one needs a fully developed context.

Another equally important way in which Gardner consistently sets up his "literary experiments" is by juxtaposing contrary ideas or principles (such as order and disorder, body and mind), watching closely to see what truths may issue from the ideational conflict. Chapter 7 is devoted to a discussion of the use of this particular technique, which I refer to as his *dialectical method*, in *Jason and Medeia*, *Grendel*, and *The Sunlight Dialogues*.

LIFE FOLLOWS FICTION

The commanding axiom of John Gardner's activities as a cultural figure is his assumption that art and life are closely connected. His work is informed by a persistent concern with the quality of life in the second part of the twentieth century. This in itself does not perhaps warrant particular attention. What makes Gardner a special case on the contemporary intellectual scene is the messianic fervor of his pronouncements on art, and the massive importance that he claims for the role of art in his own life as well as in the past and future life of humanity. In an address to the students at Rochester University in 1973 ("Life Follows Fiction"), he made a claim which was later to become one of the leitmotifs of *On Moral Fiction:* "Life follows fiction—never doubt it for a moment. Nothing in the world is more powerful than art, for good and evil" (3). To Gardner, therefore, it makes a world of difference *what* topics art chooses to address, and *how* it dramatizes these topics. This conviction on his part has greatly helped determine the direction of his own fiction, as well as his ventures into the field of aesthetic theory.

The idea that life follows fiction is something which Gardner talks about repeatedly in essays, articles, and interviews. It is not surprising, therefore, that this motif is also subject to fictional treatment on his part. Four stories which address art's potentially *vulnerary function* are "Nimram," "The Music Lover," "Come on Back," and "Redemption." These are all collected in Gardner's last book of short stories, significantly entitled *The Art of Living and Other Stories,* and they show how music and song sustain people in their efforts to cope with death as well as the pull toward nihilism that tends to accompany a heavy sense of loss. In the following I try to explain the author's insistence on such a possibility

in terms of his personal history. In the latter part of the chapter I
turn to a more specialized form of the life-follows-fiction idea:
Gardner's often repeated assertion that *art instructs.*

1

Nimram is an American conductor of national and interna-
tional fame who, on his way back to Chicago from a concert on
the West Coast, becomes acquainted with a young girl sitting next
to him on the plane. It is a stormy night, the girl has never flown
before, and in an effort to help her through the ordeal Nimram
engages her in conversation. He then finds out that she is suffering
from a terminal disease, a fact she handles with courage and grace,
largely by recognizing that in her fear and helplessness she is one
with humanity at large. She gives words to this realization by
appropriating a rather cryptic line often spoken by her uncle
Charley: "He says the most interesting thing about Noah's Ark is
that all the animals on it were scared and stupid" (23). This comment would appear to suggest a misanthropic reading of the world.
Given the context, however, it should rather be seen as a reflection
of stoic awareness on Uncle Charley's part. We learn about him
that he, too, is dying of a terminal disease. But like his niece he
refuses to sink into loneliness and self-pity; his stubbornly cheerful approach to hardships seems to spring from the life-sustaining
realization that a sense of frailty and inadequacy is an unavoidable
part of the human condition. His trials, then, inspire him not to
loneliness and isolation but to a reaching out, a call for togetherness. Thus, in the story the plane becomes a kind of latter-day
Noah's Ark. The frail, scared girl and Nimram, at any other time
the incarnation of harmonious ease but now haunted by a sense of
utter helplessness at the prospect of the youngster's death, become
representatives of interdependent mankind: through their interde-
pendence they endow each other's lives with dignity and meaning,
however transitory.
     Nimram is struck by the contrast between the rich and event-
ful life he has led and the brevity of the girl's life experience, and he
feels "helplessly fortunate and therefore unfit, unworthy, his whole
life light and unprofitable as a puff-ball, needless as ascending
smoke" (19). Understandable though this response is, the story
makes the point that Nimram's sense of guilt is not constructive,
nor does it have a basis in fact. The girl learns the conductor's
name; upon arrival in Chicago her father tells her that Nimram is

conducting the Chicago Symphony in Mahler's Fifth the following evening, and she goes to the concert with her parents. The concert in a way becomes a repetition of her experience on the plane, suggestive of companionship and togetherness on the grandest of scales. This section of the story is told through the girl's point of view and is thus controlled by her consciousness. In this way the author is better able to convey the uplifting effects of art on the mind of someone potentially ill-inclined to care about art at all. A psychologically sound reaction to the fact of imminent death could have been disillusionment and bitterness. By recreating in vivid and suspenseful images the girl's excitement at hearing her fellow traveller conduct his orchestra, Gardner succeeds in convincing the reader that the girl's enthusiastic response is also sound.

Deftly the author recaptures the marvel of Mahler's Fifth Symphony:

> Now his left hand moved and the orchestra stirred, tentative at first, but presaging such an awakening as she'd never before dreamed of. Then something new began, all that wide valley of orchestra playing calm, serene, a vast sweep of music as smooth and sharp-edged as an enormous scythe— she had never in her life heard a sound so broad, as if all of humanity, living and dead, had come together for one grand onslaught. The sound ran, gathering its strength, along the ground, building in intensity, full of doubt, even terror, but also fury, and then—amazingly, quite easily—lifted. (26–29)

This passage is indicative of Gardner's great stylistic potential, recreating as he does the girl's musical experience through onomatopoetic, symbolic, and syntactic means. The description of the orchestra playing, "serene, a vast sweep of music as smooth and sharp-edged as an enormous scythe," not only offers rich musical images, but with the many sibilants creates a musical effect while at the same time reinforcing the central image by imitating with rhythmic regularity the sound and movement of a scythe. The scythe is of course an instrument closely associated with the figure of death, and the image thus creates resonance for the death motif sounded earlier in the story. But death is transcended by the music, by that which is everlasting in art: the ability to unite people in a timeless experience of community. The note of togetherness struck by the Noah image on the plane is sustained by the orchestra's symbolical "scrunching forward and closer together" to make room for the extra instruments needed to play a Mahler symphony. Then in the music the theme of togetherness is given the widest reference possible by the orchestra's conjuring up a sound so broad that the girl can only compare it to "all of humanity, living and dead" coming together "for one grand onslaught"; the force of that experience is reflected by the sonorous vowel quality and the heavy beat of the last three words of the sentence.

No doubt Gardner chose the piece to be conducted by Nimram very carefully. Mahler reportedly intended his symphonies to be self-contained worlds, complete in themselves; they should reflect the confusion, terror, but also the beauty, of life. These are all elements of the girl's life, and the music brings them together and transforms them to a spiritually uplifting experience; the music, like the plane, that twentieth-century Ark of confusion, "amazingly, quite easily" lifts. This part of the experience is given added resonance through stylistic means: a series of short, descriptive phrases reflect the restless searching around of the music.

The conductor's name obviously became more and more important to Gardner during composition, because he first called him Amram, then changed the name to Nimram (Winther 519). Nimram brings to mind Nimrod, Noah's grandson; hence Nimram emerges as a symbol of survival through art. Nimram's life is *not* "unprofitable." He brings comfort to the girl in her distress on the plane, but more importantly he acts as a catalyst in awakening her to the purifying and sustaining force of art; and art, in Gardner's view, is man's most powerful weapon in his struggle against chaos and death.

"The Music Lover" and "Come on Back" deal with the same subject, although without quite the evocative power of "Nimram," partly because after the introductory story the other two seem slightly programmatic. "The Music Lover" tells the story of Professor Klingman, who devotes himself completely to music after the death of his pianist wife. Music is the only builder of meaning that he cares about in his widowerhood, and his rage and despair when on one occasion he is confronted with a contemporary piece in which a cello is sawed in two match Gardner's denunciation of nihilistic art in *On Moral Fiction*. "Come on Back" describes how a Welsh community in the upstate New York of Gardner's childhood combats grief at the death of one of the villagers the way the Welsh have always done: through communal singing.

"Redemption" also belongs to this group of stories which describe and explore the vulnerary function of art. The theme of this story differs somewhat from that of the other three, but the subject matter is the same: the protagonist seeks consolation in the world of music after the death of his brother. Jack Hawthorne, the protagonist, was driving a tractor when his younger brother, David, fell off and was run over and killed by the cultipacker the tractor was hauling. Driven by guilt and self-hatred, the young boy tries to deal with his confusion caused by the accident by perfecting his skills on the French horn; he uses the horn as a means of escape into self-imposed isolation, withdrawing from his family and any other company.

He is brought out of his isolation when he suddenly realizes that he will never reach the level of mastery of his teacher Yegudkin, a seventy-year-old Russian exile who has played with famous orchestras around the world. Yegudkin now teaches music but also has a set of arrogant values, constantly deriding "the herd" for failing to appreciate music at his own level. When Jack asks Yegudkin if he thinks that he, the student, will ever be able to play like the great master, the Russian scoffs at this foolish presumption. Thus, John Howell points out, Yegudkin, "'beatific and demonic at once,' has paradoxically saved [Jack] from the artistic self-absorption and isolation he has chosen" ("The Wound and the Albatross" 6). After the crucial lesson in which he is forced to recognize his own limitations, Jack's reintegration into society is described in symbolic terms. Rushing to catch his bus back home, he finds that "the crowd opened for him and, with the horn cradled under his right arm, his music under his left, he plunged in, starting home" (48). The young boy has to recognize his own limits; that is, he has to reconcile himself to the fact that the ideal (his aspirations of becoming a great musician) and the real do not always match up. Only by accepting his own fallibility and imperfections can he deal with his own guilt, become reintegrated into the community and be reunited with his family. Jack's clutching of the instrument and musical score in that symbolical final scene suggests that music will still be an important part of his life, but now more in the manner of the other three stories we have been discussing, and not as a means of alienating himself from the community.

"Redemption" warrants close attention for several reasons. The early pages in particular contain some of the most gripping lines that Gardner ever committed. The opening paragraph, describing the accident which killed Jack's brother, is unique in its control and vividness. The ensuing study of the boy's self-loathing and his estrangement from his family moves as if by its own momentum, wholly logical and with considerable intellectual and emotional authority. Part of the story's attraction, then, lies in the sheer force of the writing that went into it. But even more important are the ways in which it suggests a key to some of the chief motivating factors behind the thematic direction of Gardner's fiction. The story also helps to explain why art has become such an all-encompassing concern for this writer. These points need to be elaborated on at some length.

The centrality of "Redemption" has to do with the fact that it is one of Gardner's most strongly autobiographical pieces of writing, exploring artistically an event which left an indelible mark on him as a person and as a writer. The key event—the accident—is lifted straight from Gardner's personal history, with only a few changes of incident and names.[1] The scene was to play itself over and over again in his mind several times a day up to the writing of the story. (It was first published in the *Atlantic Monthly* in May 1977; the accident involving the death of Gardner's brother took place in 1947.) After he had written about the accident, Gardner stopped having the flashbacks, he says, confirming D. H. Lawrence's dictum that one sheds one's illnesses in art. The suicidal feelings Jack develops in the story are also true to Gardner's own experience, as witnessed, for instance, by the strongly autobiographical "Stillness" section of the posthumous work *Stillness and Shadows*, and the reason that the boy's father gives for not taking his own life—"the damage his suicide would do to his wife and the children remaining"—is the same one Gardner himself has offered for not giving in to his own suicidal inclinations. Like Jack, Gardner played the French horn, and the Eastman School of Music that Jack attends on Saturday afternoons is the one Gardner went to for his music lessons.

But the main impulse behind "Redemption" is not strictly autobiographical. We know that Gardner used writing much the same way that Jack Hawthorne used his horn, as a means of escape and as a way to combat confusion and despair. Art "made my life," Gardner has said, "and it made my life when I was a kid, when I was incapable of finding any other sustenance, any other thing to lean on, any other comfort during times of great unhappiness" (Singular 39). It seems obvious, therefore, that when Gardner claims that art has the power to console, his prime authority is his own personal history; one of his chief purposes in writing these stories must clearly have been to awaken others to the potentially beneficial effects of art.

What is of greater interest to us here, however, is the extent to which the excruciating experience of accidentally killing his brother has affected his own writings. One should tread cautiously here and resist the temptation to establish the kind of relationship between Gardner's life and his art that Phillip Young sought to set up in the case of Hemingway, arguing that the direction of Hemingway's art, in terms of theme as well as of artistic technique, was determined by his continuous struggle to cope with the psychic effect of the physical wounds he received in the course of a turbulent personal history. Nevertheless, there is surely a large degree of truth to Edmund Wilson's claims about the relationship between the artist and his works:

> The real elements, of course, of any work of fiction, are the elements of the author's personality: his imagination embodies in the images of characters, situations, and scenes the fundamental conflicts of his nature or the cycle of phases through which it habitually passes. His personages are personifications of the author's various impulses and emotions: and the relations between them in his stories are really the relations between these. (176)

Gardner has himself insisted on the close relationship between the art product and the personality of the artist: "The tensions we find resolved or at least defined and dramatized in art are the objective release of tensions in the life of the artist" (OMF 180–81).[2] One is therefore perhaps justified in pursuing the Hemingway parallel at least part of the way. The tensions that his childhood experiences engendered in Gardner evidently never lost their grip on him. As late as 1979 he stated: "You keep violently fighting for life, for what you think is good and wholesome, but you lose a lot. I think all my struggles toward anything worthwhile are pretty much undermined by psychological doubts. But you keep trying" (Singular 38). Thus Heraclitus's old maxim—"the way up is the way down"—truly holds for Gardner. This is a fact to bear in mind when assessing the existential seriousness of his life affirmation. There is nothing facile about the basic optimism that controls his books. Gardner was intimately acquainted with personal despair, and as we shall see, his affirmations take into account a number of the major arguments that are traditionally advanced to support a pessimistic view of reality.

The paradigmatic nature of "Redemption" can hardly be

exaggerated. Jack Hawthorne's self-hatred is generalized into a hatred of the total creation, man and animal. This attraction toward an absurdist view of the world (the motivating force behind Jack Hawthorne's and—presumably—Gardner's suicidal inclinations) is explored again and again in Gardner's fiction.[3] It is usually yoked with an absolutist approach to man and life, a failure to reconcile the discrepancy between the real and the ideal, and the failure to accept human fallibility, which characterizes Jack Hawthorne's initial response to the death of his brother. I am, of course, not suggesting that in everything Gardner writes lurk the shadows of his brother's death. But the frequency with which Gardner returns to situations and characters which allow him to explore this kind of tension attests to the biblio-therapeutical nature of his writings, as well as to the formative importance of the accident described in "Redemption." This is not to say that Gardner's fiction is narrowly confessional, representing a constant and obsessive picking of the scab over the wound caused by his brother's death; that would in the end have rendered his novels and stories trivial. What saves his fiction from triviality (in the sense of it being overly private) is the fact that in his personal traumas Gardner has discovered a paradigm, or a metaphor, for what he regards as the central illness of recent Western culture: the inclination to keep peering into the abyss, "counting skulls," losing oneself in a fashionable attraction toward despair.

In these four stories the answer offered to this type of dilemma is of a very general kind: art has the power to console provided one is receptive. It is probably no coincidence that for his exploration of this very general idea Gardner chose to focus on music, an art form which is almost totally abstract, speaking primarily to our emotions rather than to our intellect. But any art will not do for Gardner. When art moves into the sphere of ideas, for instance in the form of literature, it has to meet certain requirements in order to have the life-giving effect that Gardner thinks it can and ought to have. This is where his concept of moral fiction comes in, and a central axiom of this theory is the idea that *art instructs*.

2

The obvious starting point for a study of Gardner's theoretically developed views on the role and nature of art is *On Moral Fiction*. The publication of this collection of critical essays established Gardner as something of an enfant terrible in the world of contemporary American letters. Stephen Singular characteristically entitled his profile of Gardner "The Sound and Fury over Fiction"; the reviewer for the *New York Review of Books* captioned his report on the book "Good Grief"; Dick Cavett promptly summoned Gardner to his television studio to have him expound on his ideas.

There were several reasons for the minor literary tempest stirred up by the publication of *On Moral Fiction*. What initially attracted most attention was Gardner's harsh attack on a large number of his fellow writers for producing art which is "trivial or false." In Gardner's view they either "pointlessly waste our time, saying and doing nothing, or they celebrate ugliness and futility, scoffing at good" (16). The list of writers whom Gardner denounces is long and includes most of the names that make up the literary establishment of the 1960s and 1970s. His criticism of these writers takes on a number of forms, but in every case it boils down to their failure to write "moral fiction." Some, like John Barth, are guilty of "fascination with the ugly, the disgusting," and they are interested mainly in literary game playing (94). Others, like William Gass, put too strong an emphasis on "texture," striving to create linguistic sculptures. For Gass, as Gardner reads him, communication is secondary; what matters most is the writer's capacity to produce interesting language. Still others, like Joseph Heller and Kurt Vonnegut, Jr., are clever novelists, but Gardner finds that they do not care enough about the characters they create and therefore are unable "to take any bold, potentially embarrassing moral stand" (89).

On Moral Fiction is in many ways an unfortunate and unsatisfactory book. Part of the problem has to do with tone; the book is too fiercely polemical, so much so that it runs the risk of turning attention away from Gardner's key ideas. Barth has pointed to this weakness: "He's banging his betters over the head with terminology and, when the smoke clears, nobody is left in the room but Mr. Gardner himself" (Singular 15). In his book Gardner offers a justification for the aggressiveness of his message. The artist "ought not to be too civilized—that is to say, too meekly tolerant," he asserts in the chapter entitled "The Artist as Critic." *On Moral Fiction* demonstrates fully that there is much that he finds wrong in contemporary art, and the following statement seems to explain why his book took on the tone that it did: The artist "should defend—with dignity but as belligerently as necessary—the artists whose work he values and attack with equal belligerence all that he hates" (147). But surely judgment is also essential if a debate is to be meaningful, and belligerence must not be allowed to replace careful reasoning. One cannot help but think that Gardner's cause would have benefitted from less stridency of tone, especially since many of his dismissals of other writers are not based on careful analyses of their works but on very sweeping generalizations. It does not strengthen his case that some of his readings are very careless, even to the point of being misreadings.[4] What Gardner risked in couching his arguments in such bellicose terms was a hasty dismissal of his book and *all* its views.

This is not the place to engage in a debate over the present state of affairs of American letters; however, no student of Gardner's own fiction can afford to go lightly on *On Moral Fiction*. There are good reasons for arguing, as Uta Janssens does, that the chief value of the book lies in the insight it offers into Gardner's own artistry (291). There is a very direct correlation between Gardner's deliberations on literary theory and his own artistic practices. Even though *On Moral Fiction* is not in itself a successful theoretical work, we must nevertheless take time for a rather full discussion of the chief tenets of that book, since they offer key insights into the compositional methods that helped shape Gardner's art. The bold outlines of Gardner's artistic program as it is developed in *On Moral Fiction* can be sketched out rather easily because the most salient points of his thesis are reiterated with great vigor throughout the book: art *instructs;* moral art *affirms* life and *offers models* for emulation; and the morality of the *writing* of fiction resides in the *truthfulness* with which the artist engages in *the creative process.* What tends to get lost in the flak of Gardner's rhetoric are the finer nuances and modifications of these roughly hewn statements. Further modifications appear in interviews given after the publication of *On Moral Fiction* and in those fictions of his (most notably "Vlemk the Box-Painter") that deal expressly with matters of art, as well as in the writings ensuing from his medieval scholarship. What emerges from a collocation of these many sources is a coherent and many-faceted system of artistic beliefs which directly influenced his own artistic practices.

"Art instructs," Gardner asserts in Part 1 of *On Moral Fiction*, in a section entitled "Premises on Art and Morality." "Why, one may wonder, would anyone wish to deny a thing so obvious?" (39). In one of its formulations this dictum might be amended to read: art cannot help but instruct. "After Marlon Brando appeared in *On the Waterfront*," Gardner maintains, "an entire generation took to slumping, mumbling, turning up its collar, and hanging its cigarette casually off the lip" (107).[5] A literary example is Goethe's *Sorrows of Young Werther*, the publication of which reportedly spurred a series of suicide cases throughout Europe (15). Even though he fails to produce examples of similar effects achieved by contemporary art, Gardner posits a correlation between what he feels to be the predominant intellectual and spiritual climate—a climate marked by "hate and despair and indifference, violence for its own sake, sex as a proof that love is an illusion" ("Life Follows Fiction" 3)—and the cultural manifestations of the times, as instanced by the ruling taste in television, film, and literature.

In "Vlemk the Box-Painter" he offers a fictionalized version of this argument.[6] Vlemk, like artists of Samuel Beckett's mettle, for whom "the worst the universe can do becomes normative" (*OMF* 22), paints a series of pictures of the Princess. In these pictures—"reality boxes" he calls them, because everything Vlemk paints, he paints on boxes—he sets out to pursue the Princess's "worst potential," and the result is a number of pictures in which her potential states of ruin are depicted. When the Princess sees the pictures, she is impressed by their "honesty" and by Vlemk's ability "to see life as it was" (*AL* 206), mistaking his projection of dark possibilities for the real thing. She embraces this new vision of herself, thereby fulfilling Vlemk's prophecies. After a night of debauchery, she ends up in the gutter, and when the box-painter finds her there the next morning, "she looked, right down to the last detail, like a certain one of the cruel, bitter pictures he'd made of her" (216). The version of reality that for a brief spell the Princess commits herself to brings destruction rather than the life enhancement that Gardner is convinced *moral art* can bring.

Gardner's emphasis on art's suitability for instruction places him squarely in a tradition that goes back to Sir Philip Sidney and Horace. M. H. Abrams usefully dubs the ruling concept of this tradition "the pragmatic theory," inasmuch as its adherents tend to look at the work of art "chiefly as a means to an end, an instrument for getting something done," judging the value of any work of art "according to its success in achieving that aim" (15). The central conceit of "Vlemk" is a picture real enough to speak, and *The Defense of Poesie* is the most likely source: "Poesy...is an art of imitation, for so Aristotle termeth it in the word *mimesis*, that is to say, a representing, counterfeiting, or figuring forth—to speak metaphorically, a speaking picture; with this end, to teach and delight" (414). Samuel Johnson's famously clipped admonition in

"Preface to Shakespeare" states the instrumentalist precept in its most concise form: "The end of writing is to instruct; the end of poetry is to instruct by pleasing" (73).

Even though the pragmatic tradition in England was more or less eclipsed by the advent of Romanticism and Romantic criticism, its precepts to a certain extent still influenced the thinking of European artists like Goethe, Balzac, and Tolstoy. In the twentieth century, however, the call for an art whose aim is to educate its audience seems very much to have become a minority position. True, D. H. Lawrence claimed for the best novels the status of guides on how to live, but as David Lodge reminds us, Lawrence's views went against "the grain of modernist orthodoxy" (121). Lionel Trilling points out that already by the nineteenth century the intellectual authority of the pragmatic theory was at an end, "although its social authority was still very commanding." From the vantage point of the late 1960s he is led to conclude that "the idea that literature is to be judged by its moral effect has virtually no place in critical theory." But he hastens to add: "In actual critical practice, however, it has a quite considerable vitality" ("What Is Criticism?" 67).

Lionel Trilling has himself on occasion expressed views that reveal a fondness for a pragmatic concept of art.[7] So did F. R. Leavis,[8] and Wayne C. Booth has also spoken up for a response to literature which brings to bear "judgments of *ends* as well as means" (*The Rhetoric of Fiction* 378; my italics). Booth's recent book, *The Company We Keep* (1988), develops an extended case for a theory of ethical criticism. Much of what is generally referred to as Marxist literary criticism also of course advocates an instrumentalist approach to literature, as do several contemporary Afro-American writers, but one would probably have to conclude that outside these circles, the position of Leavis, Trilling, and Booth is a lonely one in contemporary letters.

John Gardner was, at least in one of his moods, clearly bent on reviving the pragmatic theory. I say "in one of his moods" because his emphasis shifted; his very pointed defense of an instrumentalist view in some contexts was toned down and modified in other contexts. However, some of his pronouncements in *On Moral Fiction* and elsewhere would appear to place him squarely in the camp of Sidney and Johnson: "Moral art in its highest form holds up models of virtue" (82). True art "designs visions worth trying to make fact" (100). "I agree with Tolstoy that the highest purpose of art is to make people good by choice" (106). "I believe absolutely that art always affects life" (Harvey 77).

These views inform Gardner's own fiction. The role he gives to the Shaper in *Grendel* conforms with his ideas in *On Moral Fiction*. Grendel, the nihilist monster, is for a while sorely tempted to believe in the visions of life celebrated by the Anglo-Saxon scop:

> It was a cold-blooded lie that a god had lovingly made the world and set out the sun and moon as lights to land-dwellers, that brothers had fought, that one of the races was saved, the other cursed. Yet he, the old Shaper, might make it true, by the sweetness of his harp, his cunning trickery. It came to me with a fierce jolt that I wanted it. As they did too, though vicious animals, cunning, cracked with theories. I wanted it, yes! Even if I must be the outcast, cursed by the rules of his hideous fable. (55)

But Grendel is convinced by the dragon's arguments that the Shaper's vision is all illusion, and he succumbs to the temptation Sidney takes issue with in his *Defense:* the temptation to see poetry as "the mother of lies" (438).

Grendel is one of several Gardnerian characters who have great trouble reconciling the real with the ideal; another one is Uncle Charley in the story entitled "Come on Back." Charley was endowed with a very good tenor voice when he was younger, never missing a Cymanfa Ganu, one of the many songfests of that part of New York State where Gardner grew up. When he loses his voice because of age, Charley becomes bitter, and his mother explains why: "Singing's got its place. But a body can get to thinking, when he's singing with a choir, that that's how the whole blessed world should be, and then when he comes down out of the clouds it's a terrible disappointment" (*AL* 250). Charley's kinship with Grendel is revealed in his interpretation of the meaning of the traditional Welsh name *Buddy:* "Means 'the poet.' They used to set great store by poets, back in Wales. Only second to kings—maybe not even second. Same thing, kings and poets. Different kinds of liars" (264).[9] Having avoided the songfests for a number of years, Charley finally goes to one; the contrast between the beauty of Welsh choir singing and his rather shabby everyday existence becomes too much for him and he takes his own life. Grendel and Charley both fail to appreciate Sidney's—and Gardner's—idea that the value of art lies not in its ability to describe things as they are but in its capacity for celebrating man's possibilities. Presumably, Grendel would have responded less scornfully to the kind of art which

Gardner indicts in *On Moral Fiction*, an art which reflects and reinforces an absurdist view of existence, an art in which "the cruellest, ugliest thing we can say is likely to be the truest." Gardner's key metaphor for this kind of art is that of man staring into the abyss, "counting skulls." But, he warns, "the black abyss is merely life as it is or as it soon may become, and staring at it does nothing, merely confirms that it is there" (126).

Gardner gives us a vision of *his* ideal artist in "John Napper Sailing Through the Universe," a story which, by Gardner's own admission, spells out his "fundamental theory of art" (Harvey 81). In his youth John Napper had painted what in "Vlemk" are called "reality pictures," "dark, furious, intellectual, full of scorn and something suicidal. Mostly black, with struggles of light, losing" (*KI* 124). But then, "at the edge of self-destruction, John Napper had...jumped back. He would make up the world from scratch: Let there be light, a splendid garden. He would fabricate treasure maps. And he'd come to believe it. How could he not, seeing how it lighted his sad wife's eyes?" (133). Napper had done what Jonathan Upchurch of "The King's Indian" is on occasion able to do: "I gaze at the dark Satanic mills... I shake my head. They vanish" (242). The old artist has not done away with uncertainty—a concern which, as we shall see, is present in much of Gardner's fiction—but he has refused to let himself be dominated by it. In Gardner's own explication: "John Napper...knows and teaches one important truth...: nothing exists for sure, until we make it; don't sit staring at the abyss, then. Make!" ("A Writer's View" 23).

In its simplest and barest form the effect Gardner is after is the one he describes in the early pages of "Vlemk the Box-Painter." The picture Vlemk paints of the barmaid is "a lie, a fraud, an outrage" because in it he has wilfully improved upon nature, making the fat and ugly woman quite beautiful (*AL* 160). The "unreality" of the picture notwithstanding, it soon begins, in true Sidneyan and Gardnerian fashion, to work its desired effect: the barmaid becomes "increasingly similar to the fraudulent painting" (161). This, then, is the aesthetic mechanism that Grendel fails to observe in his spyings on the Shaper and Hrothgar's court. He rightly finds that the scop's idealized version of Hrothgar's deeds is a lie, an illusion; but he is wrong in concluding that the Shaper's poetry, therefore, must be spurned. Even though Hrothgar and his men fall short of the ideal that the Shaper holds up for them, his poetry nevertheless has the effect of making them *try* to realize ideals. Through the acts of heroism and sacrifice to which the Shaper's poetry inspires them, Hrothgar's kingdom prospers.[10]

Gardner's advocacy of the pragmatic theory is a sustained and detailed one, then, informing his theoretical as well as his fictional work. But this is not the whole story; Gardner has on occasion modified his views. Before we turn to a discussion of these modifications, however, it may be of interest to observe that Gardner indicates great sympathy also for the other half of the Sidneyan equation, the call for an art which delights. His responsiveness to this concept helps to explain the aura of fantasy which envelops his fiction. "I really do believe that a novel has to be a feast of the senses," he told the *Paris Review* interviewers, "a delightful thing." This attraction to fictional forms which engage the imagination as fully as possible lies behind his declared disenchantment with strict realism; he feels that in writing realistic fiction too much creative energy is spent providing details which are not essential to the book's vision. His penchant for fantasy also helps to explain the genesis of much of his fiction. The *Beowulf* story, for instance, was ideal source material for him, he says, because of its powerful visual images, what with meadhalls, Grendel, Grendel's mother, and the dragon (Ferguson et al. 43–44). Gardner also partly attributes the appearance of so many grotesque characters in his work to this wish on his part to put on a good show, because "a circus needs some very funny characters." He calls this a "Walt Disney effect" (Christian 28). The allusion to Disney is significant, since Gardner has pointed to a willed cartoon effect in a good deal of his fiction, a conscious blend of exaggeration and comedy, which is meant, presumably, to engage the reader's imagination and help bring about that "willing suspension of disbelief" on which many of his aesthetic effects depend. Two characters that Gardner has identified as cartoon figures are Grendel, a monster, and Clumly, the Chief of Police in *The Sunlight Dialogues*, whom Gardner describes as "hairless, with a great big nose and perfect teeth.... Nobody ever looked like that" (Bellamy 174). The list could be extended considerably: John Horne in *The Resurrection*, Agathon in *The Wreckage of Agathon*, the Sunlight Man in *The Sunlight Dialogues*, Henry Soames and the Goat Lady in *Nickel Mountain*, Dr. Flint and Wilkins in "The King's Indian," Freddy and Bishop Brask in *Freddy's Book*, and Arnold Deller in "The Art of Living," to mention only the most conspicuous ones.[11] A sense of comedy and an acceptance of human fallibility are important elements of Gardner's overall vision, and the fact that in his circus shows the spotlight persistently veers—as if by its own volition—

to that part of the ring where the clowns huddle together contributes emotionally and intellectually to the building of that vision.

Gardner's strong advocacy of an instrumentalist approach to literature is toned down in some contexts and modified in others. It seems clear that in *On Moral Fiction* (which contains his most sustained defense of the art-as-instruction concept) the polemicist got the better of the careful analyst and literary theoretician. One point which is bound to have irked many readers is Gardner's clarion call for an art which "holds up models of virtue" (82). In our antiheroic age, such a statement is likely to cause embarrassment rather than enthusiasm. But models of virtue are not the same as paragons of virtue. Gardner's statement is tempered by his warning that these models must not be "cheap or cornball models of behavior" (18–19). They may be heroic models "like Homer's Achilles or models of quiet endurance" (82). The Homeric precept notwithstanding, a glance at Gardner's own fiction reveals that his heroes lean toward the quotidian rather than the Homeric: the timid but loyal Peeker in *The Wreckage of Agathon;* the Clumlys in *The Sunlight Dialogues,* confused but honestly struggling for ethical coherence in their lives; the "reformed" Jonathan Upchurch in "The King's Indian," who eventually decides to settle for a life of "discipline" in Illinois rather than pursue the monomaniacal philosophical quest of Dr. Flint; and Sally and James Page in *October Light,* who conduct their tragicomic battle of opinions with the shrewdness and stubbornness of Vermont farmers.[12]

In the *Paris Review* interview (Ferguson et al.) Gardner offers a welcome qualification of the idea of models. He breaks the concept of moral fiction down into three forms. The first and highest form is the one I have described already: virtuous models are held up for emulation. But Gardner here also fully accepts "indirect" models. One finds these in what he calls "negative moral fiction, or moral fiction in the tragic mode, where you want to be different than the protagonist—you want to be better."[13] An example of such a protagonist is Macbeth. Then there is what he calls moral fiction of the third degree,

> wherein alternatives don't exist. Not for fashion's sake or for the cheap love of gruesomeness, but from anger and concern, you stare into the smoking volcano.... That doesn't tell you what you should do. It doesn't tell you, I don't want to be like that. But it makes you understand and, understanding,

hunger for a world not like this. It's obviously the least uplifting of the three kinds of moral fiction, but it's morally useful. (Ferguson et al. 73)

These are indeed important modifications on Gardner's part, and one can only regret that he failed to elaborate on these ideas in *On Moral Fiction*.

Gardner has said that although his purpose in writing "Vlemk the Box-Painter" was to work out in fictional form the key ideas of *On Moral Fiction*, he found that in the process of writing he was forced to modify some of his earlier views (Winther 520). What he may have had in mind is a shifting of priorities, away from a fiction which holds up models of conduct to a favoring of art which emphasizes the need for truthful exploration. In *On Moral Fiction* he places about equal weight on these two functions of art. Alongside his persistent call for instruction, there is also a repeated warning against a didactic, or moralistic, fiction "in which the writer knows before he starts what it is that he means to say and does not allow his mind to be changed by the process of telling the story." Moral fiction "communicates meanings discovered by the process of the fiction's creation" (107–8).

Vlemk, as he emerges at the end of the story, would seem to qualify as a moral artist in the sense that he fulfills the demand for truthful exploration in art. When he first paints the Princess's picture, his painting proceeds in accordance with Gardner's description of how the true moral artist works. The object is now not to produce a model of virtue, as he was to do in painting the barmaid's picture, but to give a true representation of reality, never cheating in the creative process, because only by capturing the very essence of the Princess can he make the picture speak. But *because* he works absolutely truthfully, setting down the Princess's features exactly as they appear to him, he discovers that she is not as beautiful as he had thought her to be. The completed picture, therefore, is not the picture of ideal beauty that he had expected to paint; there are "lines suggesting a touch of meanness in her character" but lines of "kindness, too; generosity, a pleasing touch of whimsy" (*AL* 149).

In his efforts to bring the Princess, now the Queen, out of the state of despondency that the reality boxes—those artistic visions of her worst potentialities—have brought her to, Vlemk decides to try the barmaid effect on the Queen. Knowingly sacrificing his gift of speech forever, he paints over the speaking picture, producing a painting which to him seems to be "exactly like the Queen except with none of her faults" (232). But this time the intended instructional effect fails. The Queen does not respond to the picture as a representation of her possibilities; instead she is awed, much in the manner of Grendel and Uncle Charley, by the discrepancy between the real and the ideal:

> "When I saw the new picture, after you'd made it perfect, I saw with terrible certainty how far I was from the person I imagined myself.... Seeing the disparity between what I am and what I wish to be, I have come to the only happiness possible for such a wreck as I am, the sad joy of the old philosophers who at least 'knew themselves.'... That...is why I can no longer go on living and have purposely declined to this pitiful state." (237)

Both the Queen and Vlemk are wrong, of course. In painting over the speaking picture Vlemk had not changed it enough to deprive it of its ability to speak. Even when he thought he was idealizing the Queen, he was still giving a representation of her true nature, because otherwise, by the story's logic, the picture would have been silenced for ever. The fact that the picture *appeared* more beautiful only suggests that he had come to love her with her perfections *and* imperfections. The speaking picture's scheming ways, which are then also the Queen's ways, have not been mended; the picture pretends, for instance, to have become muted, to better manipulate and keep control over situations. But these blemishes only add to the Queen's charm, infusing the story with a welcome touch of humor. Since the format of the story is the fairy tale, there is the obligatory happy ending. The Queen's life is saved through Vlemk's sacrifice and comical love, and the Queen is finally able to accept her own less than ideal state.

The need to accept one's own fallibility is one of the most important thematic concerns of Gardner's fiction, and in "Vlemk" the tension which results from a juxtaposition of the real and the ideal is resolved in such a way as to favor an emphasis on self-acceptance rather than self-improvement. In this story, therefore, the predominant aesthetic code is less that of Sidney, with his call for artistic presentations of what ought to be, than the code of, say, the Gawain-poet, whom Gardner lauds for his handling of the King Arthur legend: "The concern of art is never with 'what ought to be,' in Sidney's phrase, but with the tension between what ought to be and what *can* be.... In short, a wise medieval poet...tests ideals against the possible" (*Sir Gawain and the Green Knight: Notes* 21–22). This tension is present in Gardner's fiction prior to *On Moral Fiction*, and it is therefore not surprising that it should reassert itself when he undertakes to test his aesthetic theories artistically, as he does in "Vlemk."

It should be noted that the modified version of the "art instructs" thesis which Gardner seems to have arrived at in "Vlemk" does not represent a drastic reversal of his previous stance. The modification should most properly be conceived of as a *shifting of priorities*. The value of the kind of art symbolized by the barmaid's picture is not denied by anything that happens in the story, but it seems to be relegated to a less prominent position. The story's leitmotif is undeniably the speaking picture with *its* thematic implications. There is furthermore a higher valuation of the artistic motivation behind the Princess's picture than that which lies behind the picture of the barmaid. In the latter instance the motivation is the same as the one which directs the Shaper's art in *Grendel*; in that work, too, the benevolent effect of holding up virtuous models is demonstrated, but just as Vlemk paints the barmaid's picture to get free wine, so the Shaper works for money and fame. Gardner has characterized the Anglo-Saxon scop as a "wonderful hack" (Winther 520), and that is precisely the role that Vlemk performs vis à vis the barmaid. "Vlemk the Box-Painter," then, ultimately celebrates the artist who explores truthfully, and the artist who limits his role to a mere designer of visions—like Vlemk in his early career, when he "edited Nature" (146)—is assigned to a somewhat lower, but still highly honorable, position.

Gardner thus seems to place art as process of discovery over art as instruction in the Sidneyan and didactic sense of that term, and that fact might serve to make his theory of art intellectually more palatable to a contemporary audience. Did not T. S. Eliot, that high priest of modernism, claim that a poet "does not know what he has to say until he says it" (98)? But a widespread and ready acceptance of Gardner's aesthetics is hindered by his insistence on an art which affirms life. It would seem that Gardner has placed himself in a theoretical bind here. On the one hand he calls for a fiction which "seeks to improve life" (*OMF* 5), a fiction which presents "eternal verities worth keeping in mind, and a benevolent vision of the possible which can inspire and incite human beings toward virtue, toward life affirmation as opposed to destruction or indifference" (18). At the same time moral art is not didactic because, instead of teaching by authority and force, it explores, open-mindedly, to learn what it should teach. It clarifies, like an experiment in a chemistry lab, and confirms. As a chemist's experiment tests the laws of nature and dramatically reveals the truth or falsity of scientific hypotheses, moral art tests values and rouses trustworthy feelings about the better and the worse in human action. (19)

This two-partite definition of what constitutes moral fiction—it is life-affirming *and* it states whatever the artist discovers that he can say in the process of writing—raises a problem which Gardner never defines and therefore does not address directly. If we stay with the chemistry metaphor, the problem could be stated this way: chemists sometimes help build life through their discovery of life-giving medicines, but chemists have also produced napalm and nerve gas. In both cases they reveal "the truth" rather than "the falsity" of "the scientific hypotheses" concerning the proper combination of substances for the production of these chemical compounds. Put differently: how is Gardner's definition of moral art to deal with an artist who in his writing is absolutely honest to his perception of the world, but finds that there is nothing which he *can* affirm? John Updike's response to Gardner's call for moral fiction probably expresses what many feel when they come upon Gardner's theories for the first time: "'Moral' is such a moot word. Surely, morality in fiction is accuracy and truth. The world has changed, and in a sense we are all heirs to despair. Better to face this and tell the truth, however dismal, than to do whatever life-enhancing thing [Gardner] was proposing" (Singular 15).

To say that Gardner has not addressed this dilemma directly is not the same as claiming that he has no answer to it. Gardner's predicament is not unlike that which Marxist literary critics have had to face in squaring the artistic demands of mimesis with the desire for proper ideological instruction in art. His way of solving the problem is furthermore strangely analogous to that of the Second Congress of the Soviet Writers' Union. Whereas the First Congress (1934) had demanded of Socialist Realism "truthful, historically concrete representation of reality in its revolutionary development...combined with the task of ideological remoulding and education of the working people in the spirit of Socialism," the Second Congress (1954) ruled that it is sufficient to ask that literature give truthful representations of reality. If Marxism is right in its analysis of historical development, then proper instruction will follow as a necessary consequence of these truthful representations.[14]

Similarly Gardner seems to hold that if only the artist takes care to represent human nature truthfully, then he cannot help but affirm life-enhancing values; man is a civilized animal, and it is through cultivation of certain "eternal verities" that he has been able to build a civilization in the first place. A truthful representation of man, therefore, cannot help but note his civilizing inclinations. Artistic exploration will also find in man a leaning toward disorder, and, as we shall see in a later chapter, Gardner's fiction is strongly animated by an acute awareness of the tension which is generated through the continual battle between the forces of order and disorder. But the fact that civilizations have been built proves that in a perspective which includes the Devonian fish, the forces of order have held the upper hand. In Gardner's view, this evolution is not a blind one; it is the product of a series of conscious choices on the part of man, and the root impulse, in spite of many false starts and aberrations, has always been to further what Chaucer called the "Commune profit." The evolution of civilizations could only have taken place if guided by *rational morality*. Gardner's conviction that there is such a thing as rational goodness lies behind his concept of morality, and this concept in turn informs his call for moral fiction, as regards his insistence on both instruction, or life enhancement, *and* exploration.

RATIONAL MORALITY

In one of his last public speeches Lionel Trilling gave his views on the role of "mind in the modern world." He concluded his address with this eloquent plea for faith in the possibilities of the human mind:

> Mind does not move toward its ideal purposes over a royal straight road but finds its way through the thicket of its own confusions and contradictions.... Yet we know that when we cast up the fortunes of mind at any given moment in history, what makes the object of our concern is mind as it defines itself by its ideal purposes, by its power to achieve order, inclusiveness, and coherence.... When mind, far from being ornamental, part of the superstructure of society, is the very model of the nation-state...any falling off of its confidence in itself must be felt as a diminution of national possibility, as a lessening of the social hope. It is out of this belief that I have ventured to urge upon you the awareness that mind at the present time draws back from its own freedom and power, from its own delight in itself. That my having done so is not a counsel of despair is assured by one characteristic of mind, its wish to be conscious of itself, with what this implies of its ability to examine a course it has taken and to correct it. ("Mind in the Modern World" 127–28)

Trilling's comments bear in an enlightening way on John Gardner's assessment of the predominant intellectual mood of contemporary culture. Trilling's remedy for the present spiritual malaise—the cultivation of the mind's potentials—forms one of the cornerstones of Gardner's artistic program. Like Trilling, Gardner very much feels that modern man has lost confidence in his own mental resources, that mind, in Trilling's admirable phrase, "at the present time draws back from its own freedom and power, from its own delight in itself." *On Moral Fiction* provides abundant documentation of the ways in which Gardner feels that this spiritual defeatism has affected contemporary art. And the solution he proposes is essentially the same as that of Trilling: man must, like Arnold Deller in Gardner's story "The Art of Living," resist the temptation "to back off" (AL 282).

The present course *can* be corrected, Gardner emphatically claims. In *On Moral Fiction* he speaks of the Romantic optimism of the early nineteenth century, an optimism which was based on the view that "humanity itself" was "innately good" (37). This optimism was crushed by the somber facts of political developments in Europe, and dejection became the predominant mood. Romantic theory provided an explanation for this development, Gardner argues, but the explanation went unheeded. The Romantic optimism was basically right because the imagination is "an innate faculty, but one which [requires] *exercise and training*" (38; my italics). Historical events did not prove the Romantic theory of man wrong; what they did prove was that Europe had for a while taken leave of her best senses, had begun to listen—through a failure of imagination—to the voices of unreason.

Now that dejection once again is widespread, Gardner asks us, both in working out his artistic theories and in his fiction, to take one more close look at the ways in which the human mind has been working, individually and collectively, throughout the ages. If we do that, Gardner says, we cannot help but notice that "history is progressive, that things aren't as bad as they were sixty years ago" (Christian 87). He is not blind to the very real causes of the present malaise. *The Wreckage of Agathon* was written against a background of widespread racial discrimination and unrest in the United States. In "The Art of Living" there are distinct echoes of the Vietnam War, the draft, and riots on the campuses, and Arnold Deller no doubt speaks on behalf of the author when he voices his contempt for TV, the extreme commercialization of consumer goods, and other problems. Gardner's last novel, *Mickelsson's Ghosts*, addresses the dangers of pollution and a nuclear disaster. But these ills represent man-induced deviations from a steadily rising curve of human achievement; the ills can be checked if only man will stop allowing his mind to draw back "from its own freedom and power." This fundamental optimism is based on the findings of a line of thinkers which include Charles Darwin, Alfred North Whitehead, R. G. Collingwood, and Brand Blanshard.

1

Gardner has identified the teachings of Darwin and the implications of *The Origin of Species* and *The Descent of Man* as his most important philosophical interest during the last years of his life (Winther 510). This explains why Darwinian terminology and concepts crop up in late novels like *Freddy's Book* and *Mickelsson's Ghosts*. In "The Art of Living" Darwin is referred to explicitly, and Arnold Deller fashions his program of spiritual improvement on Darwin's evolutionary theories. Gardner agrees with such an approach, in terms which to some may have seen naively optimistic in 1980 but which a decade later, in view of East European developments, have taken on a definitely prophetic ring: "I think goodness is more fit to survive than evil.... I think democracy is more fit to survive than tyranny...other things being equal, virtue is strong" (Winther 510). In retrospect it seems almost unavoidable that Gardner should eventually turn to Darwin, since so many of the other philosophers that he has taken a declared interest in— Whitehead, Collingwood, and Blanshard among them—all reveal a marked evolutionary bent.

"And when I came to Whitehead," Gardner once told an interviewer, "my head went off because...I felt he said what I would say. That is to say his world-view, incredibly, was like the world-view I had developed" (Harvey 74). *Process and Reality* is Whitehead's courageous attempt at constructing a coherent cosmology, and it is a book that Gardner has referred to approvingly on several occasions in defending one philosophical position or another.[1] Whitehead's book is very difficult to follow, dealing almost exclusively in abstracts and using a highly specialized terminology, but its main thesis might perhaps be given the following summary formulation.

The name Whitehead gives to his theories is *philosophy of organism*, and he conceives of the world as being in an eternal state of process. The first of his twenty-seven "Categories of Explanation" reads: "That the actual world is a process, and that the process is the becoming of actual entities." The basic principle of this process he calls "the concrescence of many potentials"; through "concrescence" are formed "actual entities" (loosely: phenomena), which in turn form the potentials for the "concrescence" of new actual entities, securing a continual and evolutionary process (33). Ork, the old priest whose religious beliefs Grendel inadvertently confirms by posing as Hrothgar's King of Gods, quotes extensively from *Process and Reality*, and he sums up his metaphysics in terms which reflect the evolutionary mysticism of Whitehead's scheme: "Ultimate wisdom, I have come to perceive, lies in the perception that the solemnity and grandeur of the universe rise through the slow process of unification in which the diversities of existence are utilized, and nothing, *nothing* is lost" (115).[2]

Whitehead looks to Plato's *Timaeus* rather than to Newton's *Scholium* for inspiration. His explanation for this persuasion brings out the evolutionary orientation of his philosophy of organism:

> To the modern reader, the *Timaeus*, considered as a statement of scientific details, is in comparison with the *Scholium* simply foolish. But what it lacks in superficial detail, it makes up for by its philosophic depth.... For the *Scholium*, nature is merely, and completely, *there*, externally designed and obedient. The full sweep of the modern doctrine of evolution would have confused the Newton of the *Scholium*, but would have enlightened the Plato of the *Timaeus*.... There is another point in which the organic philosophy only repeats Plato. In the *Timaeus* the origin of the present cosmic epoch is traced back to an aboriginal disorder, chaotic according to our ideals. This is the evolutionary doctrine of the philosophy of organism.

Whitehead thus places the philosophy of organism in opposition to what he calls the Semitic conception of "a wholly transcendent God creating out of nothing an accidental universe" (142–43, 146).

R. G. Collingwood and Brand Blanshard avoid Whitehead's mystical categories, but these three thinkers nevertheless share a commitment to an evolutionary view of the world. It seems that none of them would have much difficulty in seconding the basic optimism of the concluding paragraph of *The Descent of Man*: "Man may be excused for feeling some pride at having risen, though not through his own exertions, to the very summit of the organic scale; and the fact of his having thus risen, instead of having been aboriginally placed there, may give him hopes for a still higher destiny in the distant future" (2: 387). Collingwood wrote *The New Leviathan* in the early years of World War II, wanting to remind his fellow countrymen and all forces working to overthrow

Hitler that the defeat of barbarism "is always certain in the long
run" (348). The reason for Collingwood's confidence is his view of
man: human nature is such that it will always create new civilizations. Blanshard is only slightly less optimistic about the future of
man in his exploration of the relative roles of reason and goodness.
"The notion of original sin," he holds, "is a malignant myth, for
which there is no sort of respectable evidence." There is no denying that men often commit evil acts; that, however, is "no necessity of human nature, but, in general, a matter of ignorance, of special defect, or of ill conditioning.... [S]ome measure of intelligence
too is given us by nature, and the inner pressure of intelligence is
everywhere toward justice and the elimination of cruelty"
(359–60). Collingwood's and Blanshard's analyses of human nature
have a number of points in common; as Gardner suggests, they
both advocate a belief in rational goodness (*OMF* 11). And, importantly, it is to Blanshard that Gardner refers the reader for a full
defense of his own views of the moral (135, 208n). It seems clear
that Gardner's view of man owes much of its direction and refine-
ment to the philosophical inquiries of these two thinkers.

   The New Leviathan might properly be called an investigation
into the anatomy of civilization. The underlying premise of this
investigation is Collingwood's assertion that "civilization is a
thing of the mind" (2).[3] He therefore starts out by stating his theory of man's rise into consciousness and maturity, that is, his interpretation of how man *becomes* "'Man' of the mind." This theory
is—as befits the subject—a rather elaborate one; in rough outline it
could perhaps be summed up in the following terms: Man, in the
first stage of mental life, is conscious of "a confused mass of feelings.... Then he 'attends to' some element or group of elements in
this mass of feeling. That is the second stage of mental life." In
this second stage is formed what Collingwood calls "appetite,"
which he describes as a "gnawing sensation," a wanting to get
away from the "here-and-now" to a "there-and-then." At this stage
the individual does not know *what* he wants: "Nobody in a condition of wanting knows what he wants or is conscious of wanting
anything definite."

   The stage beyond appetite is "desire." In desiring, or wishing,
man "not only knows that he wants something, but he knows
what it is that he wants." Collingwood distinguishes between
"true desires" and "false desires." In the first instance you "really
want" the object of desire, in the latter case, you think you want it
but you are mistaken. In the earliest stages of mental development

man's only way of finding out what he wants is through trial and error. At later stages man is able to draw on his memory of previous experiences; through the working of reason he is able to form more reliable hypotheses as to what things or actions are likely to bring satisfaction or, conversely, prove themselves disadvantageous. Hence, one of the prime functions of reason is to analyze the potential effect of fulfilling conflicting desires. Thus reason is all-important to man in his quest for "the good," because in Collingwood's theory "good" is synonymous with "desirable" or "worthy to be desired."

In his inquiry into the foundation of rational goodness, *Reason and Goodness*, Brand Blanshard makes no reference to *The New Leviathan*, nor to Collingwood. Nevertheless, he begins his exploration of what constitutes "the good" in human lives by developing a theory of man which in its essentials corresponds with that of Collingwood. Their terminologies differ, as do their treatments of the nuances and implications of the theory, but all the stages of mental development spelled out by Collingwood are found in Blanshard's analysis as well. The first nine chapters of *Reason and Goodness* review the most prominent attempts at arriving at philosophically defensible theories of "the good" in the European history of ideas. Against this background Blanshard develops (in Chapters 11–14) his own ideas on goodness. Drawing on the findings of a host of psychologists, from William James to Freud and the Gestaltists, Blanshard starts out with the premise that "*conscious process is goal-seeking from the beginning*" (293).[4] A child does not know what it wants; it is ruled by instincts and "impulses" only (corresponding to Collingwood's "appetite"). An "impulse" Blanshard defines as "an 'urge' or felt tendency toward a certain course of behaviour." Through a process of trial and error the child forms "desires" (here the terminology corresponds exactly with that of Collingwood). "Desire" is also an urge, "but now with a consciousness of its end." Like Collingwood, Blanshard bases his definition of "goodness" on this psychological scheme: "'Good' has the meaning it does because we are the sort of beings we are. Human nature *is* essentially a set of activities directed toward ends, and human life is a striving toward these ends." "What is good is what fulfils those impulses or strivings of which human nature essentially consists, and in fulfilling them brings satisfaction."

Both Collingwood and Blanshard emphasize the role of reason in arriving at what constitutes the good for man. Collingwood's distinction between "immediate consciousness" and reason is matched by Blanshard's differentiation between "immediate" and "rational" will. Our immediate will is in operation in most cases of instant gratification. This is the will of the moment that we obey in making most of our quotidian decisions; we act, often with only a minimum of reflection, to satisfy any number of impulse-desires. But sometimes these desires are what Collingwood calls "false desires," desires we think we want to see satisfied, whereas upon reflection we find that what we really desire is something different. When the will of the moment is thus overruled, it is because man possesses both an immediate *and* a rational will. Through the working of this larger will, man arrives at an understanding and definition of "the good" which will often turn out to be an improvement upon "the good" sought by the immediate will. This improved conception of the good is achieved through reflection, and it constitutes what Blanshard calls "the rational good" for man. Much as he might want to think otherwise, no man can avoid being ruled by his rational will in a large number of situations.

Here is Blanshard's description of how any man will, at some point or other, find himself moved by the workings of his rational will:

> He continually defers present good to a later and greater good, corrects impulsive choices by reflection, recognizes the force of another's claim when at the moment he would prefer not to. In doing so, he concedes the claim of rational good upon him, a claim which, if he is consistent, he must admit to have overwhelming force in confirmation or in veto of the will of the moment. We agree that he does not know in detail the object of this larger will. We agree that it is not a will at all in the simple straightforward sense in which the will of the moment is such. But it remains a will in the extremely important sense of an ideal to which the man by implication commits himself every day of his life and whose claims he cannot repudiate without turning his back upon himself.

Collingwood and Blanshard are adamant in denying the viability of a Platonic conception of the good. Plato, reflecting on the fact that the thing one person holds to be good may be loathsome to others, was driven, in Collingwood's description, "into a wild-goose chase after some object that should be absolutely good, 'good in itself.'" On this point, Collingwood says, he respectfully declines to follow

the Greek master because "what is good is only good in some specific way: good 'as this' or good 'for that,' never just good or wholly
good or 'good in itself'" (*The New Leviathan* 80–81). Blanshard's
hero in developing a concept of the good is Aristotle. Blanshard
approaches the problem through a method "of which Aristotle was
the pioneer, a study of goodness that places it in its wider human
and biological context." Blanshard refutes G. E. Moore's "attempt
to make goodness of unvarying meaning, identical in a symphony,
a mathematical intuition and the taste of a sandwich." Such a
view of the good fails to consider how deeply goodness is "impli-
cated with human nature and faculty…. Man is a creature of
impulses, needs, and faculties; what he seems to be bent on is the
fulfilment of those impulses, the satisfaction of those needs, the
realization of those faculties…. [The] good is as various as they are,
and…to conceive of goodness rightly, when cut off from these
roots in human nature, is impossible" (291–92).

Rational goodness is so called because it is arrived at through
the workings of man's reason. Gardner reveals his faithfulness to
the theory of rational morality in that he too refuses to recognize
the existence of an "ideal good," living a life of its own in the form
of a Platonic idea. "The Good," Gardner argues, is a value which
exists "when embodied and, furthermore, [when] recognized as
embodied" (*OMF* 133). Since the point is crucial, we must allow
room for Gardner's full explanation:

> The view of the Good which I have presented denies (or at
> any rate avoids) the metaphysical assumption, seen in Hegel,
> for instance, that there are properties, subsistent entities,
> which attach to existent particulars (boy scouts, say, or mis-
> sionaries) but might without absurdity be supposed to attach
> to nothing. The idea of an imperishable form of the Good has
> always been appealing, since it keeps the Good from chang-
> ing with governments and hair styles; but actually we need
> not invent ghosts to keep things relatively stable. To say that
> by the Good a human being can mean only the human
> good—the only good he has any hope of understanding, that
> is, any hope of intuitively grasping—is not to say that the
> Good is a matter of opinion. To deduce from personal and
> cultural experience that the idea is there to be discovered,
> whether or not any man will ever have the wit to discover it,
> is to claim for the idea of the Good the same verifiable effica-
> cy, and in that sense "reality," that we claim for the struc-

ture of a properly functioning molecule. The Good is existential in the sense that its existence depends upon man's, not in the sense that it can be defined adequately by a clod's personal assertion. (137)

It follows from this definition of the good that rational goodness cannot be readily codified. Hence a system of morality which has rational goodness as its basic premise must necessarily be characterized by *nonfinality*. According to the theory of rational morality, goodness is a mental construction, and all mental processes, Collingwood points out, have an "*asymptotic* or *approximative* character." It is impossible to conceive of a mental process which "begins with pure ignorance and ends in pure knowledge. These are 'ideals': they lie outside the process of change leading toward the one and away from the other" (*The New Leviathan* 284).

Blanshard likewise insists on the nonfinality of rational goodness. He views man as a teleological being, always striving for the fulfilment of *new* desires:

What is good is what fulfils those impulses or strivings of which human nature essentially consists, and in fulfilling them brings satisfaction. The ends sought, and therefore the goods recognized, at any given time are provisional only; the fulfilment of present desire always leaves much to be desired; and hence our conception of the good is in course of constant revision. *The* good is nothing short of what would fulfil and satisfy wholly. (343)

However, no such total satisfaction is possible, and to operate with a finite conception of the good would be to go against everything we know about human nature.

Gardner is of the same persuasion: "Morality, then, describes actions or preparations for action (psychological actions); and since the possible number of actions in the universe is unlimited...morality is infinitely complex, too complex...to be reduced to any code" (*OMF* 134-35).

2

On the face of things the theory of rational goodness would seem to lead to a completely relativistic system of morality. The existence of an ideal, unchanging good toward which man can strive is denied, and each man is under the obligation to reason out what constitutes the good. In the light of these considerations, how are we to understand Gardner's claim that there are lasting values—"eternal verities"—which are valid for all men? In Gardner's mind such a claim is not a case of non sequitur. On the contrary, it follows by necessity from a proper understanding of how rational goodness works *in the context of civilizations*. In asserting his belief in universal values, Gardner once again reveals his indebtedness to the psychologically based theories of Collingwood and Blanshard: "There are principles in the world, 'eternal verities,' as Faulkner liked to say, *because of our nature*, and those principles can be discovered" (Edwards and Polsgrove 47; my italics). It is against the background of this carefully qualified belief in the existence of universal values that we should understand Gardner's confidence in the ultimately benevolent thrust of evolution. The key to our understanding of how the principle operates is the phrase *personal and cultural experience*. A collocation of Collingwood's and Blanshard's theories with that of Gardner will again help us see more clearly the philosophical foundations of Gardner's aesthetic theories.

	"How does a man become possessed of a social consciousness?" Collingwood asks in *The New Leviathan*. "How does he become able to think: 'We will'?" His point of reference in answering this question is as always his basic theory of man: "By the same process which enables him to think: 'I will.'"[5] By the time a man begins to interact consciously with other members of a community, he will long since have learned to distinguish between himself and something "not himself." "It is from experience of making this distinction, without which he cannot think of himself at all, that he comes to reflect on his own act of decision, in other words, to think: 'I will.'" For a man to have an idea of himself as a free agent he must recognize the existence of other free agents, as well as the existence of social relations between them and himself. We have already seen that a free agent is someone who is in a position to satisfy his desires. In sorting out his real from his false desires, he is aided by reason, which draws on previous experiences of satisfaction and frustration. A society, in Collingwood's definition, is a community in which members share a "social consciousness." By this term he understands "an act of deciding to become a member and to go on being a member: a will to assume the function of partnership with others in a common undertaking, and a will to carry out that function."

Collingwood's study is a descriptive one in that his aim is to give "a catalogue" of the functions of the modern European mind "as exemplified in its practical and theoretical working." This professed commitment to a historical presentation may explain why Collingwood only develops a theory of *how* a society comes into being, but does not speculate on *why* free agents should want to become members of a society. Blanshard and Gardner do offer an explanation of this phenomenon; briefly stated, their theory is that through the workings of rational will, a man seeking rational goodness will, provided his reason is sufficiently enlightened, invariably find that striving to bring about *the general good* will in the end always bring about the greatest good *also for the individual.*

When the discussion of the good is brought out of the individual and into the collective sphere, attention shifts from the *good* to the *moral:* "The Good for man is by another formulation (whenever action is called for) the *moral.* Morality is the body, or engine, of the Good" (*OMF* 134). Acting to bring about the good is thus a moral act. And the hub of morality for Gardner is the general good. Rightly understood, what is good for man "cannot be divorced from what is good for his society and environment" (134). Blanshard agrees: "*The good, in the sense of the ethical end, is the most comprehensive possible fulfilment and satisfaction of impulse-desire.* By a comprehensive fulfilment I mean one that takes account not only of this or that desire, but of our desires generally, and not only of this or that man's desires, but of all men's" (311).

How, then, is a person to achieve *coherence* in ethical behavior when he cannot refer to a universal and unchanging moral code? The theory of rational morality seeks the answer to this problem in an approach that Gardner suggests in his definition of the good cited above: by appealing to "personal and cultural experience" (*OMF* 137). Blanshard uses a similar phrase, holding that "'good' is not the name of a simple abstraction, but is, on the contrary, a term with a complex meaning that has long roots in human nature and its history" (315). For Collingwood "personal and cultural experience" is the very stuff of which civilizations are made.

The utilitarian aspect which characterizes the theory of rational goodness is an important element of Collingwood's concept of civilization; a civilization is created to work for a joint purpose, and it is a product of rational will: "The will to civilization is the will to earn one's own self-respect and the respect of the other members of one's own community; and this is done by the sheer exercise of will, joining with these others to do something about the situation in which you find yourselves."[6] It has been shown already that a person's need to consider the general good arises after rational analysis, which in turn has its base in his *personal* experiences of previous satisfaction and frustration. But *cultural* experience is an equally important element in the formation and continued life of a civilization. Without a mechanism for passing on previously established knowledge, communities would never evolve beyond the stage of instinctual animal behavior. Collingwood speaks reverently of how man first discovered, and then passed on from parent to child, the many skills necessary for an intelligent exploitation of the natural world. And the only way of ensuring that these skills were not lost was by forming communities, because no one man could retain more than the smallest share of the ancestral wisdom. A high level of civilization is therefore of necessity linked with a free flow of information. Collingwood can think on no better example of a truly civilized man than Chaucer's poor clerk: "And gladly would he learn and gladly would he teach." Collingwood insists that Chaucer's clerk is *not* an ideal figure, vanished long since. To Collingwood it is a self-evident truth that "all men have a natural desire for knowledge" and "a natural desire to impart knowledge." If this were not so, we could not explain how "any civilization, however low, ever continued in existence for more than one generation."

Brand Blanshard argues that all men have a natural desire for knowledge: "Nature itself has thus determined that we should seek certain forms of self-fulfilment.... [F]rom his very constitution [man] does and must regard knowledge and beauty as goods to be pursued. He is so made as to desire them, and fulfilling and satisfying such desires is what 'good' means" (331). *Because of their nature*, therefore, men have a number of goals in common. These are recognized through the assertion of rational will, and the creation of states is a means to the achievement and securing of these ends. Blanshard's bow to the importance of *cultural* experience shows up most markedly in his thoughts on education. Defending the need for continuity in educational policy, he reminds advocates of radical and all-encompassing scholastic reforms

that there is something absurd in asking each generation to start its experimentation afresh, that there are some things, indeed many things, which may now be regarded as settled, that there is some knowledge and poetry and music that *in virtue of having been found fulfilling and satisfying by actu-*

al ventures into it, repeated ten thousand times, may now be held without presumption to be really good, and enormously superior to some others. If experience can establish nothing, one wonders what education is for. (367; my italics)

But the importance of cultural experience is not limited to the sphere of formal education. It extends to all kinds of interpersonal relationships, and Blanshard's recognition of this fact leads to his seconding of Leslie Stephen's dictum that conscience is "the concentrated experience of the race." Conscience "makes us wiser than we know, because it is the deposit of parental example, of the instruction of teachers, and of the pressure of society, themselves in turn the product of centuries of experimentation" (33).

3

It is within the conceptual framework of a Collingwood and a Blanshard, then, that Gardner's defense of "eternal verities" must be understood. Eternal verities are "real and inherent values...which are prior to our individual existence" (*OMF* 24). Gardner, like Collingwood and Blanshard, links these values to man's nature. Bearing in mind Gardner's commitment to such a worldview, it is easy to see the philosophical reasons for the ongoing battle against existentialism in his novels. Similarly, it stands to reason that he should be weary of situation ethics: "I don't have a lot of love for situation ethics; it's no ethics. I think you have to have principled ethics which are based on a deep understanding of human nature and human need" (Christian 89). Gardner's belief in the existence of eternal verities lies behind his postulation of rational morality. The Good, he argues, "presents a goal for the human condition here in this world, a conceptual abstraction of our actual experience of moments of good in human life" (*OMF* 136). This "conceptual abstraction" is based on the conviction that there is "a significant coherence in human experience[,]...that some beliefs and attitudes are beneficial for the flowering of sensation and consciousness, while others, to a greater or lesser degree, constrict and tend to kill" (177). Gardner's novels and stories may be read as a series of investigations into the role of "eternal verities" in the lives of men (see Chapter 7), but it should be noted that the theoretical framework itself—the philosophical basis for undertaking these investigations—has also been submitted to fictional treatment. Paradoxically, we find these discussions of rational morality in Gardner's most recent work. In his earlier fiction he explores the if's and but's of specific values; in *Freddy's Book*, and particularly in "The Art of Living," he takes a closer look at the philosophical justification for defending values in the first place. In these two works his indebtedness to Darwin, Collingwood, and Blanshard shows up even more expressly than in his nonfictional comments on these matters.

Gardner has stated that *Freddy's Book* sprang from his interest in Darwinian theory and from a desire to explore the idea that "virtue is in fact more fit to survive than vice...or democracy more fit to survive than tyranny."[7] Asked about the genesis of this novel, Gardner explains that the story of Gustav was perfect for him because Gustav was the first democratic king, democratic in the sense that since all the Swedish nobility were killed in the Stockholm massacre, he had no established apparatus on which to rely in carrying out his political decisions; hence he had to depend on the consent of the people. Even though the book that Freddy gives to Winesap is entitled "King Gustav and the Devil," it is not Gustav who kills the Devil but his men, Lars-Goren and Bishop Brask, by supporting each other. So for Gardner, "and certainly [for] Freddy in telling the story, the credit goes to King Gustav, but really the credit goes to Sweden[,]...to mankind, to humanness." The Devil is "the archetypal symbol of pride, tyrannical pride," and in Freddy's allegory he is defeated by democratic forces, by democratic pride. Gardner concludes, "In other words, the greatest evil in the world turns into the greatest good in the world, and of course, that's relevant to Darwin and the notion of the survival of the fittest."

Bishop Brask's role in the overthrow of the Devil is particularly illuminating in that he contributes to it against his own better advice. Brask is one of Gardner's many skeptics; throughout the story he keeps returning to evolutionary ideas, but his interpretation of evolution is frequently in antithetical opposition to the democracy-is-more-fit-to-survive idea suggested through the book's ending. Upon first broaching the matter with Lars-Goren, the Bishop is on the "right" track. Talking of King Gustav's hobby of stock-breeding, he waxes philosophical:

> "What does it suggest, this stock-breeding? It suggests that, given enough time, we could transform the world, change every tree, every flower and insect.... Is it that that draws kings to the sport of breeding stock? Have they seen to the heart of the mystery? have they noticed that they're on to the

fundamental secret of God?... suppose it's the same with ideas, governments, even virtues?... We hear the expression 'Might makes right.' Suppose it's true—I mean *profoundly* true. Suppose there is in fact no good in the world except *that which survives*.... Create a form of government more effective than all others, in due time it will destroy or at any rate outlive all the others. What more could any king ask when he dies than to be remembered as the man who created such a government as that?" (199)

There is nothing in this little speech that contradicts the ultimate meaning of the book as explained by Gardner. In Gardner's view democracy as a form of government *is* "more effective than all others" and therefore most fit to survive. But Brask is an old political hand who has had experience with nothing but aristocratic rule, and he refuses to heed the stirrings, in his mind and heart, of a belief in benevolent evolution. Even though he is genuinely moved by the goodness of pastoral life in Lars-Goren's Hälsingland, he finds that the knight's simpleminded faith in Sweden's democratic potential is no match for the complexity of life in the cities. He fears that the lack of a strong central authority will lead to a kind of mob rule. For instance, he sees the growing influence of Luther's rebellion against papal autocratic rule as a forewarning of things to come:

"You think it's *reason* the Lutherans have introduced into human affairs? It's a new and terrifying tyranny—I think so. In the old days we knew who the tyrants were: King so-and-so. Bishop so-and-so. Queen X. Judge Y. The tyranny was official, however covert. We knew whom to watch. In the future every dog will have his plot and his secret arsenal." (221)

Outwardly Brask remains true to his skepticism till the very end. His last words are an indictment of Lars-Goren's motives for wanting to kill the Devil:

"It's for yourself you do this, my dear Lars-Goren! No one but yourself! What's your love for your children and wife but greed? What's your love of justice, your love for all so-called humanity, but a maniac's greed? Do you think they've elected you God, Lars-Goren? You're a tyrant! Mad as Tiberius! You'd kill them all as readily as you'd save them, you know

it! And if killing proves fittest, then it's killing that will survive! How can you act, then, confronted by such knowledge?
Maniac! Animal!" (244–45)

Brask's accusations against Lars-Goren are false. True, at the
moment of killing the Devil Lars-Goren is portrayed as animal-like,
proceeding as if by instinct, hardly uttering a word, thus offering a
stark contrast to the squealing of Brask, the perennial doubter and
nondoer. Having shed his knight's armor, Lars-Goren looks "like a
man from the world's first age, indistinguishable from a furry
beast" (241). But in the context this is a noble image. By killing the
Devil Lars-Goren becomes a Darwinian Everyman, symbolizing the
kind of strength, confidence, and ingenuity that have brought man
through a process of steady evolution to his present state of civilization. Lars-Goren does not kill the Devil for selfish reasons. As he
left the Lapps for his meeting with the Devil, "he was seeing his
family in his mind's eye, and rational or not, he was thinking he
must make the world safe for them" (235). Lars-Goren is not completely unmoved by Bishop Brask's doubts, but he possesses something which the Bishop lacks, what Keats termed negative capability: Lars-Goren is able to live with uncertainty and still act. When
Brask tries to demolish the knight's basic optimism by construing
hypothetical cases of the utmost ethical complexity, Lars-Goren
twice counters him by citing the Golden Rule: "One must be sure
of one's motives, needless to say. But it seems to me a man knows
when he's acting for justice, not out of personal fury—that is, when
he's acting by the Golden Rule and when he's not" (218). Darwin
called the Golden Rule "the foundation stone of morality." But the
Golden Rule—"do unto others as ye would they should do unto
you"—is nothing but another way of formulating the key concept
of rational morality, as Darwin understood in explaining how man
originally came upon the idea:

> Ultimately a highly-complex sentiment, having its first ori-
> gin in the social instincts, largely guided by the approbation
> of our fellow men, *ruled by reason, self-interest*, and in later
> times by deep religious feelings, confirmed by *instruction* and
> *habit*, all combined, constitute our moral sense or con-
> science. (1: 159; my italics)

We see that all the elements of "personal and cultural experience"
are present in Darwin's formula. Lars-Goren, for all his simplicity

in the sphere of ideas, emerges as a staunch defender of rational morality.

Finally, it should be noted that Bishop Brask's actions belie his skepticism and therefore help to prove it wrong. Even though he remains outwardly cynical to the very last, he recognizes a growing feeling of friendship for Lars-Goren. For all his protestations that their killing the Devil means nothing, he still accompanies the knight all the way. And at the very end, when he expects the usual sensation of despair, he feels joy. In spite of himself he recognizes some meaning in life: "Absurdly, for all his philosophy, he was glad to be alive and dying" (242). As Lars-Goren cuts the Devil's throat, King Gustav in faraway Stockholm suddenly has a vision; he tears up the execution orders he has been signing, thinking: "Let the Riksdag decide.... What concerns all should have the approval of all" (246). Inadvertently, Bishop Brask has contributed to the victory of the democratic forces he formerly feared.

"The Art of Living" is even more overtly concerned with evolutionary theory and the role of rational morality in the formation of civilizations. The short story is set, as has been noted already, in the United States of the late sixties: mention of TV news about the Vietnam War and campus riots helps define the mood of the story. The prevalent feeling is that "the world's in chaos" (281); the easiest thing would be to do nothing, to let the world drift. But Arnold Deller is a confessed Darwinian and refuses to back off; Deller is the central figure in the story, a somewhat comical but neverthless earnest, cook, who argues that life should be approached with the kind of care and high seriousness which a true professional—a cook, say—shows in his work. He argues for a return to rational morality in terms which strongly echo those of Blanshard: "We've got to think things out, understand our human nature, figure out how to become what we are" (282). Blanshard puts the problem only slightly differently: "Nature itself has thus determined that we should seek certain forms of self-fulfilment. It is only through the seeking of these ends that we have become what we are, only by continuing to seek them that we can become what we may be" (331).

Deller's explanation of how civilizations are formed is vintage Darwin, beginning with the assertion that man is a social animal: "It's one of those big instincts you can't get away from— comes of having babies that can't fend for themselves" (284). Darwin traces the origin of man's moral sense, a prerequisite for the development of civilizations, to "the enduring and always present nature of the social instincts," and social instincts, in turn, are "probably an extension of the parental or filial affections" (2: 374; 1: 77). Blanshard, too, propounds a view of man as a social animal: "In biological descent, and hence in instinctive complexion, we are connected far more closely with the most gregarious of animals than with the tiger or python" (359–60). Parental feelings, says Deller, evolve into love; first there was love of the child, then of relatives and neighbors, "since that also helps survival" (285). But equally basic is a feeling of hate for strangers because they represent potential threats against survival. Collingwood speaks in similar terms: Hobbes "was right to think that men are 'naturally' enemies to each other; so they are; but they are 'naturally' friends too" (*The New Leviathan* 305).

The cook's reasoning proceeds along familiar lines: man discovers that he best contributes to his own survival by devising ways in which to promote ordered social relations. Lars-Goren and Darwin speak of the Golden Rule; Blanshard talks about the rational will and the general good; Arnold Deller's name for the same principle is "love by policy" or "the art of living":

> "But what happens when Italians and Irishmen start trying to live in the same town? Or Englishmen and Welshmen, Germans, Jews, Chinamen, black men? When that begins to happen we've gotta expand our horizons, retrain our instincts a little.... We invent civilization and law courts.... That's when you've gotta use your head—you see? Love by policy, not just instinct. That's the Art of Living. Not just instinct; something you do on purpose. Art!" (286)

The theory we have been discussing throughout this chapter holds that the general good is also the greatest good for the individual; the theory further states that the evolution of civilizations is to be explained by man's recognition of, and acting on, this principle. It should be emphasized, however, that this process is *not* assumed to be automatic in the sense that once the idea of rational morality has been discovered, as it were, mankind may sit back in complacent anticipation of a steady improvement in the affairs of men. Collingwood was provoked into writing *The New Leviathan* by the perhaps most potent eruption of barbarism ever, the rise of Hitler's Third Reich. His book was clearly intended as a booster of Western morale, reminding free Europe of *how* it had come upon the gift of civilization and what truths it must never forget if it wanted to stay civilized. Blanshard reminds his readers that even though man in his finest hour will always choose to work for the general good, there is "no *compulsion* to act this way. I am free to follow the lesser good if I choose" (331).

The hub of rational morality is self-interest. This is less of a paradox than it may at first seem. As we have seen, the rational moralist argues his case by referring to the basic psychological mechanisms which govern human behavior. When he is wise— that is, when his rational will is most keenly at work—man will always work for the general good, because only then can he hope to contribute toward the implementation and preservation of a social order serving the good of the individual.

Gardner is of course also highly aware of man's propensity for erring when it comes to deciding upon what constitutes the most beneficial line of personal and collective action. "Humanness is coherent," he states in the concluding chapter of *On Moral Fiction*, "and can go right or wrong" (177). This is a most crucial point for our understanding of what motivates Gardner as a writer. His thematic concerns are dictated by his desire to contribute his ideas on how humanness can go right and wrong. However, his aesthetic theories are also greatly influenced by his commitment to a worldview based on rational morality. "Art's where it all comes together," Arnold Deller pleads (287), and nobody who has read *On Moral Fiction* can doubt that he speaks on behalf of his creator. The purpose of that book, Gardner says, is "to explain why moral art and moral criticism are necessary and, in a democracy, essential" (19).

Gardner assigns to art no less than a messianic role, thinking it *"civilization's single most significant device for learning* what must be affirmed and what must be denied" (*OMF* 146; my italics). Arnold Deller views the artist—again, we must assume, with the author's wholehearted approval—as a "model for humanity, some-one whose process could teach people the process of a higher art, the to-coin-a-phrase Art of Living" (300). Gardner is convinced that *art* is the best possible guide through what Trilling called "the thicket" of the mind's "own confusions and contradictions," and this conception of art as a *method of exploration* is one of the basic premises of Gardner's aesthetic theories.

THE AESTHETICS OF EXPLORATION: THEORETICAL CONSIDERATIONS

The dual aspect of Gardner's aesthetic credo—art as instruction *and* exploration—was largely lost in the din of the initial controversy over *On Moral Fiction.* When reviewers ignored Gardner's insistence on the exploratory, indeed epistemological, function of art, it cannot have been for its lack of prominence in the book, because Gardner makes his point again and again: "Art gropes" (9). "Art is as original and important as it is precisely because it does *not* start out with clear knowledge of what it means to say" (13). "Art is the means by which an artist comes to see; it is his peculiar, highly sophisticated and extremely demanding technique of discovery" (91). "Thus at its best fiction is...a way of thinking, a philosophical method" (107). Art, when it works properly, is an art which *explores.* The purpose of art is to instruct, yes, but instruction should come as a *result* of exploration. Whatever points of view the artist wants to put across to the reader must be duly tested, forged in the smithy of his craft.

Gardner does not provide a detailed or systematic philosophical defense for this insistence on the epistemological function of art. Considering the prominent position which this aesthetic concept is given in *On Moral Fiction,* this is a regrettable omission. However, if one collates statements made throughout *On Moral Fiction,* as well as in Gardner's other critical writings, one discovers that there exists a coherent philosophical basis also for this aspect of Gardner's aesthetic program.

1

Gardner has on several occasions identified and paid homage to the major sources of inspiration for his aesthetics of exploration. In *The Poetry of Chaucer* he cites Benedetto Croce and Collingwood as representatives of the modern view of art (modern in contradiction to the medievel view) as "a means of 'discovering' or 'expressing' reality" (369). This point is further clarified in his discussion of Collingwood's ideas in *On Moral Fiction*. In *The Principles of Art* Collingwood relates to aesthetic theory the general view of man's rise into consciousness which he outlined in *The New Leviathan*. "This rise into consciousness," Gardner says, "is in effect man's first creative act—one requiring an enormous amount of mental power—and, according to Collingwood, it is also man's first act of freedom." Gardner argues that the "creative thinking involved in art is an extraordinarily complicated version of this same activity of mind" (*OMF* 200).

A brief survey of the central aesthetic ideas of Croce and Collingwood may serve to provide a more systematically developed view of the philosophical underpinnings of Gardner's aesthetic theories than that provided by his own writings. It is not my contention that Gardner agrees with Croce and Collingwood in all the conclusions that they draw from their basic premises—many of the issues raised by their theories Gardner does not address at all—but he does share a number of their key assumptions, and it is to these that we now must turn.

In *The Principles of Art* Collingwood differentiates between, on the one hand, "magical art" (art intended to incite readers to action) and "amusement art" (art intended for entertainment only) and, on the other, "art proper." Magical art and amusement art are placed in the category of "technical" art because they spring from a means-and-ends view of the artistic process: the art object is constructed so as to produce a preconceived effect in the reader. Art proper, however, is defined as "the expression of emotion," and as such it is nontechnical because until the artist "has expressed his emotion, he does not yet know what emotion it is."[1]

Collingwood's description of the creation of "art proper" indeed draws on the categories he developed for the description of man's rise into consciousness in *The New Leviathan*. The first stage in the process of expressing an emotion is "a psychical, or sensuous-emotional experience." Any act of sensing has an emotional charge which we are vaguely aware of, but to which at the initial stage of sensing we are unable to give a name (cf. "appetite"). In the next stage consciousness allows us to "attend to" our sensations, enabling us to name them, so to speak: the psychophysical experience "is transformed from sense into imagination, or from impression into idea" (cf. "desire"; *The Principles of Art* 273–74).

This, then, is the basis on which Collingwood proceeds to make aesthetic judgment. In his mind, the phrase *good art* is a tautology, because art is by definition the expression of emotion, and to "express it, and to express it well, are the same thing." Bad art, therefore, is not an emotion badly expressed, but a failure to express emotions at all. "A bad work of art is an activity in which the agent tries to express a given emotion, but fails." Collingwood uses the term *corruption of consciousness* to describe an instance of an agent's failure to express an emotion (282–83).

Benedetto Croce is an idealist in the sense that for him nothing is real unless it is intuited or perceived by mind. Croce does not deny the existence of unperceived or pure matter the way Berkeley did, but he argues that we cannot know anything about this matter unless the impressions we receive from matter are converted into intuitions. Croce's aesthetic theories are determined by his idealist starting point; furthermore, his analysis of the processes involved in the aesthetic act corresponds very closely with that of Collingwood. Like Collingwood, Croce speaks of sensations and impressions. Where Collingwood talks of emotions (that is, emotions of consciousness), Croce uses the term *intuitions* (8), but otherwise we recognize Collingwood's scheme in Croce's differentiation between intuitions and sensations:

> And yet there is a sure method of distinguishing true intuition, true representation, from that which is inferior to it: the spiritual fact from the mechanical, passive, natural fact. Every true intuition or representation is also expression. That which does not objectify itself in expression is not intuition or representation, but sensation and mere natural fact. The spirit only intuits in making, forming, expressing.... Intuitive activity possesses intuitions to the extent that it expresses them. (56)

To Croce, aesthetics is the "science of successful expression," and like Collingwood he makes expression the yardstick of aesthetic judgment. Beauty, he says, is to be defined as "successful expression, or rather, as expression and nothing more, because expression when it is not successful is not expression. Consequently, the ugly is unsuccessful expression" (79).

The defining characteristic of this theory, then, is emphasis on expression, and, as we have seen, in *On Moral Fiction* Gardner's emphasis on the cognitive function of true art is no less strong than that of Collingwood and Croce. This does not imply that Gardner's ideas on the artistic process match completely those of Collingwood and Croce. For instance, we have no reason to assume that Gardner defines art as widely as do our two philosophers. To Collingwood and Croce any successful expression is by definition art. Carrying his logic to its utmost consequences, Collingwood declares that every "utterance and every gesture that each one of us makes is a work of art," provided the utterance is an instance of successful expression and not one of corrupt consciousness (*The Principles of Art* 285). Croce does not go quite that far, but he does hold that the distinction between art so-called and ordinary intuition is one of quantity rather than of quality, and he is led to affirm, for instance, that every "scientific work is also a work of art" (15, 25). Certain differences in method and extremity of view notwithstanding, a number of Gardner's statements in *On Moral Fiction* do seem inspired by the ideas of Collingwood and Croce, and his positions become clearer, and carry greater philosophical weight, when read through the theoretical spectacles provided by the British and Italian philosophers.

We have seen that Gardner postulates a close kinship between the creative thinking involved in art and man's rise into consciousness as it is described by Collingwood in *The New Leviathan;* in fact, he views the creative act as a refined and extended version of the same process (cf. *OMF* 200). Gardner would in all likelihood refrain from calling a scientific treatise a work of art, but he seems to share Croce's view that the difference between the kind of thinking that goes into the production of art and ordinary thinking processes is quantitative rather than qualitative. "What is generally called *par excellence* art," Croce argues, "collects intuitions that are wider and more complex than those which we generally experience, but these intuitions are always of sensations and impressions." Artists are people who "have a greater aptitude, a more frequent inclination fully to express certain complex states of the soul" (13). But the artist's raw material, the sensations and impressions, are basically the same as those that constitute the consciousness of any thinking being.

Gardner's view is similar. Using Collingwood's formula for

man's rise into consciousness as his starting point, he claims that similarly the "urgings of passion, both present and remembered, provide the poet with his 'fantasy'—the raw material of his fable" (*OMF* 200). Through a series of revisions the artist comes "to fuller and more totally conscious awareness of his feelings" (201), never knowing until his final draft exactly what those feelings will turn out to be. This hunting for the exact expression of the artist's feelings Gardner compares to the common experience of participating in a discussion, "sensing with every nerve end the truth that will not show itself, trying to put one's finger on where the speakers are going wrong, and at last, if one is lucky, recognizing, with a shock of relief, what it is that needs to be stated." Echoing Collingwood and Croce, Gardner says that a person who has had such an experience—and he claims, justifiably it seems, that we all have them more or less regularly—"could not *know* what he knew until he found words for it." For Gardner—and again we recognize Croce's phraseology—all "understanding is an articulation of intuitions" (153).

No doubt Gardner is his own prime source for generalizing in these terms about the artistic process. He has repeatedly told interviewers that his stance on an issue is always modified as a consequence of his writing about it; and in *On Moral Fiction* he gives an account of how the values and opinions he started out with in writing *October Light* proved oversimple at the end of the novel (114). However, the universality of his own experiences is borne out, he says, by his studies of literary history, a prime example being the successive drafts of Tolstoy's *Anna Karenina*, in which the initial story and its implications were turned almost completely around. In the successive drafts of works by, for instance, Dostoevski, Kafka, and Chaucer one can witness a similar process (108–9).

Croce's view that the artistic process is but a complex form of expression makes him deny that "the word *genius* or artistic genius, as distinct from the non-genius of the ordinary man, possesses more than a quantitative signification." Croce's proof is communicability. "Great artists are said to reveal us to ourselves," he says. "But how could this be possible, unless there were identity of nature between their imagination and ours, and unless the difference were only one of quantity?" (14). Gardner implicitly makes the same point when he says that a "test of creative energy is the test of efficient communication" (197). If anything, the artist's business is communication, and the whole concept of communication presupposes a belief in the existence of a communal consciousness.

From a philosophical point of view, these are important convictions because they indicate a certain ontological orientation on Gardner's part, an ontological orientation which springs directly from his epistemological persuasion. Peter Skagestad notes that Collingwood (as well as Karl Popper) is "deeply committed to the view that there is one and only one common human rationality, and that the presuppositions of alien people, past or present, are always in principle intelligible, given sufficient imagination, patience, and goodwill" (19). This conviction determined Collingwood's and Popper's approach to historical method. A similar conviction appears to have influenced Gardner's conception of the ultimate powers of art. A commitment to an aesthetics of exploration, Gardner says,

> reflects a fundamental conviction of the artist that the mind does not impose structures on reality (as existentialists claim)—arbitrarily maintaining now this, now that—but rather, as an element of total reality—a capsulated universe—discovers, in discovering itself, the world. The artist's theory, as revealed by his method (however artists may deny it), is that the things he thinks when he thinks most dispassionately—not "objectively," quite, but with passionate commitment to discovering whatever may happen to be true (not merely proving that some particular thing is true)—that the ideas the artist gets, to put it another way, when he thinks with the help of the full artistic method, are absolutely valid, true not only for himself but for everyone, or at least for all human beings. (OMF 122–23)

The idea that by mining the depths of his own consciousness the artist can discover truths that are valid for everyone presupposes a belief in the possibility of sharing experiences, a belief that human consciousness is governed by universal laws. Against this background Gardner's declared interest in the theories of Jung is easy to understand (Winther 511). The ontological basis for Gardner's trust in art's ability to produce reliable "hypotheses on the structure of reality" (OMF 120) is furthermore consistent with the concept of rational morality. According to that theory the advent of civilizations is explainable in terms of man's inborn inclination to work for the general good; such a theory would become meaningless unless it presupposed a universal modus operandi of man's mental processes.

"What kind of articulation of his intuition satisfies the artist?" Gardner asks toward the end of *On Moral Fiction*. His answer would seem impressionistic were it not for the philosophical ballast provided by the aesthetic theories of Collingwood and Croce: "The answer is, one which honestly feels to him like art" (*OMF* 169). "The meaning of art is hard to define satisfactorily," Gardner admits, but "it works or not depending on how it feels" (151, 152). When we remember the systematic thinking which underlies such a statement, we realize that Gardner does not advocate aesthetic relativism; "how it feels" is not an unruly variable but a constant which can be defined, however tentatively. Since an artist's raw material is some element or other of a common consciousness, it follows that the question "Is this a truthful expression of a given emotion?" should ideally produce the same answer in different artists. Such a view of the artistic process still does not make the question of judging artistic competence altogether unproblematic. The manifestations of consciousness, Gardner points out, are infinitely complex, and naming them requires great mental energy, sensitivity, and alertness (200).

Since Gardner's theory of art as process of exploration conforms with the theory of expression, it is not surprising that his basis for making aesthetic judgments is also identical with that of Croce and Collingwood. Croce defines beauty as "successful expression"; to Gardner beauty is "truth of feeling" (*OMF* 144). "The true critic," he claims, "knows that badness in art has to do...with the artist's...lack of truthfulness, the degree to which, for him, working at art is a morally indifferent act" (56). In this formulation one easily recognizes Collingwood's concept of "corrupt consciousness" and Croce's definition of "ugly art" as unsuccessful expression.

Gardner, like Croce and Collingwood, belongs in the camp of philosophical idealism, at least some of the time. In keeping with his idea that the world of matter possesses no other knowable qualities or characteristics than the ones perceived by the human mind, Croce argues that it is wrong to speak of *"beautiful things or physical beauty*. This combination of words constitutes a verbal paradox, for beautiful is not a physical fact; it does not belong to things, but to the activity of man, to spiritual energy" (97). Collingwood defines beauty in similar terms. He describes the aesthetic experience as an "autonomous activity." In his view, "to say that beauty is subjective means that the aesthetic experiences which we enjoy in connexion with certain things arise not from any quality that they possess, which if they did possess it would be called beauty, but from our own aesthetic activity" (*The Principles of Art* 40–41).

Idealism is of course not an unequivocal term. In calling Croce, Collingwood, and Gardner idealists, my chief concern is not to characterize their metaphysical beliefs, but to signal their epistemological orientation. Gardner's views on beauty are, for instance, not compatible with Plato's position in the *Philebus*, where the Greek idealist philosopher takes "beauty to be a property ingredient in things" whose existence "is not dependent upon, or affected by, perceiving it" (Stolnitz 266). Rather, Gardner agrees with Poe (and with Croce and Collingwood), who saw beauty not as a quality, but as an effect. In Gardner's interpretation this means that "as vibrations are not sound except when they strike an eardrum, so beauty *comes alive* in the mind of the beholder" (*OMF* 143). To recognize this, Gardner says, is "to get rid of a confusion which has plagued aestheticians for centuries.... Beauty is something that doesn't exist except in the instant it jars the soul and thus at once comes into being and attracts" (156).

2

It would seem, then, that Gardner is in agreement with a number of the underlying premises and the practical ramifications of the theory of expression. However, on one important point Croce/Collingwood and Gardner go their separate ways: on the matter of *artistic technique*. Croce argues that by the term *artistic technique* we should understand "*knowledge at the service of the practical activity directed to producing stimuli to aesthetic reproduction.*" When a would-be artist looks around for a technique to aid him in *finding* the right expression for his intuitions, he will look in vain. Expression, "considered in itself, is a primary theoretic activity," and therefore it precedes practice, that is, technique, or knowledge about ways in which to externalize and communicate intuitions or emotions. "Expression does not possess *means*," Croce says, "because it has not an end" (111–12).

Gardner takes a different approach. Throughout his career as a writer he also taught creative writing at several American universities, a practice which would seem incompatible with the precepts of Croce's aesthetics. Justifying the position that creative writing can indeed be taught, Gardner takes issue with "the tendency that fiction has developed—the notion of fiction as *just* expression...[O]f course fiction is expression, of course painting is expression; in fact if there's not expression, then it's dead. But that's not all. When you're writing a story you ought to know: now I'm at the lady-is-about-to-open-the-dangerous-door scene" (Cuomo and Ponsat 48). He elaborates on this view in *On Moral Fiction*. Developing, in true Crocean fashion, the idea that beauty is "truth of feeling," he goes on to say that the artist works his way back to moments of beauty in life by *formal* means (144). This view influences, among other things, Gardner's concept of *imitation* through the presentation and study of *character*. Fiction is a laboratory experiment, Gardner says, "too difficult and dangerous to try in the world but safe and important in the mirror image of reality in the writer's mind" (115–16). The writer works out a moral problem by examining how a character behaves when subjected to "the pressures of situation working for and against him (what other characters in the fiction feel and need, what imperatives nature and custom urge)." Suspense is an important element in the process, and it is created by the writer's "torturing" the reader with alternative possibilities, delaying the climactic action. A character's actions do not simply reflect his nature but "his nature as the embodiment of some particular theory of reality and the rejection, right or wrong, of other theories. When the fiction is 'tight,' as the New Critics used to say, the alternatives are severally represented by the fiction's minor characters, and no charactrer [sic] is without philosophical function" (114–15). In an interview Gardner describes how the enormous cast of *The Sunlight Dialogues* evolved out of the need to put ideational and emotional pressures on the central character, Clumly (Natov and DeLuca 126).

But imitation is not the only artistic road to discovery for Gardner. Another is to explore the meaning of what he calls "*symbolic association*" (*OMF* 118; my italics). Gardner's conviction that "one of the ways in which fiction thinks is by discovering deep metaphoric identities" (119) stems from his Iowa Writers' Workshop days, where the members used to play the game "Smoke." The game consisted in one person choosing a famous person, whom he would describe in terms of what kind of insect the person would be, and what kind of animal, transportation, weather, and so forth, would be likely to be associated with him. What the participants discovered was that "our associations are remarkably similar," and the game proved to Gardner "the mysterious rightness of a good metaphor—the one requisite for the poet, Aristotle says, that cannot be taught" (119). Even though Gardner

does not explain the phenomenon in those terms, this conviction
ties in well with the belief, essential to the theory of expression, in
the existence of a common consciousness, as already discussed.
For the creative artist metaphoric sensitivity of this kind is an
invaluable resource, since it provides him with a method for mining the emotional and intellectual depths of his characters while at
the same time communicating his findings to the reader. Discovering the right metaphors with which to describe a person (one that
"feels right" to the artist), placing the character in this or that setting and seeing how he fares, leads the writer, and the reader, to
discoveries about the characters that could not be made by discursive thought alone. So Grendel, the self-appointed outcast, is an
Anglo-Saxon monster; Clumly is described as a mole, stubbornly
burrowing his way through the confusions spread by the Sunlight
Man; Henry Soames agonizes in the shadows cast by the overpowering Nickel Mountains; it takes the open seas to curb Jonathan
Upchurch's youthful ambitions; and the unlocking of James Page's
heart coincides with the "unlocking" of the Vermont countryside.
Certainly, fictional practices like these are not unique to Gardner's
novels and stories, but his theorizing about them helps to explain
the welter of descriptive detail in his fiction, pointed to and
applauded by, for instance, Robert Towers in his review of *Mickelsson's Ghosts.* Gardner's strong belief in the aesthetic importance and power of symbolic association also accounts for one very
pronounced stylistic habit on his part: the merest glance at almost
any page written by this author will reveal an extraordinary fondness for the *simile.*

Gardner points to a third way in which fiction turns into a
mode of thought. It is closely related to the method of working by
symbolic association, and it consists in discovering "how one dark
metaphor relates to another" (*OMF* 120). Having worked his way
through the first draft of a story, rendering scene by scene, character by character, by means of concrete images or metaphoric
expressions (cf. symbolic association), the writer should go back
over his draft, looking for "odd connections, strange and seemingly
inexplicable repetitions," because in art, "repetition is always a
signal, intentional or not." Sometimes the meaning of the repetition will become clear to the writer, pointing to logical relationships that had so far eluded him. At other times no such overt
meaning materializes, but the writer may still decide to retain the
repetition because—and here we encounter once again the expres-
sionist terminology—it "feels right" (121–22).

Repetition in art is something that Gardner has dealt with in his medieval scholarship, and what he has to say about it in that context provides a useful elaboration on his comments in *On Moral Fiction*. In his book on Christian poetry in Old English Gardner starts out with a chapter entitled "Premises," where he adopts a wide definition of allegory, derived from Angus Fletcher:[2] "Let *allegory* be understood here as shorthand for the idea that poetry is the most suggestive of all forms of literature, enforcing its suggestions by a greater distortion of natural speech than any other genre can afford." Gardner's concern is with different ways of "poetic signaling," one of the most important ones being *"rhythmic encoding."* Poetic style "suggests more than it states, and, in large measure, its suggestion is controlled." Even though his discussion is addressed to poetry, the same principles apply to fiction. To illustrate this Gardner offers an example that bears special interest for readers of *Nickel Mountain:*

> For instance, if a novelist speaks, at several points in his narrative, of the mountains looming above his characters, the reiteration implies some meaning in the image. Whether the writer has a conscious purpose (e.g., mountains as signs of the littleness of man) or no conscious purpose, merely an unexamined nervous feeling about mountains, the image implies something, and the reader is teased toward a meaning beyond that which is stated.

Rhythmic encoding may be verbal, that is, take the form of verbal echoes, or it may consist in parallel images or events, in short, "any form of stylistic or structural repetition which...catches the reader's attention and prompts him to ask himself what the point is, or...what the connection between the disturbed details may be" (*The Construction of Christian Poetry in Old English* 11–14).

It should perhaps be noted that in his studies of medieval literature Gardner treats rhythmic encoding primarily as a rhetorical device in the classical sense of that term, that is, as a method by which the writer communicates preestablished meaning; in *On Moral Fiction* it is primarily treated as an instrument of discovery, one of several literary techniques which the writer may employ to discover subconscious and hidden connections in his own mind. Only after this process is completed does the repetition become a rhetorical device in the traditional sense in that it communicates the writer's own findings to the reader.

The repeated use of monkey imagery in the title novella as well as in several of the preceding stories of *The King's Indian* provides a good example of how rhythmic encoding works in Gardner's own fiction. The use of this imagery contributes toward the formulation of one of the central themes in the collection: man's need to accept his own fallibility.

The fallibility motif is presented with iconographic clarity in a crucial scene toward the end of "The King's Indian." In this novella the protagonist, Jonathan Upchurch, is initially powerfully tempted by the state of metaphysical certainty and harmony which is the promise of the *Jerusalem*'s quest for transcendence of the physical laws governing time and space. In the course of events Jonathan comes to realize that transcendence is not such a desirable goal after all. His acceptance of this fact is signalled by his recognition and acceptance of man's nonideal and inescapable physicality. If man is a physical being, he is also fallible, the victim of the forces of mutability. In the scene in question Coleridgean grace comes to Jonathan Upchurch and Miranda Flint when they declare their mutual love *in spite of* their physical shortcomings and blemishes: Miranda's former beauty has been transformed to physical ugliness through the violent rape committed by the ship's second mate, Wilkins; Jonathan is hopelessly wall-eyed. Both Jonathan and Miranda have been engaged in a quest for eternal verities in the form of mystical and absolute knowledge, but now they have learned to accept a less than ideal, earth-oriented, existence. Looking at Miranda's tear-streaked face after the rape, Jonathan reflects that it is no longer the face of a beautiful woman, but "a mutilated child's, a monkey's" (304). The monkey image works in its own right here, contrasting Miranda's earlier beauty with the comical face of a monkey. Furthermore, the image is given resonance by its repeated use earlier in the same story, as well as in the preceding stories, all of them concerned with themes that relate in one way or another to the themes explored in the title novella.

Wilkins is another quester after eternal truths and absolute answers. Unlike Jonathan and Miranda, he is unable finally to reconcile the real with the ideal, and in frustration and despair he takes his own life. In the story he is presented as a half-breed with many animal-like features, one of these being "his big monkey's ears" (228). A related character is Dr. Hunter in "The Ravages of Spring," who tries to achieve eternal life by recreating his own image through clones. At one point he is said to cling to the narrator's hand "like a monkey" (51). All of these characters, Miranda,

Wilkins, and Dr. Hunter, are united by their longing for transcendence. Linking them together through monkey imagery may be one way in which to universalize the nature of this quest. Making quixotic gestures as these characters do is not an uncommon human characteristic; even though the quest for ultimate answers may take different forms, it constitutes an important element of human fallibility.

The quest for transcendence is given a rather grotesque expression in the case of Miranda, Wilkins, and Dr. Hunter. But their efforts receive a touch of comedy and human warmth through three other occurrences of the same image. The first time Gardner uses monkey imagery in the collection is in the opening short story, "Pastoral Care." In this story the protagonist is a rather proud and arrogant character, the Reverend Pick, whose self-importance is underscored by his name (he picks his peers carefully). Mrs. Ellis is one of several characters in the story toward whom Pick cannot help but feel condescension. At one point she too is said to have the grip of a monkey (10). Even though Pick, the narrator, no doubt has negative associations when employing the image, Mrs. Ellis, and through her the image, is redeemed by the contrast which is established between her and the Reverend. Mrs. Ellis is comical in her naïveté concerning the role of Christian missionaries in developing countries, but she is also gentle hearted and well intentioned. For one thing she cuts a decidedly more positive figure than Pick, who says he feels sympathy with her in her distress, "but not enough sympathy to abandon [his] theology, accept her as an equal" (10).

"The Temptation of St. Ivo" gives us a central experience in the life of the proud and extremely fat monk Brother Ivo. Ivo, whose comical physical frame is emphasized (reinforced through Herbert L. Fink's highly expressive drawing), is also associated with the image, or rather, he makes use of it in talking about the parodical knight he meets in his nocturnal search for Brother Nicholas; in speculating that perhaps the knight's face inside the steel armor is that of "an evil monkey," Ivo is in reality projecting his perception of his own role vis à vis the world. His response to the appearance of the knight is determined, as he himself realizes, by habits stemming from the special form his solipsism takes, that is, his pride in his skill as a decorator of sacred manuscripts: "My mind has lost control: The rules, techniques of a lifetime devoted to allegory have ruined me" (88). Whatever ominous overtones the image "evil monkey" may have carried are effectively deflated by the ending of the story, which gives us a Cervantes-like, richly comical image of Brother Ivo hanging on for dear life to the steel skeleton containing the antiheroically trembling knight, plumes bobbing as the horse floats "through the moonlit mist" (89).

The most obvious linking of the monkey image with the idea of man as essentially comical is found in an amusing passage in "King Gregor and the Fool." King John is sent for to judge whether or not the Fool's gem of a poem ("*You think I'm small because I'm lazy; / But big brave knights get killed. That's crazy.*") is biblical, as the Fool claims in an effort to save his neck. If the poem is judged nonbiblical, the Fool's head will roll, because King Gregor thinks him guilty of spreading subversive ideas about warfare. After King John has reached his Solomonic verdict (The poem, he claims grandly, "is distinctly Biblical. Loosely."), the Fool starts to jump up and down "as if he thought he were a monkey" (169). This interlude takes place in the court of Queen Louisa, who is the true heroine of the story. She is a remarkable figure who possesses the enviable ability to change into a toad when she so wishes. In a sense she may be seen as Gardner's Everyman; even though she is highly comical, she has a potential for goodness, and she is utterly lovable.

One final word on monkey imagery. In "The King's Indian" Gardner alludes extensively to *Moby-Dick*, and knowing Gardner's propensity for literary game playing, it is not implausible to read into the pervasive use of monkey imagery in *The King's Indian* a distant echo of Melville's "Monkey-Rope" chapter. In that case the image would serve as one more reminder that we are all united by the common bond—or monkey-rope—of comical fallibility.

Having dealt with imitation, symbolic association, and repetition as means of artistic exploration, Gardner turns to "one last check on fiction's honesty: tradition." No author writes in a vacuum, Gardner reminds us:

> The medium of literary art is not language but language plus the writer's experience and imagination and, above all, the whole of the literary tradition he knows. Just as the writer comes to discoveries by studying the accidental implications of what he's said, he comes to discoveries by trying to say what he wants to say without violating the form or combination of forms to which he's committed. (*OMF* 124)

Actively struggling with literary tradition, Gardner claims, provides the writer with rich possibilities *for making discoveries* about the human condition. This is a most important observation for anyone who wants to study Gardner's trademarks as a writer of fiction, because this view of tradition has indeed greatly influenced the composition of his works.

TRADITION AND THE
ARTIST'S MOMENT

The correct assessment of literary expression, Gardner argues in *On Moral Fiction*, "cannot safely treat the work of art in isolation from its background: the tradition behind the work and the moment (time and place) of its appearance" (163). "Improving" slightly on T. S. Eliot's famous essay, he states one important reason why the Western literary tradition has come to put such an indelible mark on his own fiction:

> To speak of "tradition and individual talent" is to speak misleadingly, though not incorrectly. We would do better to speak of the convergence of tradition and the individual artist's moment. The artist is a man of maximum sensitivity, a man who sees and feels more things in more precise detail than do the people around him, partly because he has excellent emotional and intellectual equipment, including—above all, perhaps—the security which makes for shamelessness, and partly because he has special machinery for seeing and feeling: the tradition of his art. (167)

Entering into an active dialogue with the literary tradition serves a very clear and precise function for Gardner: it is one of the most important ways in which he sets out to make his literary discoveries. This involvement with tradition has resulted in two chief strategies: first and foremost, his heavily allusive style (to be discussed in Chapters 5 and 6), and his explorations of *the formative influence of genre*.

1

The first book to be published bearing Gardner's name is an anthology of prose fiction texts called *The Forms of Fiction*, and it reflects an understanding of genre which has considerable bearing on his own literary practice.[1] The texts in the collection, which Gardner edited together with Lennis Dunlap, are grouped according to certain genre categories (sketch, fable, yarn, tale, short story, and novella), and the editors' categories are indeed determined on the basis of a combination of what Wellek and Warren call "inner" and "outer" form. The rationale behind the book explains Gardner's emphasis on the formative importance of genre; in the introduction to their anthology the editors argue that although

> all good works of fiction are similar in certain important respects, they are strikingly different in others. Different basic forms of fiction select different elements and organize these elements in different ways. A reader's failure to recognize the difference between fictional forms may lead to serious misunderstanding of the nature, function, and value of specific works. (23)

This insistence on genre as a formative element in the literary process carries no special distinction in that it conforms with the credenda of several recent schools of criticism.

What makes Gardner a special case, however, is the *epistemological importance* he attributes to genre, and this orientation may explain the wide range of artistic expression that characterizes his production. Gardner calls moving from one form to another "genre-jumping," by which he also understands the crossing of one genre with another, and it is something he engages in because it gives him a new instrument with which to explore reality. Thus genre provides Gardner with yet another means of discovery:

> It basically comes to the fact for me that literature, writing, is a way of thinking about things and when you change your instrument, you see different things. The result is that when...you write a tale and cross it with the yarn or sketch or whatever, what comes out is something you never could have dreamed would come out. I mean you know the plot and the characters, but the genres you're pushing make you see things where you wouldn't have seen without them. (Harvey 79)

Some critics have explored the importance of genre in Gardner's writings, focussing especially on the author's use of *pastoral* conventions. David Cowart, in the article *"Et in Arcadia Ego:* Gardner's Early Pastoral Novels," detects elements of the pastoral not only in *Nickel Mountain,* which Gardner subtitled "A Pastoral Novel," but also in *The Resurrection, The Wreckage of Agathon,* and *October Light.*

The Prologue to *The Resurrection* describes a graveyard where James Chandler, the protagonist, is buried. In this scene great emphasis is put on the vegetation cycle, on the coming and going of the seasons. The novel proper describes how Chandler, a professor of philosophy, is confronted with the news of his imminent death, his move from California back to his native, and rural, Batavia, and his struggle to come to terms with death and mutability. He resolves the conflict, if only marginally, when he comes to realize that it is "not the beauty of the world one must affirm but *the world,* the buzzing blooming confusion itself" (229). Thus Chandler becomes reconciled with the idea of mutability through an acceptance of life as an interplay of positive and negative forces.

Approaching *The Resurrection* with a pastoral framework in mind does not necessarily serve to elicit meaning, but it provides an extra focus and a resonance for the central conflict. In the case of *Nickel Mountain* an awareness of the pastoral frame of reference helps the reader to discover connections which might otherwise have gone unnoticed. The central concerns are the same as those of *The Resurrection,* although with a different slant. Whereas James Chandler loves ideas to the point where he forgets to love his family, Henry Soames's problem is a *surplus* of love, a self-effacing willingness to take on the burdens of the whole community. The pastoral frame helps us to see Henry's role more clearly; he is, as Cowart points out, a "Pastor" for all the needy who happen to stop by his diner. But this profusion of love proves counterproductive; when Simon Bale dies in an accident caused by Henry Soames, the latter is unable to forgive himself and he sinks into a state of paralysis as a result of an overpowering sense of guilt. He is finally brought out of this state when he realizes that the point is not to achieve crucifixion. Early in the novel he makes his "pastoral" ambition quite clear: "It's finding something to be crucified for. That's what a man has to have.... Crucifixion" (42). Later he comes to see that what one should aim for instead is communion; the ideal is not to *be* Christ (the archetypal Shepherd), the one responsible for the well-being of everyone, but to be Christ-*like.* Cowart shows convincingly how the novel, partly as a result of a shift in point of view, moves from a concentration on human isolation to a sense of community, the responsibility for everyone's welfare being shared. Again the pastoral framework reinforces the meaning of the narrative, this time through a contrast which is set up between country and city. In trying to make up his mind on what to do about Simon Bale, Henry is reminded of a story he once read in the newspaper: "Some old man had been stabbed in New York City, it said in the paper, and there were fifteen people standing around and even when he asked them to, they never even called the police" (178). Willard Freund, who leaves the community for the city, is changed from a youngster full of life and enthusiasm into a cynic who feels nothing but contempt for the simplemindedness of the villagers who brought him up and nurtured him.

But, Cowart argues, the pastoral frame does not serve as a romantic gloss, turning the novel into an updated version of a sentimentalized classic pastoral: "These are real people in a real setting, their lives hard but solid," and the characters "spend a good deal of their time clomping around in 'good honest shit.'" In Cowart's reading the novel "makes no overt claims for the rural life, but as the reader comes to know Henry Soames and his community he cannot fail to recognize that these people have a sense of shared values and of community that is of inestimable value in surviving the manifold shocks of modern life" (11).

Cowart is no doubt right in arguing that Gardner does not hold up a sentimentalized version of life in the country as the one and only right way to live. However, it is possible to see the pastoral element as part of a metaphysical equation, and if we view it in that perspective, there is no doubt that the pastoral alternative has held powerful sway over his imagination. In his eloquent essay on "the Manichaean Pastoralism" of Gardner's novels, Samuel Coale makes a persuasive case for placing Gardner in an "ongoing and 'mainline' tradition" in American literature; this tradition involves writers like Hawthorne, Melville, and Faulkner, and the tension these writers treat is that which Faulkner called "the human heart in conflict with itself":

The garden and the machine confront each other anew in Gardner's fiction. The voice of the garden, linked to the pastoral impulse with its love of nature and poetic longings, confronts the voice of the machine, linked to the darker Manichaean belief that the world is mere accident, brute force controls all history, and only outright manipulation will keep things running. (20)

Coale argues convincingly that this conflict is never completely resolved in Gardner, but at least in *Nickel Mountain* the central character is able to derive some measure of peace from involving himself "with birth, death, weddings, those ceremonial rituals that come and go with the seasons" (21). "It was different in the country," Henry observes, "where a man's life or a family's past was not so quickly swallowed up, where the ordinariness of thinking creatures was obvious only when you thought a minute, not an inescapable conclusion that crushed the soul the way pavement shattered men's arches" (179). *Nickel Mountain* ends the way *The Resurrection* begins: with a graveyard scene. Henry and his son, two generations, return from hunting, with a dead rabbit in their canvas bag, and they pass by a graveyard where two old people are having their son's coffin—the son died fifty years earlier, at the age of fourteen—dug up to be moved to the graveyard where they themselves plan to be buried. Jimmy, Henry's son, is thoroughly excited about the idea of seeing a dead body, whereas the grave diggers are matter-of-fact and experts at their work, which is described in graphic detail; in the background there is the sound of a tractor plowing for winter wheat. The scene is obviously meant to underscore the inevitability, but also the ordinariness, of death, and the promise of the life cycle. The focal point of the tableau is Henry, taking pills against his heart problem, reconciled with the idea of death and instilled with a sense of "the holiness of things" and the interdependency of all nature. Never a man to find words that do justice to his emotions, Henry says sadly: "'Life goes on,'...and the words filled him with a pleasant sense of grief. He thought of his own approaching death, how Callie and Jimmy would be heartbroken for a while, as he'd been heartbroken when his father died, but would after a while forget a little, turn back to the world of the living, as was right" (308).

The tranquility which is the dominant tone at the end of *Nickel Mountain* resonates with a tradition that goes back to Theocritus and Vergil. It is, however, a mode which is difficult to maintain in the twentieth century, and Coale shows that the pastoral tranquility is shattered in *The Sunlight Dialogues*; Stony Hill farm, where Arthur Hodge, Sr., held everything together through his unified vision, *was* a pastoral garden, a place where natural scenes "shimmer with an inherent grace" (22), but is abandoned by

Hodge's descendants and ends up by being burnt down. Hodge's vision suffers fragmentation through "a kind of power failure" in his sons, an inability to unite vision and practical knowledge in the face of the pressures of a disintegrating civilization (*SD* 576). The pastoral mode reasserts itself marginally at the end of the novel, however, when Clumly addresses a meeting of farmers to explain his new vision of law and order, a vision in which the need for communal care is as important as is the meeting of the demands of the law.

In *October Light* the pendulum swings back. Initially the rural setting does not serve a liberating purpose; emphasis is placed on James L. Page's fanatical work ethic, instilled by the demands made upon him during a long life as a farmer. The "locking in" of the Vermont countryside in October matches the locking in that takes place in Page's intransigent soul. Slowly, however, the disastrous effects of Page's stubborn views begin to dawn on him; gradually he is awakened to what he is missing, being ruled by "his excessive Yankee pride in workmanship, his greed, his refusal to stop and simply look, the way Ed Thomas had looked" (432). In "Ed's Song" James sits through a sermon on the beauty of the changing seasons and the life cycle, and when the Vermont countryside starts to "unlock" in the spring, so does James's frozen heart.

Neither Cowart nor Coale counts *Freddy's Book* among Gardner's pastoral novels, but that novel also invites reflection on Gardner's handling of the pastoral tradition. Here the promise of stability and equilibrium to be achieved through a rural retreat is again muted. The book's main narrator is the mammoth son of Sven Agaard, a professor of history living in the rural outskirts of Madison, Wisconsin. The young boy's gigantic physical frame is the result of a genetic disorder. Freddy tries to protect himself from society's taunts and cruel treatment of the outsider by literally locking himself up in the house he shares with his father. He works his way out of his isolation through bibliotherapy, by writing an allegory set in the Sweden of Gustav Vasa. Freddy's projection of himself is Lars-Goren Bergqvist, one of Gustav's men, like Freddy a giant of a man, eight feet tall. Lars-Goren is afraid of only one thing, the Devil, who in the allegory comes to represent everything that Freddy fears in society. Lars-Goren tries to flee from the Devil as well as from the dangers resulting from the unsettled political situation at the time. He goes to his castle in Hälsingland, but this rural retreat offers no permanent solution. The precariousness of his situation leads Lars-Goren to fantasizing about the ultimate retreat, a pastoral landscape in extremis: the white expanses of snowy Lapland. "It's something about the simplicity," he explains to his family, "the absolute simplicity of the landscape, the light, the inescapable concern with necessities, nothing more" (149). However, Lars-Goren realizes that it is not possible to solve his problems through retreat; in killing the Devil he acts vicariously for Freddy, who through the writing of the allegory gets ready for his reentry into society. As the author has pointed out, giving his book to Winesap is Freddy's first step in that direction (Winther 521).

The final sentence of Freddy's narrative is significant in relation to the pastoral framework: "There was no light anywhere, except for the yellow light of cities" (246). The death of the Devil, as pointed out already, represents a victory for the nascent forces of democracy in a totalitarian Europe; Freddy invokes the "yellow light of cities," his symbol of hope, in the context of a vision in which the Russian tsar declares war on Poland for their "daring to think lightly of the tsar." Thus Freddy is ready to take on the confusion of the cities, signalling a newfound willingness to tackle the complexities of modern existence.

This denouement represents a reversal of the function of the pastoral element in *Nickel Mountain*. The urban alternative is presented as fertile ground for the forces of entropy in both novels. It is easy to stay virtuous in the country, Bishop Brask reminds Lars-Goren, "But who can live in Stockholm as you live here in Hälsingland?... what are the cities but hotbeds of rivalry and cunning, fear and exploitation? It's the old story—Abraham and Lot: Abraham up there with his sheep in the mountains, Lot struggling to stay honest down in Sodom and Gomorrah." After a vivid listing of the many evils that accompany city life, Bishop Brask puts down Lars-Goren's optimistic outlook with characteristic sarcasm: "Ah yes...complexity's a terrible thing" (214–15). Unlike Henry Soames, Freddy willingly takes on this complexity: he moves *from* a pastoral *to* an urban landscape. The commanding symbol of community and human interdependency is thus no longer the Catskills of *Nickel Mountain*, but the bustling cities of Gustav Vasa's Sweden.

In *Mickelsson's Ghosts* Gardner employs the pastoral framework one last time. Like James Chandler, Mickelsson, another professor of philosophy, retires to the country in a time of trial. He suffers from no physical disease, unless one counts his growing alcoholism, but he is dying a slow professional and emotional death, and his move to an old house in rural Pennsylvania is a last attempt to sort out his many problems. In this novel the expectations raised by the pastoral frame are thwarted from the very start. Mickelsson's house is haunted, the locals are constantly at each other's throats, and their few protestations of friendliness toward Mickelsson are marked by an ambiguity which he cannot help but experience as almost threatening. Mickelsson attempts to regain stability and a sense of purpose through an elaborate restoring of the old house, trying James Page's recipe of trusting in Yankee workmanship. His efforts are frustrated, however, as the work he has so expertly carried out is undone under rather melodramatic circumstances when a self-appointed son of Dan comes looking for a piece of evidence that might incriminate the Mormon sect. At the end of the novel the promise of the pastoral frame is all but crushed when evidence of illegal, big-scale industrial pollution is found on Mickelsson's very property. The Arcadian overtones of the setting in *Nickel Mountain* and *October Light* are thus nonexistent in *Mickelsson's Ghosts*; if anything, Mickelssson's experiences call up associations of Sodom, a comparison which seems all the more fitting since one expression that the protagonist's disintegration takes is an obsession with illicit sex. This point is driven home to the reader through vivid and repeated descriptions of Mickelsson's visits to a local prostitute; these scenes are rendered with a frankness that is quite unusual for Gardner, no doubt in order to emphasize the extent of Mickelsson's fall.

Mickelsson, too, is able to make a recovery, although perhaps more marginally than Freddy. In the end he does make a reentry into society. One of the many responsibilities that Mickelsson has shunned in his retreat is that of nurturing relations with his colleagues, in particular with Jessica Stark, who supports him practically and emotionally in his difficulties, but who receives little or no help from him when her job as a teacher of sociology is threatened. Jessica does keep her job, and there is a victory party to which Mickelsson is not invited. He goes to the party anyway, forces his way in, and declares his love for Jessica, who accepts his gesture. There is a love scene which may appear totally incongruous at first, with the other party members constantly coming to the door, wanting to know what is happening in the bedroom. But the scene becomes less farfetched when read on a nonrealistic level. For one thing, it is clearly meant to dramatically mark the end of Mickelsson's solipsistic retreat. Mickelsson's pride is severely wounded when he discovers Jessica making love to a colleague whom Mickelsson despises (this affair starts only after Mickelsson has broken off with Jessica), and for a long time his pride prevents him from reestablishing contact. In the final pages of the book that spell is broken, and the scene, therefore, should be seen as serving an iconic rather than a realistic function; the non-realist intention of the scene is of course made quite explicit as large white bones suddenly start to rain down around the two lovers. The white bones are possibly intended as a tip of the hat to the recognition that there are more things between heaven and earth than the analytic professor of philosophy had previously been willing to dream of. Throughout the book Mickelsson has shown a growing concern with parapsychological phenomena, as well as accounts of other improbable events; one of the spectacular events that has been referred to earlier in the book is the sudden inexplicable pouring down of white bones.[2]

Whatever the possible interpretations of that final scene, the fact remains that in his last novel Gardner moves a step beyond the position worked out in *Freddy's Book*. Now a rural setting is even denied an initial promise of stability and harmonious order, such as Lars-Goren is able to experience, albeit only momentarily, in Hälsingland. It is quite clear, then, that the archetypal conflict that gave rise to the pastoral form in the first place—withdrawal versus commitment, the simplicity of rural life versus the complexity and disorder of city life, "the garden versus the machine"— has held a particularly strong sway over Gardner's artistic imagination, influencing the conception of no less than six of his novels. His unwillingness to commit himself to one or the other pole of the conflict should be seen as yet another manifestation of the consistently exploratory nature of his art.

2

The *tale* is a traditional form that Gardner makes use of almost as frequently as he does the pastoral. His ventures into the form of the fairy tale are yet another example of his ongoing dialogue with tradition. Since the conventions here are fairly easy to recognize, this approach should enable us to discover some of the artistic resources Gardner thinks he can tap by writing in this medium. A good place to start is his children's stories, because their simplified form makes it easier to spot certain basic principles at work in the author's artistic handling of tales. Furthermore, the fairy tales we will look at for illustration contain the germs of thematic concerns that Gardner explores at length in his fiction for adults.

One of Gardner's primary reasons for turning to the fairy tale is the simplicity of the form. Tales, he says in an interview with Roni Natov and Geraldine DeLuca, usually deal with one basic idea, and in a fairy tale he can concentrate on that idea without worrying about creating a realistic setting and having to explain motivation in convincing psychological terms; in a fairy tale these things can be dispensed with because the form as such, through a practice that has been established by tradition, does not require them (119). But any literary form that has become conventionalized through a long and recognizable tradition will develop a metalanguage, a semantic frame of reference that the artist can explore; the reader will form certain expectations through his acquaintance with other fairy tales, and Gardner is able to create meaning simply by *failing* to meet these expectations.

In their illuminating discussion of Gardner's fairy tales for children, Geraldine DeLuca and Roni Natov explain how Gardner develops meaning simply by inverting archetypal fairy tale patterns ("Modern Moralities for Children"). Thus in Gardner's version of the classical story of the three brothers fighting to get half the kingdom and the Princess's hand in marriage ("The King of the Hummingbirds"), the youngest brother owes his success not to smartness but to dim-witted kindness. He wins the Princess not through an act of prowess or verbal wit, as in so many of the traditional tales, but through accidental bumbling, in which a host of hummingbirds solve his problem because in the past he has been kind to their king. By ironic reversals of this kind Gardner passes critical comment on a long-cherished fairy tale tradition of applauding shrewdness and strength, as shown, for instance, in many stories involving the Norse Ashlad figure.

"Vlemk the Box-Painter" is Gardner's most extended venture into the fairy tale mode in his "serious" fiction. Much of the humor of that novella is generated through the author's modification of traditional fairy tale role expectations. For one thing, the Princess/Queen is allowed far more space for character development than is customary in traditional fairy tales. This is shown, for instance, by the fact that the author allows her to pursue the diabolical inclinations in her character. The humor is particularly marked toward the end of the novella, where the Princess is given ample opportunity to display her comical fallibility through the playing of her charmingly wicked games designed to maneuver Vlemk into her net. The delight one experiences in reading the ending derives largely from the contrast between this eventful conclusion and the rather flat wrapping up of the traditional fairy tale, in which Ashlad routinely gets the Princess, whereupon they live happily ever after. From the point of view of the author it is perhaps unfortunate that the ending is also experienced as offering comic *relief*; most readers probably cannot help but feel that "Vlemk" is primarily an aesthetic tract, intended to spell out in fictional form some of Gardner's positions in *On Moral Fiction*. When the ending does come as a relief, it is because one forgets the author's high purpose for a moment and simply relishes Gardner's storytelling talents.

Registering this complaint does not amount to saying that "Vlemk" is an artistic failure. One of the delights of the novella is the inventive central conceit of the speaking picture, which may well explain *why* Gardner chose to work with the themes of "Vlemk" in the form of a fairy tale. It is difficult to think of another form that would accommodate so well the extended use of such a trope. A fairy tale is by convention programmed to deal in the fantastic, and the form gives Gardner ample room for exploring the possible thematic and aesthetic implications of his masterful invention.

The three "Tales of Queen Louisa" in *The King's Indian* are also held in the fairy tale mode. Gardner's choice of form for these stories was in all likelihood dictated by concerns similar to those that determined the form of "Vlemk." The Queen Louisa stories were conceived, Gardner has said, in order to illustrate the aesthetic principle he developed in "John Napper Sailing Through the Universe":

> The artist has to create new and wonderful possibilities. What happens in the Queen Louisa stories is that the princess has died; Queen Louisa has gone crazy; and, having no way to make anything out of the fact that the princess is dead and everything's awful, she in her insanity creates a new world, which gets better and better. (Harvey 81)

In order to dramatize the artistic potential of John Napper's stance, Gardner probably felt he needed a fictional universe in which everything the imagination commands can and does happen. He therefore created a Laingian court for Queen Louisa, where the supposedly mad are the sole providers of sane thoughts. The author evidently wants to pepper the readers' minds with suggestions of "wonderful possibilities," something that might have taken forever in a realistic medium. The form of the fairy tale allows him to string together in rapid succession a series of fantastic occurrences, indicative of man's capacity for willing the good. And in Queen Louisa's court everything *is* possible: chambermaids become princesses, the Queen can change into a green toad, and her husband the King, who has been transformed into an old dog by a witch spouting existentialist one-liners, is changed back to his old self on the Queen's command, to summarize only some of the more colorful events in the first of the three stories.

One can see the technical reasons Gardner had for putting the fairy tale form to these uses. The aesthetic risks are considerable, however. True, these stories have some richly comical moments, such as when King John passes his verdict that the Fool's poem is "distinctly Biblical. Loosely"; or the commotion created when the Queen commands a halt in the fighting between King Gregor's and King John's men (Queen Louisa: "'Listen, they could have *killed* each other!'" "'That's the idea!' King Gregor screamed."); or when the whole court goes skinny-dipping throughout the palace (in King Gregor's rendering: "The next minute, off they all went through the palace, reaching out like swimmers and slowly bringing their arms back and reaching out again, and sometimes giving a little kick with one foot, except for old Tcherpni's wife, who was doing the dog paddle."). The humor notwithstanding, the risk the author runs is that the stories will fail to appeal, that the events become so farfetched as to seem totally contrived and therefore lose poetic persuasiveness. Too many of the "wonderful possibilities" suggested by these narratives disintegrate into occasions of whimsy, and the fairy tale frame, in this case, defeats its purpose.

3

"The King's Indian" is subtitled "A Tale," but the conventions Gardner draws on in this novella partake as much of the *yarn* as of the *tale*. We are very fortunate in having Gardner's own description of the conventions that, in his reading, normally govern both of these forms, a description which provides us with some insight into the aesthetic motivations for this instance of "genre jumping."

"Although any adventure story is loosely called a yarn," Gardner and Dunlap say, the term properly applies to a bizarre or comic story related in a manner which suggests a storyteller working in the oral tradition, that is "spinning a yarn"—employing verbal and structural repetition, digression, asides to the reader, homely expressions, and exaggeration as he embellishes, out of memory and imagination, incidents, characters, or settings.... The narrator presents the narrative's action as frankly incredible and depends for his success upon the reader's recognition of this incredibility. (27)[3]

Compare this description with old Jonathan Upchurch's prolegomenon to his tale of youthful adventures on the high seas:

"Hoaxes! Don't speak to me of hoaxes, sir! I was part of the worst that was ever dreamt up in all history, and not free of it yet. Two old gnomes from Nantucket, some years ago.... Gnomes. Hah! Cracked checkerplayers, that's nearer the mark! Beelzebub and Jaweh! Never mind...interminable damned...Hoaxes. Hah."...

"I could tell you a tale, if ye'd understand from the outset it has no purpose to it, no shape or form or discipline but the tucket and boom of its highflown language and whatever dim flickers that noise stirs up in yer cerebrium, sir—the boom and the bottle we chase it with—fierce rum of everlasting sleep, ha ha!—for I won't be called a liar, no sir! not when I speak of such matters as devils and angels and the making of man, which is my subject, sir." (197)

It takes no crafty analysis to discover that Gardner very much wants old Jonathan to emerge as a master spinner of yarns. Nearly all the elements of Gardner's definition in *The Forms of Fiction* seem to be there already in the first few sentences that Jonathan speaks. The reader knows from the outset that this is going to be a tall tale indeed, giving him no less than the worst hoax "ever dreamt up in all history." The sheer storytelling energy of those two paragraphs ensures the illusion of an oral tradition, and there are the digressions and pauses characteristic of the spoken rather than the written word. Further on in their analysis of the formal traits of the yarn Gardner and Dunlap remark that the reader is definitely meant to realize that "the narrator is, despite his protestations, a liar." Jonathan, true to form, protests wildly, and if the exaggerations of his opening salute do not convince us of his proclivity for dressing up the truth, the warning flags are out immediately afterwards when he proceeds to give a detailed account of his own birth, an event he says he remembers, "believe it or not, with some clarity."

The narrative frame set up through the initial paragraphs is thus clearly that of the yarn. But many of the ensuing events also link "The King's Indian" to the tradition of the yarn. "Setting is often simplified," Gardner and Dunlap point out, and ordinarily "the hero of a yarn has tremendous strength, tenacity, cunning, or inventiveness, or else is an extraordinary coward, drinker, gambler, liar, bull-headed fool." A ship is almost by definition a simplified setting, and on the list of typical character traits of a hero in a yarn, about half of them apply to Jonathan.

It is of interest now to compare Gardner's and Dunlap's definition of the yarn with that of the *tale.* "The characters in a tale are...intended to be convincing without suggesting comparison with actual people," they argue. "They behave in recognizably human ways as a result of human emotions," but "they tend to be a little larger than life and may possess extraordinary powers," and "they are seldom characters from the world familiar to most readers." All of these observations fit "The Kings's Indian," with its colorful cast of pirates, slaves, and scheming magicians. Yet the main actors on board the *Jerusalem* mostly behave according to established emotional patterns; Jonathan and Wilkins are both taken in by Augusta, and she on her part shows strong filial affection for Dr. Flint and learns to love Jonathan in the end; when Wilkins commits suicide, the fact is explained by plot developments, as is Miranda's excessive curiosity. Still, the reader would never think of these characters as "actual people," so in all respects they seem to fit into the mold established by traditional tales, as defined by Gardner and Dunlap.

So does the handling of plot in "The Kings's Indian." Here is Gardner's and Dunlap's description of the characteristic function of plot in a tale:

The tale also gains its peculiar kind of credibility through manipulation of plot. In most tales the narrative begins with an extraordinary initial situation, a cause, which produces a series of effects, realistic or unrealistic, to establish a poetic logic. The plot of a tale, unlike the plot of a short story, is loosely constructed; except in its simplest forms, the tale is more often than not discursive.

Again there is close correspondence. Jonathan Upchurch's story certainly begins with "an extraordinary initial situation," not to say two or three. There is first Jonathan's calamitous visit to the Buried Treasure Inn, leading to his purchase of the sailboat *Jolly Independent*; then he survives being overrun by the whaler *Jerusalem* in midstorm; third, the *Jerusalem* is a mystery ship bound for a secret destination and is under no circumstances willing to return Jonathan to the shore. The plot of the story is definitely "loosely constructed," with a number of surprising turns of event. There is nevertheless a "poetic logic," established partly by the plot developments which result from Jonathan's relentless quest to unravel the secrets of the *Jerusalem*, and partly as a result of Dr. Flint's unwillingness to give up his search for the Vanishing Isles. Even the ending of the novella seems to fit the formula, "having a ring of finality rarely encountered in the short story." On the surface at least this is the kind of ending we get in "The King's Indian": Wolff, Wilkins, and Flint are dead, the ship is in the hands of Jonathan and his lordless crew, and sails are set for land, where Jonathan plans to settle in Illinois with his Miranda. We shall see later that the finality of the ending is undercut in various subtle ways by other elements of the narrative, but that is an effect readers may easily miss in their first reading of the novella.

Thus "The King's Indian" borrows from the tradition of the yarn *and* the tale. There are several reasons why I have gone into considerable detail about this. First of all, I want to show that Gardner is highly conscious of the particulars of traditional literary conventions. Whether or not critics will find his categories useful is here beside the point. The fact that Gardner himself cares about this type of categorization indicates that *he* sees them as bearing meaning and that he may be expected to explore these categories consciously for aesthetic effect in his own fiction. He may well have done just that in "The King's Indian."

So far this analysis of formal elements in "The King's Indian" has not been concerned with meaning; what has been ascertained is simply that in certain ways the novella employs conventions of the traditional yarn and tale. As usual with Gardner, it is to the *modifications* of traditional aspects that we must look for meaning, those places where there is a systematic deviation from a norm. Such a deviation is to be found, it seems, in the *intermingling* of the two forms. Even though the yarn and the tale may have certain things in common in Gardner's thinking about them, they are mutually exclusive in one respect: in their relation to reality. In the tale, Gardner and Dunlap argue, artistic success depends on whether or not the writer is able to bring about the reader's willing suspension of disbelief, upon "the reader's willingness to put mundane reality out of his mind altogether." Even when the tale deals in improbable events, as is its wont, "the matter of reality does not enter the reader's mind as a serious question." This is, however, exactly the opposite of the effect that the yarn is after. What marks the yarn from the tale, as well as from the short story, in Gardner's view, is the fact that "whereas the short story usually depends upon the reader's willingness to accept the narrative as entirely possible in the ordinary world, the yarn depends on the reader's skepticism." That is why the writer of a yarn is at great pains to emphasize, as Gardner does in "The King's Indian," the narrator's mendacity.

But the fact that suspension of disbelief is intended gives rise to a paradox. Why, on the one hand, would the author want to *insist* on the artificiality of the narrative by so overtly drawing attention to the yarn frame and, on the other, try to achieve the effect of the tale, which is to make the reader *forget* the artificiality? One might, of course, blame the use of these contradictory frames on incompetence, but we will see later that the pattern of vacillation between the mode of the yarn (insisting on artificiality) and the tale (suspension of disbelief) is reinforced through the use of metafictional devices as well as by the thematic implications of the narrative. The fact that Gardner has called *The King's Indian* a study in literary aesthetics justifies speculations along these lines (Harvey 81). Thus, the vacillation is no doubt intentional and serves to illustrate an aesthetic position of great importance for our understanding of "The King's Indian" as well as of Gardner's other fiction: the fact that fiction is an artifice is undeniable, and for philosophical reasons it is important that we do not forget this; but fiction also has the power to move, to affect life, by constructing visions of what we can become, and this is fiction's noblest function.

4

The Gardnerian position under examination in the present chapter is that in order to justly assess a work of art one must take into account "the tradition behind the work" and "*the moment...of its appearance*" (OMF 163; my italics). So far we have only looked at the first part of this proposition, but for the proper outlining of Gardner's artistic profile we also need to consider the second part, the importance of "moment." In this context the theoretical framework of reception analysis should be of particular interest to Gardner criticism because it is built on assumptions about the literary process which Gardner shares. Not only does Gardner view the writing of fiction as an act of exploration on the part of the artist, but he is also concerned that the *reading* of fiction should constitute a process of discovery for the reader as well: "The 'creative' aspect, then, is not merely the province of the writer during the act of fictionalization, 'closed' when the text is completed to the author's satisfaction, but, in a broader and real way, a participatory right of the reader in the act of discovery." For a literary text to be moral in Gardner's sense, it has to be the product of the artist's truthful exploration, but it must also be fashioned in such a way as to trigger discovery in its readers: "A fiction which is [moral] depends upon this multiple-dialogue between author, text and reader" ("A Writer's View" 31).

These statements suggest a tacit bow to the distinction that reception analysts make between *artefact* and *aesthetic object*. Artefact is "the literary text as it is finalized in writing or in print," whereas the aesthetic object is "the meaning correlate" or "the concretization" of the artefact in the consciousness of the readers (Fokkema and Kunne-Ibsch 143, 137). Reception theorists concentrate on the aesthetic object, and they introduce the concept of a "horizon of expectations" (*Erwartungshorizont*) on the part of readers as a determining factor in the creation of aesthetic objects; the reader's particular vantage point in terms of, for instance, intellectual climate and awareness of literary tradition decides the possible "concretizations" of any given artefact, or text (Jauss 173). These theorists further argue, and this point is particularly relevant to a discussion of Gardner's fiction, that the author's awareness and assessment of what, among others, Seymour Chatman has called "the implied reader" (that is, "the audience presupposed by the narrative itself" [148]), in turn helps determine the form and shape of the text.

Gardner always writes with a hypothetical audience in mind (Ferguson 63). The intended receiver, or the implied reader, is not always readily identifiable, but there are texts in which an implied reader *does* emerge, where our awareness of the writer's projected audience enables us, on the one hand, to formulate hypotheses concerning the genesis of that text, and, on the other, to highlight and define important aspects of the author's intention. *Grendel* is very much such a case.[4]

It has already been established that for Gardner the pressure of the artist's moment is a force to be reckoned with in the assessing of literary careers. The forms that this pressure takes will naturally vary greatly from one writer to the next; it can be political, psychological, cultural, historical, or a combination of these and others. Gardner's particular social moment has of course affected him in a number of ways, but there is perhaps one pressure that has exerted itself more strongly than all others: the pressure of a culture whose predominant commitment is, in Gardner's mind, to an absurdist view of life. In an interview Gardner offers the following interesting account of the genesis of *Grendel:*

> *Grendel* came about because I was teaching an Anglo-Saxon class, and I told the kids that the three monsters in *Beowulf* are very symbolic, and Grendel is symbolic of the rational soul gone perverse. Somebody asked me in class if that was just old-fashioned Christian talk, or was it possible in the modern world for the rational soul to go perverse. And I said "Sure, Sartre's Existentialism is perverse rationality." As soon as I said it I realized what I was going to do, and I began planning *Grendel.* (Christian 81)

In *On Moral Fiction* Gardner analyzes the spiritual malaise which he sees as governing the intellectual climate of America as a consequence, at least partly, of existentialism's grip on Western mentality. When asked in an interview if his ongoing battle against existentialism was not rather like flogging a dead horse, Gardner retorted that existentialism as a school of thought may have stopped exerting its influence, but America is characterized by an emotional commitment to the basic tenets of existentialism, even though most Americans probably are unfamiliar with the term as such (Winther 510). In the novel within the novel in *October Light* Gardner parodies a sensationalist type of literature devoted to spreading the gospel of meaninglessness, and in *On Moral Fiction* and in other contexts he constantly chides contemporary writers for their tendency to keep staring into the abyss. Speaking about "the dominant feelings of the age," Gardner leaves no doubt about how he defines the artist's moment that is his own:

> Feelings of skepticism about traditional values are the dominant feelings of the age, feelings the artist must find his way over or around or under if he's to make the affirmation which

defines him. Even if some of these feelings are wrong, mere mistaken emotion...they are the driving emotions of men and women with whom the artist is involved and for whom he cannot help but feel a sympathy which ends up confusing him. They are the artist's only available subject. (*OMF* 168)

It is against this background that *Grendel* was conceived, and, I will argue, Gardner's assessment of his readers' "horizon of expectations" has a lot to do with the choosing of artistic strategies for that book.

The implied reader that I postulate for *Grendel* is thus someone who expects another fashionably experimental novel (an Anglo-Saxon monster as narrator-hero, no less), confirming prevalent notions of absurdity, nihilism, and meaninglessness, a novel in which the viability of traditional values is passionately denied. In accordance with these expectations Gardner creates a metaphysical rebel who is sure to capture his readers' fancy in a way a virtuous hero could not have done in these antiheroic times. For our present purpose it should be noted that Grendel comes close to being a personification of Gardner's own social moment, as he himself describes it. Even though no artist can afford to neglect tradition, Gardner says, he must not pander to it, "paying no mind to the howls and whimpers and giggles of his age" (*OMF* 169). Grendel is a *charming* monster, verbally witty, appealingly self-ironical (who can resist self-irony in a monster?) and he is pitted against comically fallible humans, whose silliness somehow makes his murdering them seem almost acceptable. Furthermore, the novel is held in the first person; the narrative is controlled by Grendel's perspective, and an inside view tends generally to create sympathy and reduce the distance between the reader and the narrator. All in all, Gardner teases us toward an identification with Grendel on a number of levels. Knowing Gardner's diagnosis of the present spiritual malaise, we can assume that when the author makes Grendel into a full-fledged existentialist, this is an element of the same artistic strategy.

Philosophical systems are by definition the result of intellectual activity subjected to the tests of reason and logic, and Gardner will not deny that as such they may have their use. The reason why Gardner views existentialism as a *perverse* form of rationality is the existentialist's refusal to look outside himself for spiritual guidance. In the introduction to her translation of Sartre's *Being and Nothingness*, Hazel E. Brown, explaining Roquentin's discovery of absurdity in *Nausea*, sums up the existentialist position:

> First there is the realization on the part of the hero, Roquentin, that Being in general and he in particular are *de trop*, that is, existence itself is contingent, gratuitous, unjustifiable. It is *absurd* in the sense that there is no reason for it, no outside purpose to give it meaning, no direction. Being is *there*, and outside of it—Nothing. (xvi)

Such a position must naturally lead to a refusal to accept the rational moralist's claim that there *are* external values, constituting essence *before* existence.

From the outset Grendel shows great affinity with existentialist thought through his insistence on the meaninglessness of existence. Echoing Roquentin, he says: "I understood that the world was nothing: a mechanical chaos of casual, brute enmity on which we stupidly impose our hopes and fears" (21–22). Sartre, adopting Heidegger's concept of the "brute existent," speaks of "the brute-in-itself." From a similar premise Grendel concludes, as Millie Hodge does in *The Sunlight Dialogues* (181), "I alone exist. All the rest, I saw, is merely what pushes me, or what I push against, blindly—as blindly as all that is not myself pushes back" (22). Grendel's ontology is thus informed by Sartre's distinction between Being-in-itself ("Brute existent") and Being-for-itself, a terminology which is hilariously parodied in *The Wreckage of Agathon*.[5] Like Thaletes, the anachronistically existentialist sage in *The Wreckage of Agathon*, and Millie Hodge, the self-appointed "bitch goddess" of *The Sunlight Dialogues*, Grendel is mired in what Gardner calls "that old bog *L'etre* [sic] *et le néant*" (*OMF* 24). However, at least in the early chapters of the novel, the uninitiated reader is less likely to see Grendel, the existentialist, as a negative figure. The "corrective principle" (cf. Just's *korrektive Wirkung*) of *Grendel* is irony; the book takes "one by one, the great heroic ideals of mankind since the beginning and [makes] a case for these values by setting up alternatives in an ironic set of monster values" (Ellis and Ober 47). Paradoxically, Gardner may have done almost too good a job of making Grendel emerge as a sympathetic character, since a number of the early reviewers failed to see the irony. Auberon Waugh identifies wholeheartedly with Grendel, saying that his story enables the reader to examine "all the legends with which mankind sustains belief in his intrinsic nobility, and see the whole structure as a pack of lies" (quoted in Ellis and Ober 47). In Earl Shorris's reading Grendel is a "sentient, bittersweetly witty, and altogether lovable being," the protagonist of a novel "in which we prefer the monster to the humans" (91,90). And Jay Ruud sees Gardner's Grendel as a hero who partakes of the contemporary fiction of the absurd, and he applauds Gardner for giving us a protagonist who refuses "to accept the values of law and order in...society, in the face of what he knows to be a chaotic and meaningless universe." Grendel's refusal is justified, Ruud feels, because "in our modern world there are no set values" (3–17). However, these early failures to see the irony of *Grendel* do not necessarily show that Gardner overplayed his hand in his conception of Grendel as a sympathetic figure; rather, these cases of misreading could be seen as a tribute to Gardner's subtlety as an ironist, since, as Jonathan Culler points out, for a text to be "properly ironic it must be possible to imagine some group of readers taking it quite literally" (154).

As the novel progresses, Gardner begins to undermine the reader's sympathy for Grendel in a number of ways. For one thing, his nihilism becomes more and more frenetic, shown, for instance, in his impulse to destroy Wealtheow, one unquestioned source of good in the novel. In Gardner's own description, Grendel starts out as "a cheerful nihilist," but after a while he "begins to *dance* on his lack of faith, and play games," and then he becomes more and more a real monster (Christian 80). Ultimately Grendel is defeated by Beowulf, who kills him in the name of the positive values that Grendel has scorned: "*fingers on harpstrings* [art], *hero-swords* [idealism, commitment to a fight against evil], *the acts, the eyes of queens* [good deeds and beauty]" (150). "I alone exist," Grendel claims. "Feel the wall," says Beowulf, and the pain in Grendel's head forces him to recognize that maybe the wall exists also.

Thus the novel ends by frustrating certain expectations that the early sympathetic portrayal of Grendel has helped build in the reader. The ways in which Gardner attempts to effect an identification between Grendel and the reader become more easily recognizable if we analyze Gardner's narrative technique positing a readily definable audience, one marked by a certain metaphysical impatience, if not rebelliousness. If the novel has a flaw, it is perhaps to be found in the fact that Gardner conceived of his audience a shade too narrowly. As we have seen, Gardner himself admits that existentialism's present influence as a school of philosophy is probably negligible. It seems, therefore, that in couching some of Grendel's rebellious instincts in existentialist terms, Gardner limits his audience to certain sections of academe; when readers who are unfamiliar with the writings of Sartre and philosophers of a similar persuasion are confronted with Grendel's existentialist lingo, their main reaction is likely to be befuddlement rather than instant identification. This is, however, a minor faux pas. Grendel's rebelliousness is given many and different expressions, and readership identification is possible on a number of levels. If nothing else, the poetic persuasiveness of Grendel's inside view makes his cheerful nihilism sufficiently attractive so as to facilitate the kind of reorientation which Just discovers in Grass's *Die Blechtrommel* and which Gardner obviously had in mind for his readers. This is not to argue that the book's aesthetic appeal resides solely in this admittedly schematic formula. A main concern in this chapter has been, among other things, to look at ways in which the artist's moment affects Gardner's art, and this discussion of how he drew on his projection of a potential audience in the creation of *Grendel* is meant as a demonstration of only one aspect of his artistic method. Another is Gardner's extensive use of literary allusions, a technique which could be said to be *the* most important extension of his involvement with literary tradition.

COLLAGE TECHNIQUE I

Collage technique is the term Gardner himself uses to characterize his conscious use of literary allusions to explore and communicate whatever "truths" the process of writing permits him to affirm.[1] His allusions are principally of three kinds: (a) *Literary*, either in the form of smaller or larger sections of poetry, fiction, or drama written by others; or in the form of appropriating another artist's style; or in the form of employing motifs used in the literature of the past. (b) *Philosophical*, in the form of Gardner's adopting shorter or longer passages from the work of philosophers for use in his own fiction. (c) *Historical*, in the sense that he integrates into his own texts material from books dealing with certain historical topics.

1

There are many reasons why a collage technique should appeal to Gardner. He himself claims that the technique developed partly as a result of what he calls "a peculiar and unfortunate" quality of mind: his tendency to remember—word for word—things he has read. In creative writing courses in college he found that he reproduced long passages of earlier writers' works without realizing it; once he became aware of this unconscious habit he began to develop an allusive technique, he says, "so that nobody could accuse me of plagiarism since it's so obvious that I'm alluding" (Ferguson et al. 60).

Even though this explanation has the charm of a good anecdote, it hardly gives the full answer, as Gardner himself implies. His interest in the technique may have been reinforced by his early admiration for James Joyce, another heavy alluder.[2] However, the strongest formative influence is probably Gardner's extensive studies of medieval literature. In his "Letter" to the *Chicago Tribune,* he defends the echoic method by, among other things, referring to medieval rhetorical theory and its concept of *inventio,* that is, "the collection of old materials to be used in a new way." That term seems to overlap with the concept of "the poetic mosaic" or "interlace," a technique much practiced both in pre-Christian and in Christian poetry from Anglo-Saxon times; Gardner describes interlace as "poems made up largely of old materials woven together for a new aesthetic purpose" ("Fulgentius's *Expositio*" 235). *Inventio* was practiced by the Gawain-poet, whose works Gardner has translated. In his introduction to this translation Gardner comments on this medieval practice in terms that take on particular interest for someone wanting to discover the rationale behind his use of a similar technique:

> Borrowing plots, descriptions, even especially elegant lines from the work of other poets was standard practice in the Middle Ages—as it has been among good poets of almost every age, for that matter. At its best this borrowing becomes imperatorial confiscation. Thus Chaucer seized Boccaccio's elegant and slight *Il Filostrato* and transformed it into the greatest tragic poem in English; and thus Shakespeare transformed the curious tragedies of earlier poets into the world's most powerful modern drama.
>
> The artistry in poetic borrowing can also lie in adapting borrowed material to its new context without obscuring its meaning in the original context, for here the poet's object is not to confiscate but rather to enrich meaning by playing one context against another. (*The Complete Works of the Gawain-Poet* 24–25)

These comments begin as a characterization of an important feature of medieval literature, but Gardner quickly expands the horizon, focussing on the technique of literary allusion as an aesthetic device for all times. The important thing here is the emphasis he places on the literary possibilities inherent in the consciously manipulated interplay of texts; that perspective is also dominant in his characterization of Chaucer, the one writer he says he loves beyond all other writers (Winther 511), as a master of the noble art of allusion. Again Gardner bears quoting at length because, with a few changes of factual detail, his comments on

Chaucer's allusive technique could serve as a description of his own practice of extensive borrowing; furthermore, the passage may give us a clue to why Gardner employs the term *collage technique* to characterize his own echoic method; finally, the tribute he pays Chaucer toward the end of the passage again draws attention to the importance that he places on the role of textual interplay in literary borrowings:

> [L]et me take time here to remind the reader of how heavily dependent Chaucer was on "sources" for plot ideas, scenery, and specific lines.... [A]ll Chaucer's poetry makes heavy use of other people's writing. About seventy percent of *Troilus and Criseyde* is from Boccaccio, and at least another twenty percent—individual lines, phrases, long paragraphs from Boethius, and so on—can be traced to other sources. Even the most original of the *Canterbury Tales*...contains hundreds of allusions and borrowed images.
>
> However much or little Chaucer borrowed, his art—as he and his audience saw it—lay in the shuffling, the reworking. His poetry is like that of a modern builder of collages[!] whose main materials are other people's drawings.... But in most of his poetry Chaucer's borrowings have a virtue unusual in poetry of the time: the borrowed detail drags in its original context and either clarifies or ironically comments on the new context. (*The Poetry of Chaucer* 34–35)

There is of course no way of mapping all the possible aesthetic choices that the artist faced in borrowing this material or that, fitting it into a given context. In many cases the author himself would probably be hard put to explain the exact way an allusion is meant to work. Many borrowings are no doubt intended to suggest more than one meaning, or meanings on several levels, so there is obviously a danger of reductionism in analyzing this aspect of Gardner's art. Furthermore, because of Gardner's skill in integrating his borrowed material, a number of allusions are likely to escape even the most observant reader. And then there is the tricky question of dealing with the allusions once they are identified; how, for instance, do we decide whether a borrowing is used with ironic or supportive intent? How do we establish the author's own understanding of, and attitude to, the sources that he uses?

There is thus a host of challenging problems to be tackled in dealing meaningfully with this important aspect of Gardner's artistic method. There is very little help to be found in the existing scholarship. One of the few critics who has dealt with the matter of borrowings in Gardner's fiction is Greg Morris. In his essay on Gardner's use of material from A. Leo Oppenheimer's book on Mesopotamian culture in *The Sunlight Dialogues*, Morris concludes that the most we can say about this instance of an allusive method is that it enables Gardner to suggest certain thematic connections that the reader himself is left to work out and thus adds to the "multi-layered pleasure of the novel." And that, Morris asserts, "is the entire point of Gardner's borrowing" ("A Babylonian" 45). The present chapter and the next engage in a discussion which goes a step further than that; they are based on the conviction that an analysis of the existing material will enable us to arrive at certain hypotheses about the aesthetic mechanisms at work in Gardner's very pervasive use of borrowed material.

2

Using traditional forms and working with the literature of earlier times serve, broadly speaking, a *double* compositional function for Gardner. On the one hand, he turns to his sources as a means of making discoveries. Thus his interest in what he calls "genre-jumping" is motivated by his view of art as a method of exploration. But his interest in older forms is not limited to a wish to do battle with literary conventions. Gardner also explores what bearing the ideas and values that earlier writers worked with in their art have on his own fictional pursuits. He has addressed this aspect of his collage technique in an interview: "I incline to think out so-called modern questions in terms of archaic forms. I like the way archaic forms provide a pair of spectacles for looking at things.... When you look at your values through the eyes of a medieval courtly poet, then his values and your values are sure to be in some degree of contrast already, so you kind of triangulate the subject of the novel" (Edwards and Polsgrove 46). What goes on in the artist's mind during composition—how he makes his discoveries, what possibilities he entertained, which positions he discarded—is a private affair; this is a process that we as readers can know very little about, nor is it essential that we gain such knowledge. Our concern is the way in which the writer communicates his findings. Gardner's collage technique serves a dual function. Not only does it enable him to make important discoveries, but it is also a means by which he can bring about a similar process of discovery in his readers. Gardner emphasizes the heuristic function of art in that he wants the reading of fiction to constitute a process of discovery for the reader, and by adopting a collage technique he has fashioned a flexible instrument for involving the reader in such a process, chiefly through the creation of what Wolfgang Iser usefully has termed "gaps," that is, a place in a text where a reader perceives a difficulty or an ambiguity, some part of the text where he cannot be certain of the writer's intended meaning. The reader will try to "close" the gap by constructing his own meaning, and thus he becomes involved in the creative process, "co-authoring" one particular concretization of the text (*The Implied Reader* 33).

One effect of gaps is to point to the self-reflexivity of literary texts, achieved through the aesthetic mechanism involved in Sklovskij's concept of "defamiliarization."[3] Gardner's collage technique is one way in which he achieves defamiliarization, and part of the artistic motivation behind his many allusions is to raise questions about the epistemological status of literary texts. Gardner was sensitive to the rhetorical value of textual difficulty; repetition of imagery is one instance of what Gardner calls "rhythmic encoding" (see Chapter 3), and Gardner's definition of his term relates it to Iser's gaps: rhythmic encoding, Gardner says, is "any form of stylistic or structural repetition which...catches the reader's attention and prompts him to ask himself what the point is, or...what the connection between the disturbed details may be" (*The Construction of Christian Poetry* 14). In most cases a literary allusion will have the same effect. When the reader discovers that Jonathan Upchurch on occasion will speak the very same lines that Melville gives to Ishmael, the reader is bound to start looking for connections. This is defamiliarization on several levels: the reader will most likely read those lines with a greater attention than he might otherwise have paid to them; he is going to speculate on the situational connection between source and borrowing; he may start looking for thematic correlations between the two works, and so on.

There are of course many reasons why a writer should want his reader to take extra notice. When the author uses the words of another writer to jolt the reader into registering a difficulty, or gap, one reason may obviously be a desire to draw attention to the fact that he *is* alluding. The allusion serves as a reminder to the reader that what he has in front of him is a rendering of, not *actual*, but *fictional* reality, a reminder that the art work is a piece of fiction which frankly admits to its own artificiality, to its status as a product of the imagination. Thus the allusion also becomes a metafictional device, "insisting on the reader's awareness of the page as physical object—the book as book" ("A Writer's View" 16).

It should be noted that Gardner himself has referred to his appropriation of the styles of Poe, Twain, and Melville in "The King's Indian" as a metafictional device (Winther 512). Twain's style is evident in Jonathan's tall tale style of narration, and Poe's and Melville's styles are directly transplanted into the novella through extensive borrowings from "Narrative of A. Gordon Pym" and *Moby-Dick*. The metafictional status of the many allusions in "The King's Indian" is bolstered by the use of the most standard metafictional device of all: what Gardner calls the "obtrusive narrator." In discussing the possible artistic motivations behind the widespread use of obtrusive techniques in contemporary fiction, Gardner makes a remark which sheds light on the narrative frame he chose for "The King's Indian." The metafictional ploys of recent fiction, Gardner says, draw attention to the realization that "language shapes the reality we see: to change the language is to change the world." This realization

> puts us into a relationship with words that the self-effacing realist narrator never thought of or, if he thought of it, would be hard put to make use of.... [The] self-effacing narrator quietly, unobtrusively puts the wine on the table, seats the guests, and starts the conversation, confidently describing the world face by face, telling lies without knowing it. ("A Writer's View" 25–26)

The narrative frame of "The King's Indian" is the very opposite of the one Gardner posits for realistic fiction. In this novella the narrator seats his guest noisily, imbuing him with a highly warranted skepticism about the tale he is about to hear; the wine (or in this case spirits) is served in the most obtrusive fashion thinkable: "With dignity, an angel enters, golden-winged, and places spirits on the table between the mariner and his guest (apparently a city fellow)" (197–98).

At regular intervals throughout "The King's Indian" the reader is reminded of this frame, and on two occasions John Gardner himself joins company with mariner, angel, and guest, addressing the reader directly (Chapters 5 and 28); the nonrealist intentions of the novella are not to be doubted by anyone. In one of his asides to the reader Gardner makes the connection between the metafictional aspect and his collage technique explicit: "I, John Gardner," he says, "with the help of Poe and Melville and many another man, wrote this book." The book, as he conceives of it, is "a queer, cranky monument, a *collage:* a celebration of all literature and life" (316; my italics). Like most of Gardner's fiction, *The King's Indian* is illustrated, a practice which the author cites as yet another instance of an obtrusive, or metafictional, technique ("A Writer's View" 17). One of the illustrations gives us the author himself *qua* Jonathan Upchurch, the youthful sailor, no less (209).

The short stories and tales that precede the title novella in the collection contribute toward making the whole book a veritable literary feast; most of them imitate, or parody, the style of one literary predecessor or another, bearing witness to Donald Greiner's claim that parody is often a way of paying homage to another writer (Morace and VanSpanckeren 80). The opening story, "Pastoral Care," Gardner has said, is an attempt to deal with a topic that is central in John Updike's fiction: religious neo-orthodoxy (Harvey 81), and the crisp, rational, and realistic style of that story certainly shows affinities with the characteristic style of many of Updike's novels and stories. The narrator of "The Ravages of Spring" (he drives a horse named Shakespeare) begins his tale by saying that the story he is about to launch would be "more fit for the author of 'The Raven'" (35), thereby helping the reader to see the parallels between his adventures and those described in "The Fall of the House of Usher." But the country doctor's tale furthermore brings to mind Kafka's short story "A Country Doctor." Gardner's protagonist, too, has to go on sick call, weather or no weather; in Kafka's story snow is the problem, and in "The Ravages of Spring" the tornadoes of southern Illinois offer a backdrop for the events in which the narrator is about to get involved. The tornado also effectively contributes to the aura of nightmare that governs the story: and nightmare, Gardner points out, is the controlling mood of Kafka's "A Country Doctor" (*The Forms of Fiction* 68–73). Not only does the storm itself lead to nightmarelike experiences for Gardner's doctor, but the uncertainty and perplexity which are the sine qua non of nightmare are reflected in the doctor's many false starts and his inability to tell his story in a straightforward manner. The instances of dream imagery and imagery of drowning and of moving under water accentuate the troubled oneiric mood of the story.

The same Kafkaesque mood of unreality and nightmare haunts "The Warden"; the title of the story refers to a character who walks interminably back and forth in his chambers, seeing no one, never coming out for food or drink. In the meantime the prison must do without rule or guidance, as must Kafka's universe. The dungeons in the warden's prison come straight out of nightmare, as do the narrator's frequent experiences of being watched by somebody he never sees. The only time the warden makes an appearance is in a dreamlike scene in which "a part of his forehead was blasted away, as if by some violent explosion" (118). These and other details in the story indeed serve to pay tribute to Kafka.

3

The metafictional status of literary texts thus emerges as one of the chief concerns of The King's Indian. The battery of metafictional devices employed in the book—obtrusive narration, direct allusions, book illustrations, imitation of styles—all serve to augment the effect of the yarn frame in the title novella: exultation in and celebration of the artificiality of the narrative. I have suggested that there are philosophical reasons for this artistic strategy; basically, it springs out of an *epistemological* orientation that Gardner shares with a number of the "new fiction" writers, and he talks at length about these matters in his *Dismisura* article.[4]

The author's projection of himself into the text is one way of rejecting the realist's idea that "as a writer he ought to efface himself, 'sit like God in the corner of the universe paring his nails,' as Joyce said." The realist narrator presumes to be telling the objective truth, "confidently describing the world fact by fact, telling lies without knowing it." In the "Prologue" to The Sunlight Dialogues Gardner pokes fun at the epistemological complacency of the realist position. As Clumly leaves after a visit to Batavia's Judge, both of them long since retired, the Judge (said to be "the oldest Judge in the world") remarks to his bored male attendant: "I made that man. I created him, you might say. I created them all. The Mayor, the Fire Chief, all of them. I ran this town. I made them, and when the time came I dropped a word in the right place and I broke them" (5). Kathryn VanSpanckeren suggests that the Judge is wrong about Clumly because the Chief of Police "remade his soul in choosing to confront the Sunlight Man." VanSpanckeren thus sees the scene as a "cautionary parable about the danger and futility of solipsistic pride in the creative process" ("Magical Prisons" 128). This is a good point, and it is corroborated by connections which VanSpanckeren leaves unmentioned in her analysis.

The Judge lives in a house with bars on the windows, suggesting (philosophical?) confinement. In a room gradually growing darker, he expounds on his omnipotence from behind a cloud of yellow tobacco smoke so heavy that he is at pains to make out the contours of Clumly's head, all of which ironically comments on the limited vision of self-declared omniscience. The attendant is portrayed as the Judge's alter ego ("'I like you,' the Judge said suddenly. 'You're like a son to me.'"), and his presence evokes the Joycean self-effaced objective authorial figure: "The attendant looks at him indifferently, as if from infinitely far away" (5). The attendant is described as being strongly preoccupied with cleaning his fingernails. In the book illustration of this scene John Napper singles out this detail for particular attention; in the illustration the only thing Napper in fact shows of the attendant are his hands, drawn by the book illustrator so as to show them in the process of paring nails. This illustration was chosen for a frontispiece, so it would seem that the book's editor (and presumably the author) as well as the illustrator join in emphasizing the parallel between the enigmatic tableau given in the "Prologue" and Joyce's famous prescription of authorial aloofness.

Through verbal repetition in the novel proper Gardner further undermines the viability of any claim to omnipotence; his text implies a refutation of a simplistic notion of a necessary and ubiquitous relation between cause and effect, be it artistic or political. It takes Clumly some seven hundred pages to effect the kind of spiritual regeneration that VanSpanckeren points to. At the outset he is every bit as authoritarian as the old Judge, and at one point he speaks about an officer he has fired in terms that echo those of the Judge: "I shut down that man's *life*" (258); the book's narrator smartly torpedoes the basis of Clumly's apotheosis of self by parenthetically commenting, "It was a lie."

The old Judge's assertions in the "Prologue" are also contradicted in the narrative. In his old age the Judge has evidently forfeited a wisdom he once possessed. Asked at one point by a city official to help remove the mentally troubled Clumly from his post as Chief of Police, the Judge says that he no longer has that kind of power: "That was the old days. I've made people and unmade them, and so did my father and grandfather. But times change, Mr. Uphill. There are no more powers, principalities, gods, demigods. No more wizards, kings" (360). "The new fiction abounds in studies of aesthetic epistemology," Gardner says, and metafictional techniques—extensive and overt use of literary allusions, imitation of literary styles, obtrusive narrators—provide the author with instant access to this "central concern in nearly all modern fiction," namely "the asking of the question 'How does the artist know what he thinks he knows?'" The answer suggested by the widespread use of these obtrusive techniques, Gardner argues, is that the author cannot be absolutely certain of *any* knowledge. Many of the modern experiments with narration are retreats "from the lying authorial omniscience," and they serve to illustrate one point: "Whereas the self-effacing narrator was truthful by definition and convention, to be accepted pretty much as we accept the rules of whist, the obtrusive narrator is *somebody* (or something), therefore non-omniscient and available for questioning." It is interesting to note that Gardner's wrestling with the premises of modern experimental techniques is yet another element of his never-ending dialogue with literary tradition; some of the key issues in the modern debate over aesthetic epistemology were tackled by medieval poets who responded to the issues raised by philosophical nominalism. One of these poets was Chaucer, and Gardner's discussion of the medieval poet's artistic sparrings with nominalism sheds light on his own aesthetic strategies.

The main reason he has written at great length about Chaucer, Gardner professes, is that he is convinced that what Chaucer has to say about life and living is even more relevant today than it was in the fourteenth century:

He knew, for instance, about "uncertainty"—knew from having thought about the arguments offered by the philosophical position called nominalism, that quite possibly all truth is relative (if we use "truth" in, say, the moralist's sense), and knew that quite possibly, there can be, in the end, no real communication between human beings. He played with those ideas throughout his career, and toward the end of his life he played even with such particularly, if not exclusively, modern aesthetic problems as the unreliable narrator and the paradox we see in Samuel Beckett and many other writers of the first rank in this century, that is, the paradox of speech denying the validity of speech. (*The Poetry of Chaucer* ix)

Gardner traces the history of nominalism back to the twelfth century.[5] In the middle of the fourteenth century England witnessed a "revival, or rather revision and flowering" of nominalism due to the teachings of William of Ockham at Oxford: "He was the first to formulate the persuasive nominalist attack on universals, arguing that only singulars exist—particular cows or trees or men—and that the universal (e.g. the nature of man) has objective value or actual existence only as it is *thought up*." Nominalism came as a reaction against realism, with its theory of universals, that is, a Platonic system of thought in which only God's idea is ultimately real, and physical manifestations of ideas are but "shadows passing on a wall." The nominalists argued that "words like 'animal' (i.e., universals) are mere names we invent to express, or abstract, the qualities we have observed in particulars." This position gives rise to an important epistemological dilemma: "If ideas are abstractions from the concrete, I can neither know that my idea is 'right' nor—since you too abstract from concrete particulars—can I meaningfully communicate my idea to you."

Even though the term *relativism* was not part of the vocabulary of fourteenth-century nominalists, Gardner says, "every nominalist understood at least something of that queasy feeling we get while we laugh at a play by Samuel Beckett." Nominalists argued that "all vision, even the artist's vision, is mere opinion. One *feels* that there are truths that can be discovered, not just affirmed.... But how can one defend them?" Hence the nominalists developed the notion that "all human knowledge is suspect" and that "truth is, outside doctrine, finally unknowable."

These are problems that also worry Jonathan Upchurch as he tries to come to terms with the multilayered deceits of the *Jerusalem*. Jonathan prefaces his ruminations on linguistic uncertainty by invoking a principle which on inspection turns out to be a first cousin to Ockham's razor: "There is in all our societies, whether whistclubs or whalers, a law of sufficiency which begins by dictating what things need not be speculated on, for efficient operation of the business at hand, and ends by outlawing and angrily scorning all thought not directly productive of firm, fat bank accounts" (241–42). In Gardner's rendering, Ockham's razor states, "Multiplicity ought not be posited without necessity." Ockham's principle may seem to belie the philosophical thrust of nominalism, but it should be read in the context of his religious convictions. Ockham was a "devout churchman" and responded to the incongruity of his philosophical and religious views by abandoning "all attempts at the reconciliation of human understanding and God's mysteries. Removed to the realm of the incomprehensible, God became a baffling Absolute Will bound by no human concepts of justice or reason, a Being about whom it was futile to ruminate."

Jonathan quarrels with a doctrinaire and simplistic application of Ockham's razor; he begins by attacking the inclination to exploit the law of sufficiency for materialist gains, but he soon waxes metaphysical:

> If the whole of the mind is a grocery-store in all its liveliness and flux—ants in the bread-bin, smell of brown paper and new spring onions, string coming down from the spindle above Mr. Primrose's balding, bespectacled head—then the intellect is a cash-register, and an expressible idea is the clang of its cheap iron bell. By specialization we vivisect reality till all but the head or the left hind leg of the universe is by someone's definition industrial waste. But move the New York industrialist to Tallahassee, abandon him there to hold forth for three years on right and wrong, or move Stonewall Jackson to a Seneca Village, return in six months, and you'll find them gravely altered men. We stake our lives on nice opinions; the globe makes one half-turn, rolling up the Southern Cross, and we clench our brains against madness. (242)

Jonathan will have none of the complacency that accompanies a materialist perversion of Ockham's razor. His sea voyage is, as we shall see, above all a spiritual, or philosophical, journey, and even though in the end he achieves a reconciliation of sorts with metaphysical uncertainty, at an early point in his narrative he embraces an extreme form of nominalism. Verbally Jonathan is at his most rambunctious in expounding on these matters, but we must nevertheless allow him the floor, since his effusions possibly contain a key to the meaning (or *one* of the meanings) of the novella's enigmatic title:

> All we think and believe, in short, is foolish prejudice, even if some of it happens to be true (which seems to me unlikely). Or to make it all still more altiloquent: Human consciousness, in the ordinary case, is the artificial wall we build of perceptions and *conceptions*, a hull of words and accepted opinions that keeps out the vast, consuming sea: It shears my self from all outside business, including the body I walk in but muse on the same as I do on a three-legged dog or an axe-

handle, a slippery wild Indian or a king at his game of chess. A mushroom or one raw emotion (such as love) can blast that wall to smithereens. I become a kind of half-wit, a limitless shadow too stupid to work out a mortgage writ, but I am also the path of the stars, rightful monarch of Nowhere. I become, that instant, the King's Indian: Nothing is waste, nothing unfecund. The future is the past, the past is present to my senses. I gaze at the dark Satanic mills, the sludge-thick streams. I shake my head. They vanish. (242)

This passage is a masterpiece of artistic compression and points up some of the rich aesthetic possibilities inherent in the author's collage technique. First of all, Jonathan's oration serves to further characterize him as a great talker, a teller not only of tall tales of the high seas but a spinner of metaphysical yarns as well. The imagery ("hull of words" and "the vast, consuming sea") reinforces the philosophical voyage symbolism so central to the meaning of "The King's Indian," as well as that of the novella's three most important sources: "The Rime of the Ancient Mariner," "Narrative of A. Gordon Pym," and *Moby-Dick*. Furthermore, the passage invokes an epistemological debate that goes back at least as far as the fourteenth century, ringing as it does with echoes of the nominalist ideas entertained by Ockham and Chaucer. The novella's title is linked to this debate, and the title thus signals one of the reasons why Gardner aligns himself with the new writers and their concerns with aesthetic epistemology.

Early on in his narration Jonathan confesses to the belief that "Indians knew things...without thinking, without learning" (203). Significantly, he remarks on the Indians' intuitive bent of mind in a context which is otherwise loaded with references to his own former rationalistic and utilitarian approach to reality: he recounts his early experiences as a schoolmaster; he reports on his meeting with Reverend Dunkel, who lectures him on one of the cardinal virtues of the Protestant work ethic (Discipline), with Jonathan playing the role of obedient pupil; and he mentions his part-time employment with the Dutch butcher Hans van Klug, when he was "indifferently lopping off arms and legs, joints, rumps, and shoulders, sorting the martyrdom of nature into piles and putting prices on it" (206). Such a rationalistic, utilitarian, and matter-of-fact approach to reality implies the philosophically complacent position that truth is knowable, and that the universe is chartable and manageable. As an Indian, Kaskiwah represents another approach to reality, and one of his functions is apparently to warn against Jonathan's former complacency. The sense of philosophical security that comes with unquestioning acceptance of habits of mind, prejudices, and a belief that there is such a thing as objective knowledge of reality is all too easily shaken, Jonathan says, through sudden shifts of perspective. Jonathan himself is subject to one such shift of perspective when he experiences "the raw emotion" of falling in love with Augusta, and again (even more importantly in view of the novella's title) when he eats the mushrooms offered him by Kaskiwah. The mushrooms are said to be from a mysterious King, and the poison they contain sends Jonathan off to a different world of hallucination for three days. The title thus serves as a reminder of the *precariousness* of a reductionist approach to human knowledge: becoming a King's Indian would seem to be synonymous with accepting, or even embracing, a multiperspectival, nonrationalistic approach to reality.

The legitimacy of an intuitive, nonrationalistic epistemological orientation is further strengthened by the textual allusions at the end of Jonathan's peroration. To a King's Indian, Jonathan says, "Nothing is waste, nothing unfecund." This is only a slight rephrasing of one of the basic convictions of the medieval monk Hugh St. Victor, who in his *Didascalion* argued that "nothing in the universe is unfecund."[6] The Neoplatonic mysticism of thinkers like Hugh became part of the Romantic tradition, which produced, for instance, William Blake, who is echoed in Jonathan's image of the Satanic mills of rationalism that disappear at the shaking of an intuitive, or Indian, head. A repeated call for multiplicity of vision constitutes one of the chief thematic strands of *The Marriage of Heaven and Hell*, where the narrator explains that he has escaped the "eternal lot" of contemplating "the infinite Abyss" that the Angel assigned him to because the abyss was only there as long as the narrator accepted someone else's—in this case the Angel's—metaphysics (xxiii–xxv). The ideational cohesion of Jonathan's ruminations, Hugh St. Victor's Neoplatonic mysticism, and Blake's celebration of intuition and mulitiplicity of vision is brought out even more clearly when one remembers that the concluding lines of Blake's long poem all but repeat the essence of Hugh's vision: "For Everything that lives is holy" (xxviii).

Gardner hardly wants us to be won over to Jonathan's nominalist-inspired mysticism (see Chapter 6 this book). However, Gardner admits "to a real mystical touch" in himself (Bellamy 176), and throughout his fiction there are echoes of Jonathan's call for a multiperspectival approach to reality: James Chandler learns to affirm "the world's buzzing blooming confusion," and Henry Soames discovers "the holiness of things"; Dorkis in *The Wreckage of Agathon* speaks in unmistakably Blakian fashion when he says, "There's a sense in which nothing is evil.... To certain people, everything that happens in the world is holy" (153). And it may be Gardner's mystical inclinations that make him so responsive to Whitehead's philosophy; one of the values that Grendel inadvertently affirms for the reader is the religious speculations of Ork. The old priest borrows Whitehead's words, but the sensibility which informs his confession is closely akin to that of Hugh of St. Victor and Blake: "Ultimate wisdom, I have come to perceive, lies in the perception that the solemnity and grandeur of the universe rise through the slow process of unification in which the diversities of existence are utilized, and nothing, *nothing* is lost" (133).

Gardner does not claim that Chaucer ever became a full-fledged nominalist, but Chaucer did become, he argues, increasingly preoccupied with nominalist dilemmas, among them the unreliability of art.[7] One way in which Chaucer achieved multiple vision was through the use of unreliable narrators; in *The House of Fame*, for instance, the speaker is a "poor, proud, stupid, child-of-Adam philosopher named 'Geffrey'" (*The Poetry of Chaucer* 157), making Chaucer's poem an early example of obtrusive narration indeed. In the *Canterbury Tales* there is of course a host of narrators, all of them more or less unreliable. These narrators are portrayed as fallible characters, and, Gardner argues,

> their human limitations, since they are storytellers, suggest limitations in art itself. The idea, grounded in nominalism, that art is futile—either wrong or incapable of communicating—will become increasingly important in the *Canterbury Tales*.... [U]nreliable narrators one after another force us to face the question squarely, ultimately casting such doubt on art's validity as to bring on Chaucer's *Retraction*. (*The Poetry of Chaucer* 157, 298–99)

Gardner may have had similar reasons for turning Jonathan into such a blatantly unreliable narrator. Being a spinner of yarns he is, as we have seen, by convention not to be trusted. In the context of Jonathan's deliberations on nominalism, Gardner subtly reminds the reader of the young man's unreliability, presumably in order to extend to art the relevance of Jonathan's epistemological skepticism. On his way to the Captain's cabin, he says about blind Jeremiah: "He knew by second sight, he claimed, where the whales was playing. And he knew more than that, or so I've ended up believing. He may have fooled us—there's always that suspicion. But if all his skills was mere showmanship...then all I can say is, that man was the slickest impostor that ever was created" (241). The narrator's unreliability does not stem from his withholding of information—the privilege of any storyteller—in the interest of suspense; but Jonathan's use of tense ("*I've ended* up believing"; "He *may have fooled* us—there's always that suspicion") is directly misleading since he *knows* Jeremiah's true identity all along, as well as the extent of his magical tricks. In this involuted story about appearances and deceits, Gardner lets his narrator add to the confusion by having him entertain possibilities that are flatly illogical. The result is a further difficulty for the listener/reader and a reminder that the text we have in front of us is not the truth but one speaker's wilfully manipulated opinion.

Unreliable narration is thus one aspect of the novella's self-reflexivity, raising questions about the epistemological status of the narrative. Gardner further demonstrates a Chaucerian (and nominalist) awareness of the unreliability of artistic expression by making "The King's Indian" a subject of parody in *The Smugglers of Lost Souls' Rock,* the novel within the novel in *October Light.* This, however, does not indicate a disenchantment with his earlier fiction, Gardner says; rather it is meant to suggest that "anything language can do is open to legitimate distrust" (Winther 519). This comment (as well as the wider issue: Gardner's recognition of epistemological uncertainty and the unreliability of art) seems especially important coming from a value-oriented author, a writer whom many perhaps associate primarily with a fiction that preaches, or moralizes.

The chief vehicle of the parody is the parallelism of character distribution and plot in the two stories. Peter Wagner, the protagonist of *The Smugglers of Lost Souls' Rock,* is picked up by the crew of the *Indomitable* much the same way that Jonathan Upchurch is saved by the *Jerusalem* after his newly purchased sailboat (the *Jolly Independent*) is overrun by the whaler. Upon coming to on board the *Indomitable,* Peter Wagner feels "oppressed by a sense of *déjà vu,* then remembered: all that was happening had happened in some novel he'd read about a hoax" (84). (The first word Jonathan utters in "The King's Indian" is "Hoaxes!") Later we learn that the Police found a paperback book in Wagner's car, "something about an Indian" (174). As he regains consciousness on board the *Jerusalem*, Jonathan is told that he has "'jined with a company of deadmen, ye see'" (216); Peter Wagner tells the crew of the *Indomitable:* "'We're on the Ship of Death'.... Another line, he remembered, from the novel about the hoax" (113).

Captain Fist of the *Indomitable* is clearly Captain Dirge, alias Dr. Flint, resurrected, both of them wearing a black coat and hat, their hair long and white (like Gardner's). At one point Peter Wagner reflects that "in German 'Fist' was 'Faust'" (97) and there is certainly much that is Faustian, not to say fustian, about both captains. Luther Santisillia (he has a first name in common with Dr. Flint) characterizes Captain Fist by saying that he had "made a deal with the Devil" (275). Of course, neither Fist nor Flint has any of the dignity or complexity of Goethe's hero, but they *are* driven by Faustian pride in a more or less perverted form, and they possess a relentless will to pursue their own monomaniacal aims.

At one point in his story Jonathan says about Augusta that at times she was an "emblem of virginal simplicity and goodness" who made him understand "the medieval image of Virgin Mary" (258). Captain Fist does not have a daughter, but also on board the *Indomitable* there is a girl, adding to the symmetry of the two texts. The plot of *The Smugglers of Lost Souls' Rock* leaves no room for a character of Dantesque dimensions like Augusta. Instead we get Jane, a plain all-American girl, forever wearing her red, white, and blue cap. Captain Fist nearly chokes from laughter at the irony of his own description of Jane's role vis à vis the crew of the *Indomitable:* "'What was Guinevere to King Arthur's court, or the Virgin Mary to the Christian religion? The coronet! The jewel that gives it all meaning!'" (98).

On board the *Indomitable* Peter Wagner is treated to a sample of the crew's choice marijuana (cf. Kaskiwah's mushrooms), and in a reefer dream he imagines himself on board a ship called *The New Jerusalem* (98). Minutes earlier Captain Fist has told him that the *Indomitable* is "like a society in small" (97); by and by the smugglers are joined by two blacks and an Indian (whose taciturnity matches that of Kaskiwah in "The King's Indian"), and the multiracial mutiny spurred by Captain Fist's autocratic ways mimicks the uprising against Captain Dirge on board the *Jerusalem.* The orgiastic nature of the revolt in *The Smugglers of Lost Soul's Rock* is a travesty of the democratic euphoria experienced by Jonathan's lordless crew in "The King's Indian." Jonathan's nakedness at the end of his story is symbolic of spiritual rebirth; in learning to care deeply for Miranda he sheds his former solipsism, and his running out naked to help the crew set sails to benefit from the sudden wind lends an Edenic touch to the novella's denouement. In *The Smugglers of Lost Souls' Rock* the object of nakedness is fornication, and the apocalyptic ending, what with earthquakes, the drug squad's B-52 bombers, and UFOs approaching, sets up an ironic alternative vision to the celebratory projection of democratic possibilities offered at the end of Jonathan Upchurch's narrative.

The self-reflexivity of literary creation—art's flaunting of its own artificiality—is thus not only an important element of Gardner's artistic strategy in writing "The King's Indian"; it is also a concern that carries over into other works as well. I have argued that the act of alluding is in itself a way of signalling artifice in that it establishes as a point of reference, not reality, but someone else's fictional invention. The echoic method also helps to underscore Chaucer's point about the unreliability of art. Integrating elements from other people's writings into his own, Gardner implicitly comments on the nonobjective status of literature: there is no such thing as an omniscient work of art. Parodying one of his own earlier works is an extreme way of demonstrating his commitment to multiplicity of vision, as opposed to the belief in the possibility of omniscience, which is inherent in the artistic strategies of writers in the realist tradition. Awareness of epistemological uncertainty is thus a determining factor of the highest order, both as concerns the *content* of Gardner's fiction and the *fictional strategies* he employs in dealing with that uncertainty. This dual aspect is nowhere more prominent than in "The King's Indian," where there is a multilayered textual interplay between Gardner's own narrative and his extensive borrowings from authors who are concerned with similar aesthetic and philosophical problems.

COLLAGE TECHNIQUE II:
A CASE STUDY

In one of his asides to the reader in "The King's Indian," Gardner makes no bones about his indebtedness to a number of literary forebears; the book has been written, he says, "with the help of Poe and Melville and many another man" (316). This indebtedness takes on many forms. "The Rime of the Ancient Mariner" serves mainly as a kind of ideational and compositional backdrop for the novella; there are only a few direct references to it in "The King's Indian." "Narrative of A. Gordon Pym" and *Moby-Dick* likewise provide a general narrative and philosophical frame of reference; but from these texts Gardner also borrows liberally in terms of plot, distribution of characters, and symbolism, as well as a number of individual scenes and lines.

1

The outstanding common feature of the four texts is that they describe a sea voyage of multiple philosophical import. Jonathan tells his story in the capacity of an old mariner who, he says, is not free of his tale yet (197). Coleridge's Ancient Mariner confesses in like manner to the Wedding Guest: "Since then, at an uncertain hour / That agony returns / And till my ghastly tale is told, / This heart within me burns" (VII, ll. 582–85). In "The King's Indian," as in Coleridge's poem, there are albatrosses and phantom ships, and the *Jerusalem* is halted in its path by a complete calm which is lifted only after Miranda blesses Jonathan unawares.

Captain Dirge's whaler, the *Jerusalem*, is out of Nantucket, as is the *Grampus*, which carries Pym and his friend Augustus to their wild adventures on the high seas. In recounting the incident which led to his being overrun by the *Jerusalem*, Jonathan borrows a number of phrases and passages from the *Ariel* episode in Poe's novel.[1] Several other key episodes in "The King's Indian" are likewise lifted straight out of "Pym." Jonathan's reflections when nearly falling from the masthead bring to mind Poe's concept of "the Imp of the Perverse," and in fashioning this incident Gardner avails himself of Pym's breathless description of his near fall from the mountainside on the island of Tsalal.[2] Furthermore, the cataclysmic mutiny that Pym witnesses on board the *Grampus* is the direct source of Jonathan's description of the crew's revolt against Captain Dirge on board the *Jerusalem*.[3] Finally, and most significantly, Gardner uses the eschatological ending of "Pym" as a backdrop for the denouement of "The King's Indian"; in fact, an important part of the intention behind Gardner's ending is lost unless it is read with Poe's text in mind. Toward the conclusion of his narrative, Pym finds himself driven by a strong current into a cataract into which he is engulfed. Gardner transposes the milky white sea and the vapor of Pym's polar region to his own novella, even to the point of having the vapor change into a mysterious shrouded human figure.[4] Gardner borrows but *modifies*, and the aesthetic significance of his modulations will be explored shortly.

Setting out to sea in the little sloop he has "bought" from Pious John and company, Jonathan waxes theatrical and begins to cite lines that he remembers only imperfectly. Those lines originally were given to Ishmael, and by putting the words of Melville's narrator into Jonathan's mouth at this early stage of the narrative, Gardner establishes *Moby-Dick* as an important instrument for the reader in his attempt to navigate the artistic waters of "The King's Indian."[5] It is noteworthy that in this important early scene, as well as in the later, equally crucial, mast episode,[6] the literary ghosts of Poe and Melville perch *jointly* on Jonathan's shoulders, creating an ideational tension and an artistic compression which are richly suggestive. Even though the individual lines or phrases that find their way from *Moby-Dick* into "The King's Indian" are fewer than those of "Pym," the points of contact between Gardner's text and that of Melville are legion.

For instance, Gardner was obviously inspired by his New England predecessor in conceiving of Captain Dirge, alias Dr. Flint. Flint has none of Ahab's tragic stature, but his name, although devoid of the biblical resonance of the name Melville chose for his captain, is every bit as suggestive of spiritual obduracy as is

Melville's allusion to the idolatrous Old Testament king. The portrait whose riddle Flint is trying to solve by seeking out the Vanishing Isles, is the magician's pasteboard mask, as well as that of his daughter and his crew. Flint proves an adept student of Ahab's tactics by imitating his Fedallah trick, bringing his own longboat crew of slaves to help him in his fanatical scheme. In *Moby-Dick* the dangers of a monomaniacal quest for transcendence—the desire to unravel the secrets of "the Beyond"—are mainly brought out through Melville's description of Ahab's tragic fall. Flint serves a similar purpose in "The King's Indian" in that he refuses to turn around long after the crew members have realized the futility of the expedition; Flint, like Ahab, shows no concern for the welfare of his men, and the ultimate consequence is of course the very nasty mutiny, bringing about the death of Flint.

Ahab and Flint are both intensely proud men, even though they may differ with regard to how their pride is motivated; Stanley Geist points out that Ahab's pride springs "not out of conceit or vanity but out of suffering" (36). In Flint's case a kind of suffering may be involved, but chiefly that which results from a bruised vanity. An important part of the motivation for his quest has to do with his pride in his skills as a magician; Flint suspects that the story about the portrait, the ghost ship, and the Vanishing Isles might be a hoax, and Wilkins explains that a strong reason for the expedition was Flint's "professional" interest: "If somebody's tricking him, his arrogance demands that he spy out who" (308). In the end both Flint and Ahab are consumed by the passion of their pride. As Georg Roppen points out, Melville links Ahab's consuming passion to his fire worship: "He worships in defiance a cosmic force he knows to be solely destructive, one which consumes and blinds, yet he begs it to come in its 'lowest form of love,' so that he may kneel and kiss it" (153). Gardner may have been thinking of this "very heart of darkness in Ahab's mind" when he conceived of Flint's spectacular death by spontaneous combustion as fitting for a man consumed by internal fires.

Much of the narrative tension in *Moby-Dick* springs from the affinity which the reader perceives between the natures of Ishmael and Ahab. As W. E. Sedgwick, among others, has pointed out, Ishmael's story "turns on his mortal need to maintain himself against the strong drag he feels toward Ahab" (120). Hence Melville gives to Ishmael an early premonition about Ahab. Prior to his first encounter with the captain of the *Pequod*, Ishmael learns about how Ahab lost his leg to Moby Dick, and he tells the reader that "what had been incidentally revealed to me of Captain Ahab, filled me with a certain wild vagueness of painfulness concerning him. And somehow, at the time, I felt a sympathy and a sorrow for him, but for I don't know what, unless it was the cruel loss of his leg" (79–80). For a while Ishmael also becomes obsessed with Ahab's purpose. After the quarter-deck episode he exclaims: "I, Ishmael, was one of that crew; my shouts had gone up with the rest; my oath had been welded with theirs; and stronger I shouted, and more did I hammer and clinch my oath, because of the dread in my soul. A wild, mystical, sympathetical feeling was in me; Ahab's quenchless feud seemed mine" (179).

There is, then, a close spiritual kinship between Ishmael and Ahab, as there is between Jonathan and Flint. Just as Ahab is totally absorbed by his desire to capture the White Whale, so Flint is engrossed with the notion of finding the Vanishing Isles. What these isles are to Flint, the *Jerusalem* is to Jonathan; he becomes obsessed with unveiling the secret of the whaler's mission. This obsession on Jonathan's part serves to propel the novella's action and thus helps to establish a logic for the plot. But there is more at stake in Jonathan's story than mere adventure; even though outward action is important in the novella—it is, like "Pym" and *Moby-Dick*, also an adventure story—the ultimate significance of plot in all three stories is its philosophical import. Jonathan's strong desire to know the secrets of the *Jerusalem* is a logical extension of a metaphysical bent in his character. This essential aspect of his psyche is adumbrated by the story with which he launches his tale: his first visit to one of Dr. Flint's "mesmeric demonstrations." The suggestiveness of Flint's magical tricks sends Jonathan into a frenzy; when the conjurer, using his daughter Miranda as his medium, takes his audience back in time to "the earliest dwellings of man, the dripping caves," Jonathan suffers a powerful hallucinatory experience worthy of a Hitchcock movie: "Great gabbling birds flew all around me, purest white, darting, dipping, plunging, screeching, their wingtips stretching from wall to wall as they warred, all eyes, steel talons, and beaks, with the writhing serpents on the balcony around me" (200).

This childhood experience has made a lifelong impression on Jonathan. The Dr. Flint episode is doubly important; it prepares the reader for later plot developments, and it highlights what proves to be one of the chief motivating factors in young Jonathan's life: his fascination with "the Beyond," those aspects of existence that do not lend themselves to ready answers. As the

Flints begin to drop "from the circuit," Jonathan thinks he has cured himself of their influence over him, "their power to frighten and draw [him], suck [him] out toward unearthly things" (201). His encounter with the Flints proves to him that "there are deadly, enslaving attractions that might laugh at even winds and tides, unhinge the swing of planets," and he is certain "the old gray sea was involved in it" (202). This explains why, to Jonathan, Miranda's entrancing face, "with its oversized, mournful eyes, was like the moon reflected in the wine-gray sea" (200).

But even though Jonathan decides to keep "to landside" to steer clear of these "enslaving attractions"—attractions which to him take on the threatening aspect of Milton's Hell "from whence deep thunders roare" (201)[7]—his reasons for doing so show that the cure has not been successful. He decides to start saving money to buy a farm in Illinois, a project which particularly appeals to him because it would take him close to wild Indians. As we have seen, it is Jonathan's theory that Indians, like Luther and Miranda Flint, know things that are hidden to ordinary mortals, the difference being that the Flints owe their knowledge to magical skills, whereas Indians possess gifts that allow them knowledge "without thinking, without learning" (205). Jonathan's desire to learn the secret of Indian intuitive wisdom and insight indicates that his Illinois project does not represent a turning away from the attraction of otherworldliness, but rather is a subconscious attempt to get at the riddles of existence by a different route.

When Jonathan's project flounders, this seems to be a matter of chance, to the extent that chance and raw gin have anything whatsoever to do with one another. On the face of things it is Jonathan's working late one evening and nothing else that makes him visit the Buried Treasure Inn, landing him in the genial company of Pious John and his crew. But, Jonathan's protestations at the time notwithstanding, fickle-fingered fate is not at all the agent of Jonathan's fall. He is later convinced by Billy More that he may himself "have been somewhat a party to the cheat. The mind runs deeper than its schemes, could be" (211). Jonathan falls an easy prey to the pirates' hoax because his own subconscious wants him to, and part of the reason is evidently his desire to be reunited with Upchurch, Sr., a sailor of long standing: the deal with Pious John et al. is settled while Jonathan speaks tearfully of his love for his father. Whereas Jonathan is impervious to his mother's pleas for his affection, his emotional ties to his father are strong, for reasons that become quite obvious as the story progresses. We learn

that Jonathan's father takes a fiendish delight in Flint's machina-
tions, and the young boy's attraction to the magician and to his
father are but flip sides of the same coin. Jonathan's father is also a
trickster; he is a great manipulator of words, driving his wife into a
rage of jealousy with his stories of how he sported with mermaids
off the coast of Gibraltar; to while away the time on board
whalers, he had turned himself into an expert sleight-of-hand man.
Jonathan takes after his father (and therefore, indirectly, Flint) in
imitating his many magical tricks, and the fantastic yarn he is in
the process of spinning bears ample witness to his storytelling talents. Like Flint, Jonathan is a crafty manipulator of other people,
constantly putting his fellow crew members on, and in the end he
outwits even Dr. Flint, the archtrickster. At times he speaks of
himself in terms which might have been equally descriptive of
Flint, the ultimate virtuoso of theatrics:

> "Who are you?" I asked... "Who are *all* of you? Where the
> devil are we shipping?" At the sound of my own grandiose
> theatrics—questions tinged, in my own ears at least, with
> dark metaphysical overtones—my fear leaped to new intensi-
> ty. "What ship *is* this?" I asked. I spoke louder now, the
> silence of the ship all around me like the silence of a black-
> draped hall when a medium begins, and my question self-
> conscious despite my urgency, as if I were delivering lines
> long rehearsed. (234)

Little wonder that Jonathan warms to the occasion of finding himself on board a mystery ship bound for the nebulous Vanishing
Isles.

The *Jerusalem*'s true mission is not whaling, then, but discovery. The multilayered philosophical significance of Jonathan's
sea voyage is in great measure dependant on Gardner's exploitation of his sources; by having "The King's Indian" resonate with
the ideational opposition of sea versus land that is central to the
narratives of Coleridge, Poe, and Melville, Gardner imbues
Jonathan's voyage with a mythopoetic quality which serves to universalize the tensions and conflicts of the novella.

It is at sea that Coleridge's Ancient Mariner gains insights
which were kept from him while ashore, and the nature of those
insights shows up the one crucial common denominator of the
four texts we are discussing. Reviewing the central issues in
Coleridge criticism, James D. Boulger notes, in his introduction to

Twentieth Century Interpretations of "The Rime of the Ancient Mariner," that the poem has been seen to treat, among other things, "the creative artist and his place in the world" (8). Coleridge, forever struggling to free himself and his contemporaries from the intellectual straitjacket of empiricism, takes his mariner on an imaginary voyage where he must "give up all fetishes of the common sense...to make contact with spiritual reality" (17). "Before the Mariner can accept faith, repentance, and a true sense of the spiritual order behind phenomena or objects," Boulger reminds us, "he must be frightened out of the easy, vulgar, and commonplace assurance of the 'reality' of things" (16).

Even though in important ways Coleridge and Gardner fight different philosophical battles in their narratives, both writers question the epistemological assurance of an empirical or realist approach to knowledge; in "The Rime of the Ancient Mariner" and "The King's Indian" alike, the protagonists must go to sea to make this realization for themselves. The Mariner's blessing of the water snakes is a gratuitous, nonrational act, liberated from the cause-and-effect mode of thinking that governs life on land, and it is this imaginative act which saves the Mariner, bringing redemptive winds. Similarly, winds come to the *Jerusalem* when Miranda and Jonathan learn to give up their quest for total knowledge and instead settle for limited vision. Jonathan bestows blessings on Miranda by declaring his love for her in her new condition of non-Dantesque ugliness; as we shall see, this ugliness is an emblem of human fallibility or imperfection. Recognizing man's imperfection also involves realizing that man cannot achieve perfect or objective knowledge of the world. In Jonathan's case, too, the act of blessing is a gratuitous act: having declared his love for Miranda, Jonathan remarks, "My voice was shaky, and where the words came from, Heaven knows" (317). Similarly, Miranda blesses Jonathan "unaware" by expressing her love for Jonathan in full recognition of his fallibility: "'You're so *wall*-eyed!'... 'Jonathan, I love you,' she whispered. 'You're grotesque'" (322).[8] The reason Miranda gives for loving Jonathan of course comically reverses traditional and rational expectations; and then, the next moment there is wind.

Daniel Hoffman calls "Narrative of A. Gordon Pym" Poe's "Total Voyage of Discovery" (265). Edward H. Davidson lists the novel as a prime example of Poe's many "excursions into a philosophy of knowledge" (222); for Poe the "poem, the short story, the novel like 'Pym' became the symbolic enactment of man's search for logic and meaning" (44). Poe's initial purpose in writing "Pym," Davidson argues, was to capitalize on the widespread interest in sea adventure stories at the time, especially those that took their readers to Antarctica, but the project grew, and soon Poe found himself "probing for some 'deep axis of reality,'" employing the happily hit-upon sea voyage as his frame of investigation (159–60). One crucial element in all the adventures that befall Pym is *deceit:* things are never what they appear to be. Throughout the story the characters constantly try to deceive each other; actions taken very often fail to produce the intended effect. What Pym slowly comes to realize, Davidson reminds us, is that this "theme of deception is applicable not only to the lives of men, but...to the very construction of the world itself" (168). In "Pym," therefore, Poe is out to create a mood not unlike that which rules in "The Rime of the Ancient Mariner," a mood governed by a strong awareness of the unexpected and the nonrational. Davidson therefore seems justified in claiming that "Pym"

is truly a symbolic parable of how the mind moves from an assumed coherence and reality of things to a recognition that everything, even the most logically substantial, is an illusion; the mind makes its own reality. And the perceiving mind fails to act with precision only when it takes for granted a "reality" which is not real. (169)

Since part of Gardner's purpose in writing "The King's Indian" was to explore some basic principles of aesthetic epistemology, there are thus good reasons why he should want to enter into a dialogue with Poe and Coleridge: this dialogue provides him with ready access to the epistemological debate of Romantic aestheticians. Actively exploring the relevance of Poe and Coleridge to his own purposes in "The King's Indian" enables Gardner to address in fictional terms some of the problems that the Romantic aesthetic tradition has confronted. It is clear from what we have said already that he sympathizes with Poe and Coleridge in their formulation of epistemological dilemmas; we shall see that he comes to question some of the solutions that Romantics have offered to these quandaries.

Recognition of epistemological uncertainty takes on a number of expressions in "The King's Indian"; Jonathan's part-time allegiance to a nominalist view of the limitations inherent in any cognitive process was discussed in the previous chapter. Further resonance for these ideas is created in that Gardner weaves ideational patterns from "Pym" into the artistic fabric of "The King's Indian." Deception is widespread in Jonathan's story, as it is in "Pym." In addition to Jonathan (and his father), Dr. Flint, Augusta/Miranda, and Wilkins are tricksters and deceivers, and much of the suspense in the novella stems from the reader's continued puzzlement as to who is at any given moment tricking whom. Flint's and Augusta's motivation for going to sea in the first place springs from their wish to penetrate a mystery which proves to be nothing but a hoax; Jonathan never quite gets to the bottom of the *Jerusalem*'s many secrets (did Miranda kill one of the sailors, or didn't she?); the first mutineers are outwitted by yet another set of mutineers. This parallel insistence on a pervasive pattern of deceit in the two texts helps to underscore the precariousness of the cognitive processes that govern people's lives.

Yet another parallelism serves to reinforce this point. Gardner obviously borrowed from "Pym" in giving Miranda the alias of Augusta. Gardner may similarly have had one of Poe's subtler narrative schemes in mind when conceiving of Wilkins. The name offers no clue in this case, but Dirk Peters as well as Wilkins are half-breeds; in both texts their animal-like physical frames are emphasized, and on one level of the narrative it is possible to see their functions as parallel. Daniel Hoffman has shown that Augustus and Peters are reflections of Pym's self, providing not one but two alter egos for the narrator. Augustus, the name in all likelihood intended to evoke the Augustan Age of Reason, reflects Pym's intellectual powers: it is Augustus who concocts the many plans that determine Pym's early life at sea. But most of these plans land Pym in trouble, and at a point when physical skill and duress are needed to save Pym from the dangers that his rationalistic self has brought him into, Augustus dies, and Peters—Hoffman calls him Pym's "more atavistic alter ego"—takes over as Pym's companion and helper (269).

For a long time Gardner's working title for his novella was "Augusta" (Howell's *Bibliographical Profile* xviii), a fact which signals the thematic importance of this character and, presumably, her name. Grace comes to Augusta (now Miranda) and Jonathan alike, but only after they have shifted their philosophical priorities; their developments are parallel, strengthening the case for reading Augusta as Jonathan's spiritual double. The logic of the plot is strongly similar to that of "Pym"; as long as Augusta and Jonathan are governed by their rationalistic inclinations, the consequences of their actions are calamitous.

Augusta, initially working in close allegiance with her father, at one point reveals to Jonathan the rationalistic and epistemological presumptuousness of the *Jerusalem*'s mission: "We've come to...understand...*everything*" (291). Flint and his daughter are ready to go to extreme lengths to fulfill their philosophical ambitions. Like Ahab, they will jeopardize the safety of ship and crew to penetrate the mask of the inscrutable. Jonathan, likewise, is characterized by an irresistible urge to know, and understand, the *Jerusalem*'s secrets. The most dramatic outcome of his rationalistic hubris is the death of the Negro slave, whom Jonathan unceremoniously commits to his bunk as part of his effort to spy on Captain Dirge and Jeremiah when they go over to the Pirates' ship. Somebody kills the black man, presumably mistaking him for Jonathan, and thus Jonathan's curiosity exacts a heavy price.

Just as Peters is an atavistic alter ego for Pym, so Wilkins acts as a double for Jonathan's physical and animalistic self. Wilkins is variously likened to a monkey, an albatross, a frog, a crow, and a lizard, and he thus brings to mind Caliban, half man, half animal, who likewise had rapist designs—albeit unfulfilled—on Shakespeare's Miranda. In satisfying his long-cherished dreams of possessing Miranda, Wilkins acts vicariously for Jonathan. Upon first meeting Miranda on the *Jerusalem*, Jonathan cannot help but feel his "maleness quicken," and he is hard put to conceal "the terrible hungry expansion" in his trousers (253). These sensual inclinations are kept in check for a long time, however, giving precedence to spiritual and Platonic expressions of affection in keeping with the cerebral bent of Augusta's and Jonathan's quests for knowledge. Wilkins's rape of Augusta/Miranda creates the emotional and intellectual climate which makes possible Jonathan's and Miranda's redemption through a mutual recognition of their physical nature. Jonathan acknowledges this acceptance of physicality brought about by the rape when he lies down naked on the berth next to mutilated Miranda. Initially he takes care not to suggest sexual desire, revealing insight into the psychological traumas surrounding rape. Finally he touches her breast, however, and Miranda seals this tacit recognition of their essential physicality by declaring her love for wall-eyed Jonathan. A prerequisite to their redemption is thus a subjugation of their one-sidedly rationalistic selves; in like manner Pym's survival depends on the emergence of Peters as first helper and companion.

Moby-Dick also deals with problems of epistemology, and again a sea voyage serves as vehicle for the author's probing of philosophical questions. Charles Feidelson, Jr., has put the matter most succinctly: "Ishmael opens his narrative by identifying voyage with vision: the field of man's vision is the sea.... The attraction of the mind to the sea is life itself as a quest for knowledge" (28–29). Those lines of Ishmael's that Gardner gives to Jonathan as he is about to embark upon his first nautical experience in the *Jolly Independent* speak to this point, and the author of "The King's Indian" thereby signals that his primary interest in *Moby-Dick* is epistemological. Finding himself alone on the wharf by the abandoned lumberyard of Pankey & Co., Jonathan is unable to resist the allure of the kind of "water-gazing" that so fascinates Ishmael in the first chapter of *Moby-Dick*, and he suddenly decides that he wants to "be there," despite his sensible plans about going to Illinois: "In landlessness alone lies the highest truth, shoreless, indefinite as God!" (212) In formulating his resolve Jonathan borrows Ishmael's famous line in "The Lee Shore" chapter in *Moby-Dick*. At this point in his career, however, Jonathan does not share Ishmael's serious interest in philosophical matters; in reasoning Ishmael-like about the attractions of the sea, Jonathan is hard put to reach beyond the stage of whimsical metaphysical posturing, a point Gardner effectively makes by having Jonathan break off in the middle of his recitation of Ishmael's apotheosis of Bulkington: "Better to perish in that howling infinite than be...something or other. (I forget my phrase.)" (212).

Jonathan's ficklemindedness notwithstanding, the relevance of the problems Ishmael confronts in *Moby-Dick* to the kind of intertextual ideational interplay Gardner establishes between "The Rime of the Ancient Mariner," "Narrative of A. Gordon Pym," and "The King's Indian" is clear: *Moby-Dick*, too, raises questions about the relationship between words and objects, about man's ability to know the phenomena and processes of the world. If readers of *Moby-Dick* were asked to recite the first line of the novel, many would probably think immediately of that famous phrase, "Call me Ishmael." However, as Tony Tanner points out, that is not the opening line; the very first word of the text is *Etymology*, and then follow a number of definitions of the word *whale* provided by an "old usher"; after that again come a series of "Extracts" which also address various aspects of the whale. "All in all," Tanner says, "it is a very 'bookish' beginning, reminding us comically yet seriously of documents as well as whales. It makes us aware that what we are holding is just one more document, and that Melville himself is a kind of usher or librarian handing to us his own very special kind of lexicon" (21–22). Tanner's reminder is especially interesting because his reason for talking about Melville in a book about American fiction published between 1950 and 1970 ties in with Gardner's observation about recent American writers and their concern with aesthetic epistemology. American postwar writers, Tanner argues, have been inordinately occupied with the relationship between words and so-called reality, and this is a traditon which dates back to the American Renaissance writers (21–27). Of the three novels that Tanner cites to argue this thesis, two have become major sources for "The King's Indian"!⁹

2

Gardner thus draws upon Coleridge, Poe, and Melville in developing and supporting one of his central purposes in "The King's Indian"; with their help he wants to question the notion that objective knowledge is accessible to man, as well as the claims to omniscience implied by the literary strategies of writers in the realist tradition. Epistemological uncertainty naturally constitutes a particularly sticky problem for literary artists. Coleridge and Poe on the one hand, and Melville on the other, go their separate ways in dealing with this problem, and we shall see that Gardner—through the use of irony and parody, and through modulations of the fictional logic established in "Narrative of A. Gordon Pym" and *Moby-Dick*—places himself in the philosophical camp of Melville in tackling epistemological uncertainty.

Poe demonstrated the limits to human cognition in story after story; he came closest to finding a way of dealing with those limits in "Pym" and "Eureka." What he tries to achieve in these two texts is a literary expression of transcendence. In so doing, he took his philosophical pointers from that species of Romantic aesthetic epistemology which Coleridge developed.[10] Poe read Coleridge at an early stage of his career, and he slavishly adopted central parts of Coleridge's analysis of the creative process. The tripartite division of human mental faculties into fancy, the primary imagination and the secondary imagination that Coleridge establishes in *Biographia Literaria* corresponds almost exactly to the scheme which Poe lays out in "The Philosophy of Composition," albeit with a slight change in terminology. Although all men possess imagination in the sense that they combine and order sensory data (primary imagination), only the precious few possess the secondary imagination, which is a prerequisite to poetic creation. The secondary imagination "both orders and destroys; it goes through the world of reality or 'selfish solicitude' and conceives some comprehensible reality which only the rhetoric (Poe thought of it as music or poetry) of the imagination may express or convey." Coleridge and Poe were idealists who believed words to be signs of essences and absolutes; the imagination offers "enticements to and then visions of the infinite, the ideal." In "The Poetic Principle" Poe speaks of an "immortal instinct, deep within the spirit of man," which is the "sense of the Beautiful." He calls this instinct "a thirst" and he likens it, unforgettably, to "the desire of the moth for the star. It is no mere appreciation of the Beauty before us—but a wild effort to reach the Beauty above" (273). More often than not Poe's poems and stories convey an impassioned sense of frustration at the impossibility of bringing this "wild effort" to fruition. Coleridge once remarked, "My mind feels as if it ached to behold and know something *great*, something *one* and *indivisible*." Poe fervently shared this sentiment, and it is generally agreed that "Narrative of A. Gordon Pym" and its companion piece, "Eureka," are his most ambitious attempts at giving expression to the experience of transcendence that he longed for all his life.

David Halliburton says of "Pym" that there "is perhaps no more interesting attempt, in American literature, to render pure transcendence" (278). He makes his remark after an analysis of the novel's ending, in which the increasingly pacified Pym suddenly sees—he is at this point rushing into "the embraces of the cataract," where a chasm opens to receive him and Peters—"a shrouded human figure, very far larger in its proportions than any dweller among men. And the hue of the skin of the figure was of the perfect whiteness of the snow" (242). Some critics have read this ending as another version of the apocalyptic conclusion that we find in "MS Found in a Bottle." Thus F. O. Matthiessen speaks of "the horror of its unrelieved light, which is the main intention of Poe's climax"; S. Foster Damon likens "the horrible whiteness" of Poe's polar region to the whiteness which, "incarnate as Moby Dick, rose from the depths and all but killed Ishmael."[11] More convincing are those critics who stress the positive notes struck by the ending. Pym's passage from Tsalal into the whiteness of the cataract should be read as a *release* from the evil of blackness. Charles O'Donnel reminds us that to Poe white is "the omnicolor," that is, "the perfect blend of all colors, and broken up it becomes the separate colors, just as God broke up the unity of unparticled matter into the disunity of particled matter, which then struggles

again toward reunification with the full design" (40). As Sidney
Kaplan points out, "Pym feels no terror; unlike the hero of 'MS
Found in a Bottle,' who descends in horror into the whirlpool, Gordon Pym, lulled in warm milk...rushes away from the Black into
the embracing arms of the comforting White, while the gigantic
birds shriek God's 'Tekel' and Nu-Nu dies of fright" (160).

Poe permits Pym to survive his polar descent, but he does not
give him the floor to reveal what he saw there. The standard, and
convincing, reason critics offer for this omission is Poe's inability
to find words for his vision of transcendence. In "Eureka," published the year before he died, he made a concerted effort at giving
words to what he was only able to suggest in "Pym"; in this
extended "prose poem" of more than one hundred pages, he undertakes to speak of "*the Physical, Metaphysical and Mathematical—of the Material and Spiritual Universe:—of its Essence, its
Origin, its Creation, its Present Condition and its Destiny*" (185).
"Eureka" is, in Davidson's apt description, "a treatise in 'scientific
religion'" in which Poe attempts "to make the universe an
'unknown known'" (227). Using as his point of departure the most
recent findings of contemporary physicists concerning the secrets
of electricity, Poe develops a cosmology in which he posits a distant epoch of Unity, in which everything was gathered in the One.
This Unity was broken up when unparticled matter became the
particled matter of atoms, that is, the physical universe as we
know it. Atoms and particled matter struggle back to the center,
and so does the human mind, moving "toward the primal order of
final being" (231). Hence we get Pym losing himself into whiteness, the "omnicolor" symbolical of ultimate Unity, or the One.

Jonathan, too, is fascinated by "the Beyond." Initially, as
shown in the Boston theater incident, Dr. Flint's mesmerizing
powers imbue him with fear of the unknown; convinced that the
sea is involved with the "enslaving attractions" of the visions suggested by the Flints, he decides to keep to landside. But once his
defenses are down—he is now the owner of the sloop, the *Jolly
Independent*—he succumbs to the temptations of "water-gazing,"
and suddenly he finds himself enthusiastically embracing the possibility of putting out to sea, where, as he says, the spirit of Plato
and Plotinus rules (212). Throughout his narrative he is again and
again strongly moved by a Pymlike temptation to lose himself in a
mystic union with the ocean. The single most important of these
experiences is his near fall from the mast. In fashioning this incident, Gardner fully explores the rich artistic possibilities of his

collage technique. This scene is borrowed almost in its entirety from "Pym" and *Moby-Dick*; thereby Gardner imbues his own narrative with some of the high drama of the sources. But the true genius of this subtle instance of literary grafting lies in Gardner's combining two episodes which not only are crucial in their separate contexts but which also push in completely opposite thematic directions. The result is a remarkable compression of ideas and of significant action; in addition, the selection of details included in the scene serves the author's purpose of characterization.

Trying to patch one of the *Jerusalem*'s sails near the crow's nest, Jonathan makes the mistake of looking down, and suddenly he becomes the victim of the impulse which Poe so strikingly has labelled "the Imp of the Perverse," that is, the desire to do just the opposite of what good reason tells you to do:

> I found myself thinking of the distance between me and the deck, and the dangerous mutability of rope, my ladder back to safety. In vain I struggled to be rid of such thoughts. The more earnestly I labored not to think, the more busily my mind went spinning toward disaster. In no time, the crisis was solidly upon me—the anticipation of the feeling of falling; the giddiness, the struggle, the headlong descent—and then the mysterious *longing* to fall, the hunger to sink into the absolute freedom of suicide. (253)

Jonathan's experience in the mast is for all practical purposes identical with Pym's near fall from the mountainside on the island of Tsalal. But Pym, always the reporter rather than the interpreter, does not stop to analyze the importance of this event. Gardner gives it an ideational context by linking it to Ishmael's reflections on the dangers involved in manning the masthead. Jonathan suddenly finds that he is not afraid: "It was as if I had lost identity, become one with the mystic ocean at my feet, image of the deep-blue bottomless soul that pervades all mankind and nature like Cranmer's ashes" (237). He has become one of those young Platonists that Ishmael (rhetorically) warns the Nantucket fishowners against enlisting in their fisheries. Ishmael has a sound piece of warning for the Platonists as well:

> But while this sleep, this dream is on ye, move your foot or hand an inch; slip your hold at all; and your identity comes back in horror. Over Descartian vortices you hover. And per-

haps, at mid-day, in the fairest weather, with one half-throt-
tled shriek you drop through that transparent air into the
summer sea, no more to rise for ever. Heed it well, ye Panthe-
ists! (159)

The juxtaposition of these two sources puts Jonathan's—and
Pym's—experience in a proper perspective. Through his identification with Ahab's purpose, Ishmael reveals that he also is tempted
by the allure of "the Beyond"; he, too, feels the desire to penetrate
the mask of the inscrutable. But unlike Ahab, the "incurable tran-
scendentalist,"[12] Ishmael knows better than to allow himself to be
consumed by this desire; in time Ishmael pulls back, and survives.

Pym, on the other hand, apparently takes no warning from
his near fall. He is rescued by Peters, lies down for fifteen minutes,
and finds, on recovery, that his trepidation has vanished completely: "*I felt a new being*" (230; my italics). The experience thus
appears to be a *positive* one for Pym. The reason is, Daniel Hoffman suggests, that the fall, like the criminal's longing to reveal
himself in "The Imp of the Perverse," is "*the longing of the living
body to die,* of the organic to become inorganic, of the differentiat-
ed consciousness in the agony of its separateness to experience the
frightening ecstasy of reintegration into the unity from which it
has been exiled—the unity of personal annihilation" (273). Pym's
experience on the mountainside is an adumbration of the ending,
when the reintegration into unity is achieved.

The mast episode also serves the purpose of characterization.
Not only does Jonathan in that scene become one of Ishmael's
"sunken-eyed Platonists," but he partakes of a Neoplatonic sensibility as well. Plotinian *unio mystica,* Gardner explains in his
study of Chaucer's poetry, is a phase in which "the individual
loses all consciousness and unifies himself with the 'ground of the
world.' The sinking into the all-one is 'the salvation and the
blessedness of the individual'" (*The Poetry of Chaucer* 369, n. 20).
In his transcendental euphoria in the mast Jonathan even glimpses
"the faintest conceivable shadow of some ultimate idea" (237).
Like Pym, Jonathan fails to become educated by this experience.
The only pain he feels is that of battered ribs after Billy More's dramatic rescue operation and the embarrassment at having revealed
himself to be less than the seasoned seahand and pirate that he had
pretended to be.

The author goes to great lengths to suggest that Jonathan's
involvement with transcendental speculation is far from over as a

result of the mast episode. Major vehicles for these suggestions are the sundry allusions to several Poe texts, among them "Ligeia." Augusta is not only Jonathan's rationalistic alter ego; she is also the focal point of his idealistic inclinations. His view of her changes—he is also aware of her imperfections, her potential for evil—but what makes him love her initially is her Dantesque qualities; her beauty is to him "unearthly, as though her small and perfect body were the house of some Plotinian spirit come down from a paler world to spy" (252–53). When she is good, she is "the emblem of virginal simplicity and goodness" who makes him understand "the medieval image of the Virgin Mary, and not as some vulnerary hope for the desperate but as an actual human possibility, a fleshed ideal" (279). The extent of Jonathan's idealist infatuation with Augusta is shown in his associating his love for her with his experience of near *unio mystica* in the mast:

> The world I must endure in separation from Augusta—stars, dark water—had an aliveness I had not observed in it before. It was her counterpart, her extension. As I'd considered falling from the rigging once, I could now toy, unseriously, with sinking peacefully, even joyfully into the waves, my element, my brother. (262)

It is perfectly consonant with Jonathan's idolizing of Augusta that upon first meeting her it is in Augusta's *eyes* that he finds "her chief beauty and the source of her impenetrability. They were the shining gray of storm-charged twilight, larger even than the gazelle eyes of the tribe in the valley of the Nourjahad" (252). Readers of Poe's tales will realize that these are the very same words that the narrator of "Ligeia" employs in his laudation of that perhaps most ideal of Poe's many beautiful ladies, the lady Ligeia, whose beauty is "the beauty of beings either above or apart from the earth" (251).

In their art and in their aesthetic deliberations, the Romantic poets tried to restore unity to the split world which Cartesian dualism had left behind. How to restore unity between the "I" and the universe? As we have seen, "Pym" and "Eureka" deal with this problem, and in Gardner's reading of "Ligeia," so, too, does this Poe story. On the allegorical level, Gardner argues, the meaning of "Ligeia" is "that to capture the ideal one must kill the real" (*The Forms of Fiction* 9). Lady Rowena must die so that the ideal lady Ligeia can be resurrected. This split between the ideal and the real, matter and mind, soul and body, troubles several characters in *The King's Indian*. Their fates are related, and their manner of resolving, or failing to resolve, the conflict has bearing on the denouement of the title novella; in every instance there lurks in the background the ghost of Poe.

The narrator's antagonist in "The Ravages of Spring" is Professor John Hunter, a geneticist who anachronistically has solved the riddle of cloning. But John Hunter is also the name of a contemporary of Coleridge. He was one of the so-called dynamic physiologists whose findings Coleridge drew on in developing his organic theory of art. Davidson thinks Hunter's ideas are part of the tradition behind Poe's belief that "the Idea and especially the Idea of Beauty manifest themselves in shape and form," hence the many botanical references in Poe's poetry.[13]

The real Dr. Hunter is thus associated with a Platonic tradition, and so is, in a perverted way, his fictional namesake. Seeing mind and matter as one, Gardner's Dr. Hunter seeks to transcend the laws of mutability by recreating identical matter; through eternal cloning he hopes to live on forever in copies of himself, seeing each clone as his own father, himself, and his own son. Little wonder Dr. Hunter feels compulsion to talk to the story's narrator about, not Descartes, but the Gnostics, who in the second century "separated body and mind," thereby causing the world to go "stark, raving mad" (52). Dr. Hunter seeks an answer to the split in an affirmation and embracing of matter: "Suppose all goodness is immanent, buried in matter—in animal spirits, the humours, in cryptarch, inorganic atoms—buried there since Time began, where it labors to be born?" (52). His solution is thus the opposite of the one prescribed by the idealist tradition, but the desire for unity is the same: "Suppose you and I should deny God's existence, crush the mad poets' idea of Soul. Would we not have at last made life whole again?" (52). There is therefore an intriguingly ambiguous irony in the fact that Gardner gives to Dr. Hunter Ligeia's/Augusta's "enormous gazelle eyes" (49). The representative of sanity in the story is the narrator, who begins his Usherlike tale by stating that he is not, "like Mr. Poe, a Platonist," and who goes on to say that he cannot share "the Platonistic predilection for Eternity as opposed to Present Time" (35–36).

In "The Warden" there is also a Professor, who likewise addresses the split between matter and mind, but with a diametrically opposite tack from that of Dr. Hunter. The lecture he gives to anyone who cares to listen is entitled "Matter and Mind," and long parts of it have migrated directly from a letter Poe wrote to

James Russell Lowell; the content of the letter conforms with the central precepts of "Eureka."[14] The topic is again unity: "Our present incarnation is progressive, preparatory, temporary. Our future is perfected, ultimate, immortal. The ultimate life is the full design" (96). For the Professor the full design is what matters; his present physical, and therefore rudimental, existence he likens to the condition of the worm, whereas the complete or ultimate life corresponds to the situation of the butterfly; death is but "the painful metamorphosis" between these two conditions. The fact that the Professor maintains this philosophy after living for years and years in abject misery—he is one of the forgotten prisoners in the Warden's dungeons—aligns him with the twelfth-century Albigensians, who, according to Dr. Hunter, had carried the Gnostic separation of body and mind to its logical conclusion by claiming that "flesh was worthless and meaningless" (52).

The philosophical predicament that Dr. Hunter and the Professor in "The Warden" try to escape in their different ways also strongly puts its stamp on, and creates resonance for, the denouement of the titular novella. Wilkins, we have noted, performs functions in Gardner's novella which are similar to those that Peters performs in "Pym." Peters is Pym's atavistic alter ego, taking over as Pym's companion and helper when Augustus (representing Pym's rational faculties) dies; similarly Wilkins acts vicariously for Jonathan in raping Augusta, marking a subjugation of the rational to the physical. But Wilkins is Jonathan's alter ego not only in this respect. Wilkins is another divided character, part Caliban, but also part Ariel, as it were. Like Jonathan, Wilkins is strongly attracted by the prospect of transcendence, of unity, of living the full design. Wilkins's quandary, and the cause of his despair, Jonathan comes to realize, is that he cannot reconcile the real and the ideal; he is "caught in awareness of his imperfection, and as tortured by it as he would have been if he'd had some god he could stand back-to-back with for measurement." Wilkins's tortured state proves to Jonathan that it has "never required enduring forms to make the world Platonic; it requires only inescapable pain" (305–6). Wilkins finds that life, when gauged with a Platonic yardstick, is a paltry thing indeed. Envious of the butterfly, he wants to escape the condition of Poe's worm, wants to "'become one with the universe, undo the separation that makes sinners of us all.'" Wilkins carries his quest for transcendence to what is for him the only logical conclusion, and his dead body sinks down next to "the crudely carved but ornate memorial of some mortal

presumably dead long since, returned to the universe...: A.G.P."
(309–10). Wilkins's gateway to transcendence is less spectacular
than Arthur Gordon Pym's white cataract, but the governing
impulse of their quests is identical.

Gardner signals an affinity between Pym and Wilkins
through that neatly placed carving on the bulkhead of the
Jerusalem. But Pym, we have argued, is but a vehicle for Poe's own
transcendental inclinations. By adumbrating Wilkins's dilemma in
those earlier stories—Poe always in the wings—Gardner further
links Wilkins to the philosophical nexus of Poe's artistic universe.
That link is cemented by the fact that the author lets Jonathan
elaborate on his definition of Wilkins's dilemma in terms that
come straight out of "Eureka":

> So Newton teaches. *Every atom, of every body, attracts every*
> *other atom, both of its own and of every other body, with a*
> *force which varies inversely as the squares of the distances*
> *of the attracting and attracted atom.* If I venture to displace
> by even the billionth part of an inch the microscopic speck of
> dust which lies on the palp of my finger, I have done a deed
> which shakes the moon, and causes the sun to shudder in its
> path, and alters forever the destiny of the myriad stars and
> planets that roll and glow in the majestic presence of our
> insatiable desire. (306)[15]

The issue is again unity, or the full design. Jonathan thus postulates for Wilkins a reading of the world which seems identical
with that of Poe in "Eureka"; in both cases ultimate transcendence
is a motivating factor of the greatest consequence.

Wilkins's demise is the catalyst that brings about Jonathan's
redemption. Jonathan's initial response to Miranda's rape—this is
before the implications of Wilkins's dilemma are revealed to
Jonathan—is revulsion:

> But the image more terrible than all the rest was that of
> Miranda Flint as I'd found her, raped, ruined, in her cabin....
> Each time I touched that chilly flesh, my hand shrank back
> as my mind shrank back from the recognition that sooner or
> later I must face: She was no longer beautiful. The swelling
> might go down, the bruises fade, but the ugliness would
> stay—missing teeth, stooped shoulders, the beaten, cunning
> look of old beggar women. Inescapable. (300)

Jonathan's revulsion is partly motivated by the contrast between his earlier, courtly (in the medieval sense of the word) view of Miranda and the wreck he sees before him; the real and the ideal again fail to match up. Jonathan now comes to understand that his earlier Dantesque vision is merely a product of artistic invention. He realizes that Miranda is, always was,

> mere girl, mere woman, humanity's showpiece, transformed by nineteen centuries of pampering to a stage creation, tinseled puppet painted, taught speech by troubadours—championed by knights who knew her lovely and probably unfaithful—philosophized by painters and jewelers and poets—and now the theater had collapsed on her, ground her to the staddle, revealed what she was. (304)

Jonathan's revulsion in turn leads to a sense of loss; he mourns the loss of his innocence, and he hopes that Miranda will die rather than live on in her imperfect state.

However, once the ramifications of Wilkins's suicide have begun to register themselves firmly in Jonathan's mind, his attitude changes. We now get the scene in which Coleridgean grace comes to Miranda and Jonathan through a mutual recognition of their fallibility. We should dwell on that scene one more time, because it takes on added philosophical and artistic significance in light of the Cartesian split we have been discussing in these last few pages. It is Gardner's telling invention that whereas grace is bestowed upon Coleridge's Mariner when he recognizes the *beauty* of the water-snakes, Miranda blesses Jonathan unawares when she discovers fully his physical ugliness. It is only after Jonathan and Miranda have accepted their essential physicality that their former solipsism changes into love. The artistic intention behind the scene is obviously to refute the notion that a recognition of Cartesian dualism must result in a position of either/or, a renunciation either of matter or of mind. By an adept ironic reversal of the ending of "Ligeia," Gardner subtly reinforces the point that it is by recognizing, and accepting, their physicality that Jonathan and Miranda are able to develop the spiritual aspects of their nature. At the end of Poe's story, the ideal suppresses the real; lady Rowena dies so that lady Ligeia can transmigrate into her body. A sign that this is about to happen is the sudden turning of lady Rowena's own fair hair from yellow to lady Ligeia's black. In "The King's Indian," however, Jonathan is made to observe that Miranda's "dyed black hair was coarse and scratchy, but at the roots it was yellow and delicate, a coming of spring" (317).

In "The King's Indian" we witness, then, a gradual shifting of philosophical allegiance. Initially Gardner makes what we might call affirmative use of all his sources; by employing for his own narrative the sea motif which is a common denominator of all three sources, Gardner establishes epistemology as a major topic of his novella. The fact that he plays the yarn frame against that of the tale, but also the mere fact that he *is* alluding, along with his introduction of elements of the age-old nominalist debate, help to warn the reader against epistemological complacency and belief in the possibility of achieving absolute knowledge. This is a point which must of necessity affect one's view of the creative process and the status of the finished literary product.

Gardner and his predecessors thus share an interest in aesthetic epistemology. But Gardner attributes a wider meaning to the term *aesthetics* than the one given in encyclopedias of literature. He has offered the following interesting account of his purposes in *The King's Indian:*

> The whole book is a study in aesthetics—aesthetics I think in the only sense that really counts, as it expresses people through a theory of beauty. Aesthetics can never be completely abstract, it has to be derived from the physical expression of a theory in people's feelings and lives, so that to study it you make up characters and you show what happens if they shape their world by this aesthetic standard or by that one—this idea of the sublime or that one—and hopefully what you come to is true art, which everybody can share in. It puts all artistic approaches into perspective.... So basically it's a book about aesthetics, a subhead under metaphysics. It *is* my book about aesthetics. (Harvey 81–82)

There is thus more at stake in *The King's Indian* than aesthetics narrowly conceived, as, of course, there is in Gardner's sources. Gradually Gardner nudges his readers into seeing that his initial allegiance to Poe's philosophical convictions stops at a certain point. Much as he admires Poe's artistic daring and willingness to experiment with fictional form, he takes, as we have seen, exception to Poe's attempts at making the unknown known. By working elements of Poe's fiction into his own narrative, Gardner dramatizes the potentially dire effects of Poe's particular "aesthetic standard," Poe's "idea of the sublime."

3

Having dealt in a serious manner with the implications of Poe's philosophical convictions, Gardner can allow himself to poke gentle fun at his predecessor in the final pages of "The King's Indian." There is much in the ending of "Pym" to tickle Gardner's imagination. As he himself points out, "The King's Indian" is, among other things, a celebration of democracy (Harvey 81), and he turns the ending of his own text into an occasion for reversing some of the "anti-democratic" patterns of "Pym." Sidney Kaplan reminds us that Poe took an active part in the public debate over the virtues and vices of slavery as an institution, and that he came down heavily on the side of Southern plantation owners. His arguments were based on what he saw as the "'peculiar nature' of the Negro." In a review of a book entitled *Slavery in the United States*, Poe concludes a long harangue to this effect with this, for him, very obvious truth: "*Our theory is a short one.... It was the will of God it should be so.*"[17] This interpretation of the nature of the black man informed Poe's writing of "Pym," and his Tsalal is an inversion of the Garden of Eden, peopled by blacks of unsurpassed savagery. Poe turns these blacks into the Devil's own servants; they are unfearful of the serpents that cross their paths, and they pronounce their name with a "prolonged hissing sound." It has been noted earlier that Pym's passage into the white cataract is a release from, among other things, the black hell of Tsalal.

Poe's representative Tsalalian is Nunu (which in Hebrew means "to deny," Kaplan informs us) and he reemerges in "The King's Indian" as the black harpooner Ngugi. Nunu is one of several Tsalalians participating in the butchery of Pym's fellow crew members. Ngugi, on the other hand, is the first one to effectively curb the slaughtering in the mutiny that takes place on board the *Jerusalem;* throughout the novella the black harpooner's tolerance and very humane nature are strongly emphasized. But Gardner's rewriting of "Pym" does not stop with the transformation of Nunu to Ngugi. Whenever the Tsalalians see the color white, they cry in fright, "Tekeli-li." Kaplan plausibly reads this as a play upon part of God's warning to Belshazzar, as interpreted by Daniel: "'Tekel'—'Thou art weighed in the balances, and art found wanting.'"[18] Poe thinks this a fitting judgment on Nunu and his kind, and he lets the man die in abject terror at the appearance of the pallid, white birds crying their eternal "Tekeli-li." Gardner obviously does not share Poe's impatience with black people, and in his version the mysterious "Tekeli-li" is reduced to the crew's imperfect rendering of Jonathan's sailorly command, "Tack-alee" (322–23). As an antidote to Poe's implied defense of "pigmentocracy," Gardner gives us Jonathan's Whitmanesque apotheosis of the democratic potential of his "Lordless crew": "Homewards, my seawhores.... Homewards, you orphans, you bandy-legged, potbellied, pig-brained, belly-dancing killers of the innocent whale! Eyes forward, you niggers, you Chinese Irish Mandalay Jews, you Anglo-Saxons with jackals' eyes. We may be the slime of the earth but we've got our affinities!" (323).

Gardner's major reservation against the ending of "Pym" seems to focus on Poe's projection of ultimate vision: the shrouded white figure. For the sake of collation, we need to cite Pym's last lines one more time: "But there arose in our pathway a shrouded human figure, very far larger in its proportions than any dweller among men. And the hue of the skin of the figure was of the perfect whiteness of the snow" (342). Gardner's version is decidedly less awestruck: "The whiteness of the sea to southward darkened; a huge sad man rose up from the water, standing on newly emerged dry land, his arms laid out lightly on an oak tree's limbs and his antique garb as white as snow." Poe's mysterious vapor is likened to a theater curtain in Gardner's version, linking Pym's vision to Flint, that master of stage-craft manipulation and shows empty of meaning. Jonathan is little impressed by this projection of absolute unity, and he cheerfully tells the white figure off: "So it's thee our Captain came to hail! *God bless you and good day!*" (323) The lightness of his tone notwithstanding, Jonathan seems to adopt a philosophical position tortuously worked out by Melville, who in one of his letters to Hawthorne declared, "If any of those other Powers choose to withhold certain secrets, let them; that does not impair my sovereignty in myself" (*Letters* 125). Jonathan bids a determined adieu, at least for the time being, to mystical voyages and metaphysical speculation, trading Antarctic waters for Illinois.

"A wise man," Jonathan comes to realize, "settles for, say, Ithaca" (303). His Ithaca is Illinois, at a safe distance, he thinks, from the sea and temptations as potentially dangerous as any of those Odysseus met with on his way home from Troy. Thus for the time being Jonathan is won over by what William E. Sedgwick (talking about Ishmael) calls man's "land sense" (123–24). In "The Castaway" chapter Ishmael tells the story of how Pip for a while was left swimming in the open ocean. Pip is unable to bear the "intense concentration of self in the middle of such a heartless immensity" and "from that hour the little negro went about the deck an idiot" (414). From then on Pip became "a living and ever accompanying prophecy of whatever shattered sequel might prove" the *Pequod's* own (411). Having thus sensed the dangers involved in Ahab's relentless quest to penetrate the inscrutable mask of the White Whale, Ishmael in the following chapter gives us his reflections while squeezing the sperm of the whale that nearly caused Pip's death. Ishmael in his next chapter turns the experience into a lyrical celebration of that "interindebtedness of man" which Ahab curses, and it provides him with a new perspective on the *Pequod's* mission:

> I forgot all about our horrible oath; in that inexpressible sperm, I washed my hands and my heart of it.... Would that I could keep squeezing that sperm for ever! For now, since by many prolonged, repeated experiences, I have perceived that in all cases man must eventually lower, or at least shift, his conceit of attainable felicity; not placing it anywhere in the intellect or the fancy; but in the wife, the heart, the bed, the table, the saddle, the fire-side, the country. (416)

By telling the white shrouded figure the time of day at the end of "The King's Indian" and setting sails for Illinois, Jonathan shows that he has lowered *his* "conceit of attainable felicity," resisting the temptation to go for the absolute vision offered by the likes of Pym and Ahab.

But the Illinois which is meant to be Jonathan's new seat of attainable felicity is the country of tornadoes that is so vividly captured in "The Ravages of Spring"; Jonathan refers to it as "Illinois the Changeable." Exhorting Miranda to come with him, he describes it as "a whole new geography, beyond philosophy and stabilizing vision" (321–22). In allowing his land sense to reassert itself, Jonathan does not settle for philosophical complacency, but he takes a rest from the allure of Flint's "mystical voyages." The largest paradox in *Moby-Dick*, Feidelson has said, is "the necessity of voyaging and the equal necessity of failure" (35). One is reminded of Ishmael, who likens the mist of a whale's spout to "the dim doubts" of his mind, the mist now and then shot through with divine intuitions:

> And for this I thank God; for all have doubts; many deny; but doubts or denials, few along with them, have intuitions.

Doubts of all things earthly, and intuitions of some things
heavenly; this combination makes neither believer nor infidel,
but makes a man who regards them both with equal eye. (374)

Ishmael sets out to sea again, proving Feidelson's point about the
necessity of voyaging; but it would seem that his experiences on
board the *Pequod* have made him better equipped to deal with
epistemological uncertainty in the future.

Jonathan tells his story in the capacity of old Mariner, so presumably he, too, puts out to sea again. Like Coleridge's Mariner,
old Jonathan says he is still not free of his tale, and this shows that
he also recognizes the necessity of voyaging, the necessity of forever revising one's interpretation of the world. Ishmael's adventures
as a member of the *Pequod*'s crew taught him to regard his doubts
of things earthly and intuitions of things heavenly "with equal
eye." This capacity for dual philosophical vision is something that
also Jonathan acquires in the course of his experiences; Gardner
captures this very essential element of his literary intentions in
"The King's Indian" through a highly imaginative handling of one
of the novella's most pervasive motifs: Jonathan's wall-eyed glance.

The symbolical significance of Jonathan's bad left eye is first
adumbrated in the second paragraph of the novella, where
Jonathan is described as a "crafty old loon with his left eye cocked
to the northwest corner of the universe" (197). A point of reference
for the meaning of that characterization has been established
already in "The Ravages of Spring," where the country doctor narrator proves himself to be a true humanist of great philosophical
equanimity with reservations against the "Platonistic predilection
for Eternity as opposed to Present Time." His humor is a welcome
antidote to the monomania of Dr. Hunter, as seen in the country
doctor's remark that "what I chiefly know about absolute values is
that they do not necessarily aid the digestion, but frequently
impair it" (35). It is this man of charitable common sense who
clears up the debris of Dr. Hunter's wild quest for absolute unity:
at the end of the story we see him assume the care and responsibility of Dr. Hunter's baby clones. The country doctor's actions lend
philosophical authority to his thoughtful recognition of the
inscrutability of existence:

I stand pretty firmly where I happen to be put, and I ponder
things. I do not necessarily learn anything. But pondering is
good for the constitution: it lends a wise calm to all bodily

parts and lends to the mind and soul a special dignity, like that of an old Red Indian sitting in a tree. I like things done properly—even tortuously, when that's what's required—but done by a man who's got one ear cocked toward the infinite. (36)

Whether one cocks an eye or an ear does not much matter in this context; in symbolical terms the important thing is the use to which that eye or ear is put, and the danger lies in letting the odd eye control one's vision, that is, one's outlook on life. That is what happens in the Boston theater scene, where Jonathan is taken in by Flint's intimations of the possibility of "mystic voyages." Flint's mesmerizing tour back through history makes Jonathan begin "to feel something going wrong with [his] vision." He starts to see birds of the kind he later learns to laugh at in the parody of Pym's apocalyptic vision, and unable to control himself, he screams frantically. Jonathan's explanation of what happens is significant:

> I had seen all my life (I was then about nine) queer shadows at the edge of my bad left eye. Fraud though Lord knows he had to be, Flint had made them solidify a little. I was now convinced those shadows were real as the Parthenon, and a man like Flint, if he ever got his claws on me, could populate my world with such creatures. (200–201)

Jonathan's words prove prophetic, of course. As we have seen, his feeble attempts at escaping Flint's influence are futile, and in the mast episode his susceptibility to the lure of "the Beyond," symbolized by his left eye, nearly kills him: it is out of the corner of his wall-eyed glance that he glimpses "the shadow of some ultimate idea."

But Jonathan watches Wilkins die, begins to realize fully the dangers involved in the *Jerusalem*'s mission, and now the wall-eyed glance is what saves him: Flint is unable to hypnotize Jonathan because he does not know which eye to look in! It saves him again later—salvation now in the sense of redemption—when grace comes to Miranda and Jonathan alike through Miranda's acceptance of Jonathan's grotesque physical appearance, the wall-eyed glance thus becoming an emblem of his physicality.

And then, in the final pages of his narrative, Jonathan's wall-eyed glance comes to represent the sum total of his experiences on board the *Jerusalem*. Having turned his back on the white shrouded figure, Jonathan remarks: "I kept my right eye steady on the bowsprit, the solemn white monster blurry in my left" (323). Whereas Melville gives to Ishmael "an equal eye" with which to regard his doubts and intuitions, Gardner endows Jonathan—literally and metaphorically—with dual vision. With one eye Jonathan looks toward Illinois the Changeable, and with the other he keeps watch on the doppelganger of Poe's projection of ultimate vision, presumably in order to see if further philosophical temptations are forthcoming from those quarters.

In his *Dismisura* article ("A Writer's View") Gardner makes the following comments on the relation between philosophical uncertainty and literary creation:

> Once you've discovered atoms, discovered that the universe has more holes in it than motes, you can never again lean on an innocent wall. But whereas fiction in the forties and fifties was overloaded with worries about such things, most fiction today takes the healthy view—though a view that can easily be carried too far—that wringing one's fingers and exclaiming "What is real?" is a tiresome thing to do; better to get on with our civilized and civilizing business, merely registering our knowledge that our knowledge may be faulty by parody of the old uneasiness. (23)

Even though Gardner makes rich use of "The Rime of the Ancient Mariner," "Narrative of A. Gordon Pym," and *Moby-Dick* in working out his own dramatization of an old philosophical dilemma, there is a world of difference in tone between the novella and its sources, and this difference seems important. Whatever their affinities, Jonathan is not Ishmael resurrected, nor is Gardner Melville. In terms of philosophical sensibility, Gardner seems to be closer to Melville than to Coleridge and Poe. Even so, "The King's Indian" never comes anywhere near to approaching the epic grandeur, the philosophical intensity, or the tragic weight of *Moby-Dick*. "The King's Indian" is characterized by greater playfulness and a higher degree of literary self-consciousness than we find in any of the sources. The comments of Gardner's just cited go a long way toward explaining this difference in tone. A program adopted by many new fictionists, he says, is to register our awareness of the fact that our "knowledge may be faulty by parody of the old uneasiness." This seems to be a fair description of his achievement in "The King's Indian." But there is another aspect of the program which is dearer still to Gardner. Rather than despairing at the elusiveness of philosophical Truth, writers should get on with their "civilized or civilizing business." Even though writers can never hope to achieve philosophical certitude, rational morality provides an empirical and pragmatic basis for the furthering of civilizations (cf. my Chapter 2). As for Gardner's own efforts in this regard, in borrowing plot lines, symbols, and motifs from his predecessors in "The King's Indian," he implicitly pays tribute to their civilizing contributions; the artistry with which he turns these materials into a totally new creation—richly imaginative, marked by a contagious playfulness and the verbal pyrotechnics of his style—is his own civilizing gift to the reader.

4

"The King's Indian" is a prime example of Gardner's sustained use of sources; from beginning to end in this novella he plays the context of his own fiction against that of other literary works. But often he makes a more isolated use of allusions in the sense that a certain literary echo may be meant to demonstrate or underscore a specific idea but is not given enough semantic space to determine in any substantial way the thematic thrust of the narrative. Since the thematic weight of these *supportive* allusions is so slight, their meaning can only be determined contextually; that is, we have to establish the wider meaning of the surrounding text before we can begin to analyze how the allusions are meant to operate in that context.

While Gardner was working on "The King's Indian," he was also revising his manuscript for *The Life and Times of Chaucer* (Howell's *Bibliographical Profile* xix). Knowing Gardner's approving view of Chaucer's heavy reliance on other poets, and knowing also Gardner's own proclivities in that regard, we should not be surprised to find throughout "The King's Indian" a series of motifs and symbols whose function and meaning we can best make out by consulting Gardner's writings on Chaucer and other medieval poets. This is an allusive activity which is different from the one we have been discussing so far. In working parts of the texts of Coleridge, Poe, and Melville into "The King's Indian," Gardner relies on the *total* context of these materials. This is normally not the case with Gardner's use of medieval materials. These allusions are usually of a conventional kind; that is, they consist of motifs and symbols that have been used by a number of poets, and their meaning is predetermined by tradition.

Even though these allusions may not in themselves be so prominent as to significantly determine the thematic direction of "The King's Indian," several of them support and give resonance to the themes which the author develops with the help of his nine-teenth-century forebears, a resonance which supports Gardner's broadest literary aims. By bringing into play a literary tradition which spans six hundred years or more, Gardner adds one more dimension to his celebration of art; his medieval allusions also help to further imbue Jonathan's story with universal significance in that they establish a fairly well defined traditional context for Jonathan's adventures and deliberations.

A case in point is Gardner's choice of ships' names in his story. An important part of the action in "Pym" takes place on board the whaler *Grampus;* for instance, it is on board this ship that the butchery takes place which inspired Gardner's description of the mutiny in "The King's Indian." The *Grampus* reappears in Jonathan's story, but only parenthetically as the ship which report-edly salvaged the portrait of Flint after the *Jerusalem,* the ghost ship, went down. Another ship mentioned in "Pym" also crops up in Gardner's novella, but this time the loan is a straightforward one; blind Jeremiah at one point identifies himself as "one-time first mate to Captain d'Oyarvido on the good ship *Princess* that found out the Vanishing Isles of the South Pacific" (234). This is the geographical destination of Captain Dirge's/Jeremiah's/Flint's voyage on board the *Jerusalem,* which explains why Flint, alias Jeremiah, chose this identity for himself. Still the question remains, why bother to change a name in one instance, while keeping it in another? And why, after naming Captain Dirge's ship the *Jerusalem,* keep the *Grampus* in the story at all? One reason for this game of musical names may be that Gardner wanted to draw particular attention to the only new ship's name in the novella: the *Jerusalem.* And a probable key to the name's meaning may be found in Gardner's medieval scholarship, where the idea of Old Jerusalem/New Jerusalem occurs frequently.

In his commentary on the "Pearl" poem by the anonymous Gawain-poet, Gardner explains the function of the Jerusalem motif in medieval literature:

The contrast central to the poem as a whole, the contrast between the mutable and discordant, on one hand, and the immutable and ordered, on the other, now takes emblematic form, becoming a contrast between the old Jerusalem and the

New. In the Old, Christ, though guilty of no crime, was murdered; in the New, Christ rules.

In "Pearl" the Gawain-poet gives this English translation for the name Jerusalem: "To two moated cities my Lord has come / And Jerusalem is the name of both / For in English the word has the meaning *Home / of God* and, also, *Vision of Peace.*"[19] There is thus a solid medieval tradition for associating Jerusalem with transcendence. Flint's choice of alias may be significant in this context; Gerhard von Rad reminds us that the biblical Jeremiah prophesied that the members of Israel living in exile were to return home and that Jerusalem was to be rebuilt (181). Through the resonance that allusions of this kind create, Flint's monomaniacal urge to solve the riddle of the *Jerusalem,* the ghost ship, is universalized to suggest any quest for transcendence, a desire to cross the border of sensory experience and achieve a vision of "the Beyond." Wilkins's description of Flint fits this interpretation: "He's hunted all his life for some holiness past magic" (308).

Gardner may have wanted to reinforce this point by having Billy More describe Captain Dirge's white house—the place where the *Jerusalem*'s mission was first conceived of, Flint and Miranda lurking in the wings—as a "big house looking down on the Cove.... It was lovely.... A house to rule an empire from, so enormous you couldn't get warm in it" (285). This description brings to mind a medieval castle, and in medieval literature, Gardner informs us, white castles are usually emblematic of the New Jerusalem.[20] Even though the color of Dr. Hunter's house is not given in the short story, he too lives in a castlelike building: "Tall and morose, with heaven knows how many rooms, and a soaring blunt tower" (46). It seems perfectly consonant with these many allusions for the author to have Jonathan at one point associate the whaler's rope work with Jacob's ladder, that classical image of Christian and Neoplatonic transcendence (215).

Yet another possible reinforcement of this reading may be found in a reference in the novella to the biblical story of Noah. In his commentary on "Purity" by the Gawain-poet, Gardner refers to Augustine's interpretation of Noah as an adumbration of Christ (344–45), and in *The Life and Times of Chaucer* Gardner cites this story as an example of how the Bible is sometimes read on an *anagogic* level, "wherein Old Testament and New Testament events are found to be harmonious, the Old Jerusalem foreshadowing the New, as when Noah's ark is recognized as an ante-type of the Body of

Christ" (81). Crawling around on the *Jerusalem*, and suspecting that the ship and its crew are hiding the real purpose of their voyage from him, Jonathan notes to himself, "Such stories are as old as Noah's Ark" (233). Jonathan thereby inadvertently associates the *Jerusalem* and its crew with yet another biblical story so closely linked to, and foreshadowing, the eternal Kingdom of Christ, perhaps the most powerful emblem of transcendence in Christian literature.

A central philosophical problem for many characters in "The King's Indian" is the split they perceive between man's spiritual and physical aspect. A prerequisite for Jonathan's philosophical change of heart is an acceptance of his essential physicality. In Gardner's fiction much artistic energy is spent on dramatizations of man's need to come to terms with his fallibility. *Physicality* and *fallibility* are not synonymous terms, but in a metaphysical perspective they have sometimes been seen as very closely related. The one thing that makes man less than a god, less than perfect, is the fact that he is made of flesh and, therefore, is a prisoner of the forces of mutability. There is thus a medieval tradition for seeing wounds or scars as emblematic of human fallibility. Jonathan makes much of Miranda's wounds and the change she has undergone because of the rape, going from ideal beauty to physical ugliness. Maybe the author had the Gawain-poet in mind when choosing to belabor this point in "The King's Indian." "No child of Adam is capable of perfection," Gardner says in relation to the central conflict in "Sir Gawain and the Green Knight," and therefore Arthur's court don the same green baldric that Sir Gawain wears to hide his wound; he received the wound because on one single occasion he had failed in relation to the medieval code of knighthood. They do this, "not out of an anguished sense that they share Gawain's spiritual weakness, but joyfully, granting glory to the girdle" (*The Complete Works of the Gawain-Poet* 81). It is an acceptance of this kind that enables Jonathan and Miranda to accept their common frailty.

In thinking up the special nature of Miranda's wound, Gardner may have been inspired by Chaucer in yet another attempt to lend resonance and universality to his tale. In the Alcyone story in *The Book of the Duchess* Juno's messenger is sent to Morpheus's cave, and when the messenger wakes him, the god of sleep looks up with only one eye. On the allegorical level, Gardner explains, this is "the natural or fleshly eye, since as a pagan [Morpheus] lacks the eye of spirit" (*The Poetry of Chaucer* 12). By giving Miranda a damaged eye, Gardner may have wanted to reinforce the idea that through the rape, which caused the damage, Miranda is shown to be a mere human, in her own as well as in Jonathan's perception, and that physicality is an undeniable aspect of the human condition. Jonathan's earlier view of her as the embodiment of a Plotinian spirit is revealed to be an illusion, and once again the ideal and the real do not match up.

One of the myths that Ishmael cites in explanation of his fascination for the wide seas is the story of Narcissus. There is a strong element of solipsism in Ishmael's earliest philosophical meanderings, "the drizzly November" in his soul making him a self-appointed spiritual outcast. But Ishmael meets Queequeg, is gradually cured of his narcissism, and, as many a commentator has pointed out, *Moby-Dick* gives us the story of Ishmael's "journey toward plenitude."[21]

Jonathan undergoes what is in many ways a similar development. We have seen that at the end of the novella he emerges as an enthusiastic celebrator of the democratic potential of the *Jerusalem*'s crew; at the outset, however, it is the image of Narcissus which best captures the state of his emotions. Self-love is early on established as one of the chief forces in the building of Jonathan's character. It shows up, for instance, in his lack of love for his mother; declaring his intentions of going to Illinois and thereby abandoning her, he responds to her many protestations with typical offhandedness: "Is it Christian charity to be chained up in other people's foolishness?" (206). Describing the attitude of his pre-*Jerusalem* days, Jonathan brags, "I was not, Heaven knows, a democrat" (205). It is hardly accidental that the author puts him to sea in a sloop named the *Jolly Independent*.

It is in keeping with these tendencies that Jonathan misreads Boethius in the early days of captivity on board the *Jerusalem*. Presumably viewing himself, rather grandly, as a prisoner in the manner of Boethius when he wrote *The Consolation of Philosophy*, Jonathan perverts Boethius's religiously founded stoicism into a credo of individual superiority in which friendlessness and unwillingness to love are basic principles. Sneering at the interindebtedness of the *Jerusalem*'s crew members, Jonathan remarks, "As even Boethius had understood—though he'd turned it rather pious—a man like myself was outside the web that entrapped their kind" (225). He feels quite safe in his indifference toward other people; no one will be capable of moving him emotionally.

Events show that this is a false sense of security, as Jonathan himself would have understood if he had read his Boethius with greater discrimination. In his biography of Chaucer, Gardner discusses in some detail the influence Boethius had on the medieval poet, and in so doing he gives us some very good pointers as to how we are to understand his use of Boethius in characterizing Jonathan. The part of Boethius that evidently catches Jonathan's fancy is his stoicism, but Jonathan fails to see that this stoicism is based on faith in the ultimate benevolence of the Prime Mover; this faith, Gardner argues, is what made Boethius so palatable to the disaster-ridden fourteenth century: it provided a possibility to reconcile one's private misfortunes with a belief in a sensible overall plan for the universe, because "God's domain and the soul's possibilities are larger than we see." What Jonathan also fails to appreciate are the further implications of Boethius' worldview:

> One single principle, according to Boethius, governs everything that exists, from winds and tides and inanimate matter to the Prime Mover's character, namely, the principle of universal attraction degree by degree—the inherent love of "natural place" and overall accord which "inclines" or encourages stones to move downward and souls to fly upward, establishing the stable and orderly ladder of existence, "the fair chain of love."... One may, with mad obduracy, deny the principle, closing up one's heart into selfishness and envy, resisting one's natural, spiritual place, thus stepping outside the universal order and losing its benefits. (*The Life and Times of Chaucer* 78)

Jonathan is indeed driven by "mad obduracy," leading to selfishness, and even when he later yields to what he calls his love for Augusta (this is prior to the rape), it is not love in the Boethian sense, but rather one more expression of his solipsism. He is cured, later, of his narcissism, but in his own early characterizations of the attraction he feels toward Augusta, he again betrays his sinning against the Boethian concept of love. Like Chaucer's Troilus, Jonathan is able to follow Boethius only part of the way, as witnessed by one of his characteristic self-important laments: "Such was my anguish, sneaking like a thief toward the object of my desire, a girl I'd never seen" (233). Gardner explains Troilus's failure to comprehend the full implication of Boethian love in words that are echoed by Jonathan: "As Scipio learned, man has the freedom to serve the common profit—in Boethian language, the freedom to accept the bond of love which relates him with the whole order, not merely some particular object of desire" (*The Poetry of Chaucer* 142). Jonathan's "love," like that of Troilus, is selective, and hence the "common profit" takes second place to the satisfaction of his own personal desires; love is perverted into love of self, and Jonathan falls into what Chaucer considered to be the chief evil of man: the evil of nonlove, which leads a man to think about nothing but himself (*The Life and Times of Chaucer* 310).

A first cousin of self-love is pride. Arrogant pride is certainly one of the first attributes one would use in describing Flint, and the magician and Jonathan, we know, have many and strong affinities. It is possible to read into "The King's Indian" an attempt to universalize and give mythological resonance to the motif of pride by seeing Jonathan as a latter-day Jonah. In addition to the fact that there is one direct reference to the Jonah story in the novella (228), there is an obvious parallelism of names. Furthermore, Jonathan is picked up by a whaler and tested in its "womb," as is Jonah in the whale's belly. They are both of them proud (or, as the Gawain-poet would say, "impatient") men, and both of them learn "patience," although in different ways: Jonah through repentance and the grace of God, Jonathan through the grace of love.[22]

The Jonah legend is one of several biblical stories that were retold by the Gawain-poet. In his commentary on "Patience" Gardner interprets Jonah's role (and this is also Father Mapple's point in *Moby-Dick*) as that of the ordinary, sinful Christian; transferred to a universal, and not specifically Christian context, he can be seen as Everyman, a true representative of fallible man, "at once comic and pathetic, foolish and admirable." These are adjectives which are suited to a description of Jonathan as he emerges at the end of the novella, and Gardner's comment that he is "struck throughout by the rather engaging wilfulness" of Jonah seems to apply equally well to Jonathan.[23] The concept of "Patience" as it is used by the Gawain-poet mirrors that of Father Mapple, although with the medieval poet the emphasis is on the blessing to be achieved through a show of patience, whereas Father Mapple's emotions are stirred primarily by the hardships involved in obeying God's command: "But all the things that God would have us do are hard for us to do—remember that—and hence, he oftener commands us than endeavors to persuade. And if we obey God, we must disobey ourselves; and it is in this disobeying ourselves, wherein the hardness of obeying God consists" (42–43). The allegorical relevance of the Jonah story for "The King's Indian" rests on the difficulty Jonathan has in obeying a truth larger than

himself; his special form of impatience in this non-Christian sense
is his pride in self, his seeking the satisfaction of the needs spring-
ing from his solipsism, rather than meeting the demands made
upon him by a concern for "the common profit."

5

   Julia Kristeva, a theoretician with a strong interest in literary
borrowing and intertextuality, has pointed out that the allusive
method, or "paragrammatisme," of the French poet Lautréamont
presupposes a simultaneous reading of both text and intertext; the
reader has to collate Lautréamont's poems with their sources in
order to fully explore their meaning (255–56). Her observation on
this score gives rise to some reflections concerning the limitations,
and potential dangers, of a collage technique.
   In his letter to the editor of *Chicago Tribune* Gardner defend-
ed his echoic method in the following terms:

Collage technique, the technique I practice, has nothing to do
with plagiarism. In every phrase, every nuance, it acknowledges its dependency. To the ignorant but good-hearted reader it gives a rich and surprising prose style—an interesting
story filled with curious odds and ends that make a scene
more vivid, a passing idea more resonant. To a knowledge-
able, sophisticated reader it can give an effect of dazzling texture and astonishing intellectual compression.

Gardner here implicitly makes a crucial point concerning the literary effectiveness of intertextuality: in order for his collage technique to work qua echoic method, the reader *must be made to recognize* the text's dependency on another text. In other words, the
author must in some way signal to his readers, "Now I am alluding." One should of course not expect the writer to footnote his
every allusion. Frequently we will be content to spot an allusion
as an allusion, without asking for the exact source. A case in point
is Ork's speech in *Grendel*. "The King of the Gods," the old priest
proclaims, "is the actual entity in virtue of which the entire multiplicity of eternal objects obtains its graded relevance to each stage
of concrescence. Apart from Him, there can be no relevant novel-
ty" (132). The involuted style of this passage suggests that it is a
loan—or a parody—but apart from the trained reader of philosophy, few will be in a position to locate the source of the allusion

(Whitehead's *Process and Reality* 248), which is a dense, and highly specialized, study in cosmology. The inaccessibility of the intertext does not in itself deprive Ork's speech of its artistic effectiveness. The primary purpose of Gardner's extensive use of Whitehead in fashioning the old priest's theological deliberations is apparently to characterize Ork as a man of high spirituality; Ork is a representative of serious religiosity in the novel and not a spokesman of *one* particular school of theology. The artistic value of Whitehead's statements as they are transposed into this particular context thus springs from their prophetical tone rather than from their paraphrasable content; the specialized jargon of Whitehead's presentation simply makes it impossible for the unprepared reader to adequately judge the theological content of these allusions. Hence in this case the *tone* of the allusion is the most significant artistic fact; the referentiality of the borrowings is secondary, and aesthetically unimportant.

The relative importance of referentiality in different cases of allusion can best be determined by considering the level of intentionality behind borrowings; by "level of intentionality" in the context of allusions I understand the extent to which the author allows the meaning of his own text to be intertextually defined. "The King's Indian" is thus marked by a high level of intentionality as regards the author's use of Melville and Poe. The importance of referentiality in this case is demonstrated most dramatically by the novella's ending; the thematic and symbolic weight of the white shrouded figure is greatly reduced, not to say nullified, if one fails to spot the connection with "Narrative of A. Gordon Pym."

When we look at Gardner's use of medieval allusions in "The King's Indian," we find that here the level of intentionality is much lower. These are, after all, supportive allusions and chiefly serve to underscore or create resonance for ideas or narrative patterns that are already established by the internal structures of the novella. Discovering how these allusions work may add depth to our understanding and appreciation of the work, but it will not significantly *change* the direction of that understanding.

When the level of intentionality is high, it seems that the author defeats his purposes unless the reader is given some clue or other about the source of the allusion(s). An intentionalist approach implies a perception of literature as a communicative act, and in order for communication to be successful, the receiver must have access to what semiologists call "the sender code." If the intertext is a well-known work like *Moby-Dick*, the source will be readily identified by readers and no overt clue is needed. "Narrative of A. Gordon Pym" is less widely known, but here we get a number of direct references to Poe in the novella as well as in the other stories in the collection. Thus by the time the reader gets to the ending of "The King's Indian," he has been provided with ample access to the code needed to decipher the thematic significance of the white shrouded figure.

If the writer fails to provide even the slightest clue to the sender code, he runs the risk of irritating rather than intriguing his readers, and if umbrage is the result of an allusive technique, communication will of course suffer. Gardner comes perilously close to sinning in this regard in *The Sunlight Dialogues*. Early reviewers were exasperated by the author's many cryptic chapter headings, headings that are never explained by the narrative itself. What is the innocent reader to make of chapter titles like "Lion Emerging from Cage," "Hunting Wild Asses," "Winged Figure Carrying Sacrificial Animal," when no creatures remotely answering these descriptions make an appearance in the novel? Greg Morris has shown that these chapter headings do make sense, provided the reader takes the trouble of familiarizing himself with A. Leo Oppenheimer's book *Ancient Mesopotamia*. It turns out that the titles originally served the function of photograph captions in Oppenheimer's book, the photographs depicting Assyrian palace reliefs. Gardner also directly appropriates sections of *Ancient Mesopotamia* for Taggert Hodge's lectures in the four dialogues he has with Clumly. Some of the existential problems keenly felt by the Babylonians are strikingly modern, Morris points out, and Gardner's many allusions to Oppenheimer's book derive their chief thematic logic from this shared sensibility across the centuries ("A Babylonian in Batavia" 29–30, 33).

Gardner escapes opacity regarding his Babylonian allusions because he does include the information needed to crack the code. For one thing, Taggert Hodge's long-winded perorations on Babylonian modes of thought quickly lead the reader to suspect that some cultural history book or other is lurking in the background; and then, in the epigraph to Chapter 4 of Gardner's novel, Oppenheimer's book is cited directly (179), providing the reader with the clue he needs to decipher the meaning of those enigmatic chapter titles.

On the whole, Gardner avoids the danger of inaccessibility; when his allusions are marked by a high level of intentionality, he usually makes it possible for the reader to identify the intertext, sometimes by direct reference in his own text to the writer or the source in question, but also by prefatorial acknowledgment. It is characteristic of his care in this regard that when he does make a faux pas, the level of intentionality is nil. In his *Chicago Tribune* review of *Freddy's Book*, William Logan shows that in rendering the factual historical material of the Vasa era in Swedish history that he needs for his fictional purposes, Gardner reproduces, with very minor modifications, long sections of Michael Roberts's *The Early Vasas: A History of Sweden, 1523–1611*, as well as passages from an English translation of Ingvar Andersson's *A History of Sweden*. The author makes no explicit acknowledgment of these sources in his book, and in this particular case it seems that Gardner's echoic method does partake of plagiarism. In his answer to Logan's broadside in his *Chicago Tribune* letter, Gardner says there was no need for an acknowledgment in this case because he took from these history books "nothing of special interest in itself." Rather than refuting Logan's criticism, this statement would appear to be an inadvertent admission of guilt. Gardner is right in suggesting that it would not benefit the reader's understanding to know that these passages were lifted from elsewhere; nor would any compilation of the different texts shed extra light on the novel. Precisely for that reason the unacknowledged borrowings seem unnecessary; if the intertext adds nothing of artistic value to Gardner's novel, the readers have the right to expect from him that he give his own, artistically adequate rendering of the historical facts relevant to his narrative. And when he did decide to cite texts that he could hardly expect his readers to be familiar with, it seems that plain courtesy, if nothing else, should have prevailed upon him to give due recognition to his cowriters.

Lapses like these are rare in Gardner's canon, however. Gardner's heated defense of his confiscatorial practices in *Freddy's Book* notwithstanding, his next novel, *Mickelsson's Ghosts*, contains a very detailed list of acknowledgments; this may have been intended as an ironic play on his earlier practice of not citing all his sources, but it could perhaps also be interpreted as a peacemaking gesture on the part of a writer who may have felt a little uncomfortable after all with the complaints of plagiarism directed against an earlier novel. And normally the notion of literary larceny will be far from the minds of Gardner's readers. A more likely response to this author's handling of a collage technique is a sense of delight at his frequent successes in achieving the effect which, by his own admission, he seeks: "a surprising prose style" as well as "dazzling texture and astonishing intellectual compression."

7

DIALECTICS

In *The Poetry of Chaucer* Gardner remarks that the *Canterbury Tales* is characterized by a "profluence" which is "dialectical": the pilgrims "offer rival points of view on a series of traditional topics." Thus the aesthetic model of the *Tales* "is not simply the 'collection'—the form represented by the *Decameron*...but the 'collection' form combined with the medieval 'debate,' represented by *The Owl and the Nightingale*." *The Owl* is one of several medieval poems translated into modern English by Gardner, and he explains the prevalence of this open-ended form in the Middle Ages by suggesting that the "original assumption...was that the reader will come to the right decision and that it will be orthodox; but the form allows the widest possible latitude to conflicting ideas and emotions and had from the beginning the potential of becoming truly dialectical" (223–24). Gardner has repeatedly impressed upon his readers that he views Chaucer's poetry as peculiarly modern, if not in form, then in sensibility. He points out that Chaucer is a master of "counterpoise"; that is, the medieval poet would set one system of values in counterpoise with another system, as he does, for instance, in the *Book of the Duchess* or *Parliament of Birds*, "setting love and religion (or art and life, or some other opposition) in ironic balance and thus writing in a more modern way, not simply ornamenting old ideas but testing them, forcing some compromise, reaching toward insight" (72).

1

Gardner's fiction, too, is dialectical in the sense of the term that he establishes in talking about Chaucer's poetry. In fact, his collage technique and a penchant for testing ideas, or values, through counterpoise, are the two most distinct figures in the car-pet of his fiction. This chapter will map out the basic pattern, and some of the ramifications, of this dialectical method. Quite schematically, we may say that in practically all of Gardner's nov-els and short stories we find a pattern of *thesis, antithesis,* and *synthesis.* One idea is routinely matched by the opposite idea, and his fictions almost without exception move to some sort of middle ground, or synthesis. *Synthesis* seems a particularly appropriate term in that the "new" position worked out on the basis of the juxtaposition of antithetical ideas nearly always preserves some element or other of both thesis and antithesis. Put differently, it appears that Gardner seldom or never introduces ideas in his fic-tion simply in order to attack or denounce them; even though the antithetical ideas do not "survive" in their original form at the end of the fiction, initially they always seem to hold some measure of attraction for him. Furthermore, Gardner's insistence on epistemo-logical uncertainty and the unreliability of art makes this a truly dialectical approach in that the position, or synthesis, ultimately arrived at in a given text is always viewed as tentative, and there-fore subject to further artistic and philosophical exploration.

Gardner seems to have been temperamentally predisposed to a dialectical approach to fictional inquiry. We will see that a num-ber of dominant thematic concerns in his fiction can be traced back to one set of antithetical ideas: *order* versus *disorder.* In his fiction, he says, there is characteristically "a battle...between the hunger for roots, stability, law, and another element in my charac-ter which is anarchic" (Ferguson et al. 58–59). Thus Gardner obvi-ously projects an important part of his own personal experience when he lets the boy narrator of "Come on Back" (one of several stories in *The Art of Living* using the rural New York of Gardner's childhood for its setting) complain, "I disliked change, hated to see any slightest hint that the universe might not be orderly to the core, as smooth in its operations as an immense old mill" (261). This basic tension in Gardner's own psyche has filtered down into his fiction. In the opening chapter I cited Gardner to the effect that all affirmations in his fiction were undermined by psychological doubts. Hence we get a constant reexamination in his art of his basic positions. We have seen that the promise of the pastoral alternative in his early books is thwarted in later texts. The fairly confident affirmations of novels like *Nickel Mountain* and *Octo-ber Light* are modified by the marginal affirmations of books like *Jason and Medeia* and *Mickelsson's Ghosts,* not to mention his opera libretti; one of these (*Frankenstein*), Gardner points out in the preface, "celebrates values in the tragedian's way, by showing the horror of their loss" (ii). However, an affirmation of sorts is always achieved in Gardner's art, and his artistic habit of arriving at some kind of synthesis stems from his deepest philosophical instincts and commitments.

The controlling axiom of Gardner's practices as a writer—art as exploration—is also the underlying premise of his dialectical approach to narrative strategy. Commenting in an interview on the fact that in writing fiction he always starts out with a position that he later discovers to be too simple, Gardner says that he tries to think of "ways of dramatically setting up contrasts so that [his] position on a thing is clear to [him], and then [he hounds] the thing till it rolls over." The artistic motivation behind his dialectical approach is a familiar one: the need for truthfulness in exploring. If the artist "favors the cop," Gardner says (as he himself eventually does in *The Sunlight Dialogues*), "he must understand the arguments for life on the side of the robber" (Ferguson et al. 53, 67).

Our author's dialectical method serves the purpose of discovery in yet another way, and this is an aesthetic effect which is closely analogous to one achieved by his collage technique. The collage technique, we have seen, is an instrument with which the writer himself makes discoveries, but it also helps bring about discoveries for the reader by creating gaps or textual difficulties that provoke him into creative, or recreative, activity. Similarly, Gardner's dialectical method is a means by which he himself tests certain ideas, but it is *also* an important way in which to involve the reader in creative activity. Setting up his fictional experiments in terms of thesis and antithesis, the author constantly confronts the reader with opposing ideas on a variety of subjects, and while trying to sort out the many if's and but's of one or several ideational conflicts, the reader will almost inevitably become involved in a very direct way in the fiction's battle of ideas. There is, however, a peril to this artistic method, a peril which Gardner does not always avoid. The pattern of thesis, antithesis, and synthesis is so ubiquitous in his fiction that it runs the risk of dulling the reader's attention. Once the reader has identified the antithetical ideas (or set of ideas), he may sit back in fairly confident anticipation of the synthesizing resolution of the ideational conflict. Especially in his more conventionally realistic novels—I am thinking of *The Resurrection*, *Nickel Mountain*, and *October Light* in particular—Gardner comes close to sinning in this regard. However, this dulling

effect can be counteracted by the author's ability to move his readers by dramatic and mythopoetic means, and in most cases Gardner manages to do just that.

The true subject of his fiction, Gardner points out, is "human
history—the conflict of ideas and emotions through the ages" (Ferguson et al. 63). In this context, too, the aims of his collage technique and a dialectical method can be seen to converge. Using traditional literature as source material for his own fiction provides
the author with instant access to the ideational and emotional
concerns of earlier writers. Frequently he draws on several sources
for one of his own texts, sources whose ideas and emotional commitments are themselves in conflict with each other, and Gardner
thus achieves an artistic and intellectual compression which is
aesthetically highly satisfying. In Chapter 6 one instance of such
an opposition was discussed, namely the ultimate thematic counterpoise of "Narrative of A. Gordon Pym" and *Moby-Dick*. In the
following it will be shown how he weaves the totally opposite
worldviews of Dante and Malory into the fabric of *The Sunlight
Dialogues* and, similarly, how he, in *Grendel*, draws on the ideas
of the Beowulf-poet and Blake to create a stimulating ideational
dialectic. Thus, frequently in Gardner's works the collage technique and his dialectical narrative strategy can be seen to work
hand in hand to produce some of his most rewarding fiction.

The purpose of Gardner's dialectical method, then, is to test
and to work out a synthesis of opposing ideas. However, to Gardner ideas are of no interest unless they are placed in a human context, be it private, social, or political. In other words, Gardner studies ideas for the effect that they have on people's lives. The
dialectics of his fiction, therefore, is always a dialectic of *characters* as they embody values or ideas, which are tested through their
actions. In a typical Gardner novel we get protagonist matched
with antagonist, each holding a more or less clearly defined view
of the world. Thus we get the anarchistic and nihilistic Sunlight
Man versus the law-abiding (and law-enforcing) Clumly, the political and metaphysical rebel Agathon versus the timid and unso-
phisticated Peeker, the materialistic and misanthropic George
Loomis versus the sensuous and altruistic Henry Soames, the
obsessively cerebral Jason versus the hyperemotional Medeia, the
self-righteously conservative and puritanical James Page versus the
liberal and "progressive" Sally, and the cynical and perversely
rational Bishop Brask versus the gentle-hearted ignoramus Lars-
Goren. The other typical pattern is that of the protagonist torn

beween conflicting alternative intellectual and emotional commitments. The classic example is of course Grendel, who hangs "balanced, a creature of two minds" (110). At times he is powerfully
tempted to believe in the existence of meaning, as shown in his
attraction to the Shaper's poetry and the beauty of Wealtheow; at
other times he gravitates relentlessly toward the Dragon's nihilistic vision of total meaninglessness. Similarly, "The King's Indian"
is peopled with torn characters struggling to sort out the emotional confusions resulting from the lure of conflicting ideas.

    True to his dialectical persuasion, Gardner describes how
these characters change in the course of their respective fictions.
In the first group of novels the "hero" normally survives and experiences a spiritual resurrection of sorts by moving to a middle position as a consequence of his meeting with, and exposure to, the
ideational universe of his antagonist. The antagonist, however,
succumbs to the excessive demands made upon him by his intellectual commitments and suffers defeat, usually in the form of
death. Thus Clumly abandons his strict law-and-order position and
becomes a spokesman for an enlightened view of justice and compassion, whereas the Sunlight Man dies because he cannot resist
the temptation to play one last trick on a representative of ordered
society. Agathon likewise suffers death because he is unwilling or
unable to relinquish his philosophical rebelliousness, whereas
Peeker takes on Agathon's familial obligations. But Peeker, too, is
changed as a result of his long affiliation with Agathon; at the end
of the novel we see him comically appropriating mental habits and
tics that he had earlier despised in Agathon. In the case of the torn
characters, they are either redeemed by achieving some measure of
balance between their conflicting inclinations, or else they suffer
dramatic defeat. Grendel goes through a conversion, albeit
marginal, when at the end of the novel he is able at last to affirm
the ordering power of art and traditional values; Jonathan and
Miranda retire to Illinois the Changeable. Wilkins, however, is
unable to live with the knowledge of "the separation that makes
sinners of us all" and commits suicide.

    Gardner's handling of character is of course not as rigidly
schematic as these introductory remarks might indicate. Thus the
confrontation between Clumly and the Sunlight Man, as Judy
Smith Murr points out, "is more than a simple one between order
and disorder" (104). Gardner makes a point of showing us that
Clumly is a man with secret longings for anarchic freedom, and
the Sunlight Man's program of destruction is partly motivated by a

strong sense of frustration at the lack of total order in the universe. (Most of the other characters in his fiction are likewise endowed with some measure of conflicting ideational sympathies.) Also, Gardner gives us Tag Hodge's tragic private history in highly vivid and heart-rending images, so that even though the alternative represented by the Sunlight Man in the novel is eventually denounced through plot developments, the author creates considerable sympathy for this character and the traumas that motivate his outrageous behavior.

Subtlety of characterization notwithstanding, there is no question but that Gardner's characters tend to gravitate toward fairly distinct ideational alternatives. Therefore, our best strategy in trying to map out the dialectical pattern of his fiction will be to watch very carefully how his characters work out their existential differences.

One central opposition of ideas in Gardner's works, then, is that of order versus disorder. This fundamental conflict finds many different expressions. Very often the tensions involved in this dichotomy spring from a concern with order and disorder on a *metaphysical* level. It is commonplace among reviewers and critics to remark that Gardner is a "philosophical" writer. However, since philosophy is only of interest to this author insofar as it affects the lives of men, he always takes care to show how ontological convictions translate into action. The following discussion of three representative texts will show how the characters' involvement in a dialectic of order and disorder on a metaphysical level manifests itself dramatically on the personal and social level: *Jason and Medeia, Grendel,* and *The Sunlight Dialogues.* The chapter closes with some remarks on the ways in which another, but related, dichotomy—*body* versus *mind*—establishes yet another pervasive dialectical pattern in several Gardner texts.

2

Jason and Medeia is in some ways Gardner's most baffling artistic creation.[1] This epic poem, in long parts a direct translation of the two related classical texts, Appolonios Rhodios's *Argonautica* and Euripides's *Medeia,* is set down by a twentieth-century poet, in the best of the medieval tradition which Gardner knew so well, as an oneiric journey through the mythological landscapes of ancient Corinth, Kolchis, and Iolkos.[2] Since the story is a dream vision, the author and narrator are at liberty to roam wide, a freedom they exercise with great relish, mixing traditional myths (for example, the king of Thebes, Kreon, reappears here as the king of Corinth) and paying frequent visits to Olympus to spy on Zeus and his unruly court of gods and goddesses. The result is a rich narrative, marked by great persuasiveness and a strong dramatic force.

Some 450 pages into the recounting of his sprawling hexametric dream vision, the narrator of *Jason and Medeia* is taken on a horse ride up a hill which is "dimly visible, impossible to name, / changing, shadowy, deep as the ancestor of all that lives, / awesome and common" (305). Trying to explain the meaning of his vision to the driver, he at first finds his head filled with ideas as "clear as day, but jumbled— / images that had no words for them." But then, he says, "I concentrated, clarifying what I saw by explaining / to the stranger as I looked. And now suddenly things grew much plainer. / I now understood things never before expressed—inexpressible..." (305). The narrator, by Gardner's own confession a fictionalized projection of himself ("A Writer's View" 21), here neatly summarizes his creator's often rehearsed conviction that true art is art-as-exploration. When we begin to examine the narrator's recounting of his dream vision, we soon find that his route to discovery, his increased understanding of "things never expressed—inexpressible," is marked by a constant shifting and reshifting of his emotional and intellectual allegiance to the two principal actors. Jason and Medeia in complex ways embody forces conducive to both order and disorder, and the narrator's coming to terms with the philosophical and ethical implications of the traditional story forces him to consider a wealth of conflicting ontological positions and value judgments.[3]

The intensely dialectical approach of *Jason and Medeia* may account for the length of the narrative. This epic and *The Sunlight Dialogues* (both of which are characterized by a highly complex literary structure) are the best examples in the Gardner canon of how a dialectical approach can perform a heuristic function for writer and reader alike. Both of these texts are ambitious attempts at moving to what the driver in the scene just described calls "the heart of things." The writer explores the problem he is investigating by sending his characters into a minefield of conflicting theories, finding his own way according to how these characters behave under philosophical pressure. The reader in like manner watches the characters and is swayed in opposite directions depending on who holds the floor at the moment. Thus the primary aesthetic justification for the great length of these narratives would appear to be subject matter: complex topics demand a complex form.

In recounting his experiences on board the *Jerusalem*, Jonathan Upchurch embarks on an epistemological voyage: one of the purposes of his narrative is to chart the boundaries of man's ability to know. Jason's retelling of *his* quest on board the *Argo* similarly becomes an *ontological* voyage. The Greek Prince seeks to navigate metaphysical waters that philosophers have sailed since the dawn of human understanding: is the true name of the universe *order* or is it *disorder, meaning* or *meaninglessness?* In a passage which reveals how closely related Jason's attempts at pinning down ontological truth are to Jonathan's epistemological voyage, golden-tongued Jason speaks with characteristic flourish:

> We sail between nonsense and terrible absurdity—
>   sail between stiff, coherent system which has
>   nothing to do
> with the universe (the stiffness of numbers,
>   grammatical constructions)
> and the universe, which has nothing to do with the
>   names we give
> or seize our leverage by. (269)

The *Argo*, together with the crew, he comments elsewhere, was "a thing puzzling out / its nature, its swim through process" (161). Jason retells his story at the court of Corinth in an attempt to prove himself the most worthy pretender to old Kreon's throne. In an important elaboration on the traditional story, the author pits Jason against sea kings from near and far in a contest of words for the hand of Pyripta, Kreon's daughter, and thus ultimately the stewardship of Corinth.[4] The elaboration is important for two reasons. First, it highlights the ethical implications of the story: Jason's willingness to break his vows of everlasting fidelity to Medeia. Second, it provides a narrative rationale for having Jason tell his story in retrospect, allowing him and others to judge the significance of that multilayered narrative.[5]

In telling his story, Jason assumes a perspective which is absent in Appolonios's version, the perspective of a metaphysical sceptic. This scepticism in turn is a direct consequence of that overpowering impulse which governs Jason's every thought, feeling, and action: his rationalism. When we consider that his antagonist is Medeia, obviously a representative of intuition and emotion, we see how the dialectics of this text contribute to a Chinese box effect: within the larger dialectical pattern of order versus disorder there is layer upon layer of ideas and principles placed in antithetical juxtaposition. In his own description of what he has tried to achieve in *Jason and Medeia*, Gardner offers yet another insight into the aesthetic motives behind his collage technique:

> [In] retelling a classical myth...one of my interests was in trying to understand—imaginatively, *from inside*—our civilization's archetypal and probably oldest myth of male and female, darkness and sunlight, reason and intuition—not to impose by wit and raw power my own romantic vision on a grumpy universe but to understand those mysteries centuries of relatives have found, or imagined they've found, in the visions and revisions of Appolonios and Euripides. ("A Writer's View" 23)

As always, Gardner emphasizes here the necessary relation between his collage technique and exploration. One of the ways in which he enters into a dialogue with those early masters is thus to have Jason elaborate on the meaning of his experiences. Jason's analysis of the relationship between himself and Medeia eloquently points up the dialectics of character in the epic:

> As the raging sun reaches
> for the pale-eyed, vanishing moon, so Medeia's burning heart
> reached for my still, coiled mind; as the moon reforms the light
> of the sun, abstracts, refines it, at times refuses it,
> yet lives by that light as memory lives by harsh deeds done,
> or consciousness lives by the mindless fire of sensation, so I
> locked needs with Medeia, not partner, as I was with Hypsipyle,
> but part. (252–53)

These are the terms, then, in which the dialectics of order and disorder in *Jason and Medeia* are worked out. Jason is cast in the mold of the archrationalist, a figure associated with the male principle, with forces of darkness, and, ultimately, Hades, that is, death. Medeia is pure emotion, associated with fire and light. On the whole Gardner was very loyal to the original sources when writing the epic. He frequently added and omitted, but rarely did he alter *facts* given in Appolonios or Euripides. Alterations, therefore, when they do occur, take on added significance, such as when the author improves upon Jason's genealogy by making him the grandson of Dionysos, "Lord of the Underworld" (167), elsewhere described as "majestic lord of the dead, son of Hades" (23). Appolonios offers a much more prosaic pedigree, citing Cretheus as the grandfather of Jason (105). For Medeia, however, no such improvement is necessary, since she is the rightful granddaughter of Helios, the god of the sun. She, unlike Jason, always acts in accordance with her heart rather than her mind.

Jason and Medeia is a study of vicious circles on the grandest of scales. Because of their respective natures—excessive reason and excessive emotion—the two protagonists end up positing a meaningless universe. This metaphysical orientation on their part results in actions productive of disorder on a human scale. Lack of meaning and coherence on the human level is then in turn seen as an argument in favor of an absurdist view of the world.

In the case of Medeia the dire consequences of a life ruled by passion alone are obvious enough. In her attempt to win, and then keep, her husband's love, she brings about the death of her brother and Pelias in a signally cruel fashion. When Jason betrays her, her passionate hatred leads her to even grosser crimes: the incredibly gruesome poisoning of Pyripta and Kreon, and, more abhorrent still, the killing of her own children. Medeia, in the old slave woman's description, is unable to control her "old bile of guilt, self-hate, pride, love" (48). Unchecked by reason, she cannot think "past the bouldered hour / that dams the flow" of her mind (47). Howling for justice, Medeia interprets the world exclusively in terms of her own experiences and sees nothing but meaninglessness:

> O, the plan
> is plain as day, if anyone cares to read. In the shade
> of the sweetly laden tree, the fat-sacked snake. Good, evil
> lock in the essence of things. The Egyptians know—with
>   their great god
> *Re,* by day the creative sun, by night the serpent,
> mindless swallower of frogs, palaces.

Her value orientation is dictated by this negative reading of the world:

> Let me be one
> with the universe, then: blind creation and blind destruction,
> indifferent to birth and death as drifting sand. (49)

Jason's approach to the world is the very antithesis of Medeia's rampant emotionalism. His rationalistic perspective commands the reader's attention throughout most of the highly convoluted plot and thus warrants a somewhat more comprehensive analysis than the one afforded Medeia's rather more clear-cut stance. When undertaking such an analysis, we do well to take note of Elzbieta Foeller's perceptive comment on Gardner's (and Barth's) use of mythological characters:

> The mythical heroes of Barth and Gardner, unlike their tradi-
> tional counterparts, do not follow their destiny with a firm
> conviction of their worth; they are doubting protagonists who
> move through life painfully, stumbling and groping for its ulti-
> mate meaning. Facing a seemingly indifferent universe which
> houses immense possibilities, they cling to the mythic pat-
> tern as a guideline in the bewildering experience of life. (194)

Jason is *not* cast as the epic's great villain. Even though the narra-
tor is moved to intense pity by Jason's victimization of Medeia, he is also deeply involved, emotionally and intellectually, in Jason's quest for meaning. "The son of Aison," he states early on,

> was a man sensitive to pain. It was that, past anything else,
> that set him apart, made a stranger of Jason wherever
>   he went.
> He suffered too fiercely the troubles of people around him.
>   It made him
> cool, intellectual...
> I was moved, watching from the shadows. He was a man
>   much wronged
> by history, by classics professors. (62)

Even though Jason's golden-tongued oratory may at times lend a touch of complacency to his character, he is nevertheless, like Medeia, a troubled human being. "I'd been, all my life / on a mission not of my own choosing," he confesses, "a mission I was pow-
erless to choose against" (111). He is himself his own best diagnos-
tician, complaining to the blind seer Teiresias, "How can man trust anything, then, / beyond his own poor fallible reason?" (23). Jason's problem is thus a failure of faith, a failure to accept those aspects of existence which are not so readily testable by the mind of man. Hence his marriage to Medeia was doomed from the start:

There could be no possibility now of harmony between us;
no possibility of marriage. We must either destroy each other—
struggling in opposite directions for absolutes, thought
    against passion—
or part. (269)

    The direction of Jason's quest is foreshadowed early on in one
of the narrator's many startling visions. With the narrator present
there appears in the hall of the Greek gods a holy child who has
seen the coming and dissolution of countless universes. He
reminds the head of the Greek gods that the reign of a single Zeus
is but a fraction of a day and night in the "Unnamable Mind." In
such a perspective, he appears to argue, the concept of value is
meaningless, and his advice is, "The wise / are attached neither to
good nor to evil. The wise are attached / to nothing" (40).
    This attitude of cosmic indifference is very similar to the one
that Jason adopts in the course of his experiences. At one stage of
his education he receives instruction from Phineus. The old seer
has had more than his share of misfortunes, and his hardships have
made him sensitive to the vision of another great sufferer, Oidipus.
As the former king of Thebes sees the universe, it is controlled by

                dark gods,
conflicting absolutes, timeless and co-existent, who battle
like atoms seething in a cauldron, each against all, to assert
their raucous finales. Gods illogical as sharks. (139)

On the basis of their life experiences, Phineus and Oidipus have
developed a tragic view of man's existence:

                In his very loneliness,
his meaningless pain, he finds the last values his soul
can still maintain, drive home, construct his grandeur by:
the absolute and rigorous nature of its own awareness,
its ethical demands, its futile quest for justice, absolute
truth—dead-set refusal to accept some compromise,
choose some sugared illusion! (141–42)

    There is much in Phineus's and Oidipus's definition of man's
tragic lot that speaks to Jason's questioning sensibility, committed
as he is to tracking truth "to whatever lair it haunts" (181). However, he fails to accept the ethical implications posited by the two

sages. He sees in Phineus's tale nothing but "inescapable senseless-
ness" and heartily applauds mad Idas's heated questions: "Why?—
Why soul? Why values? Why greatness?" (141, 142). Ever the keen
rationalist, Jason cannot even accept the marginal faith of a
Phineus or an Oidipus. His empirical mind will only permit him to
state that the world "was a harmless drunk" and that "life itself, all
our pain / is idiocy" (146, 150). Much as man may want to think
otherwise, he is "not the invisible player / but the player's pawn"
(269), at the mercy of inscrutable powers beyond his control.

The literary effectiveness of *Jason and Medeia* is to no small
degree to be attributed to Gardner's considerable allegorizing talents. Hence, in his version of the Jason story, the Wandering Rocks
become, in Argus's explication, emblematic of "all Time-Space in
a duckpond.... See how it moves / by law, yet unpredictably"
(243–44). When Appolonios fails to provide suitable raw material
for allegory, Gardner deftly turns to Homer, stealing from him the
Odyssean horrors he needs to complete his allegorical plan. Jason
is spared the trial of Skylla and Kharybdis in *Argonautica*, but in
Gardner's tale he has to negotiate that formidable strait: "On one
side, / sheer rock cliff, on the other the seething, roaring mael-
strom." Jason, who screens his every experience for philosophical
import the way a philatelist examines his most precious stamps,
immediately interprets the event: "On the left /...call it death by
rectitude. On the right side.../ death by violence, / bottomless
shame; between—barely possible—death by indifference, / soul-
suffocation in the corpse that stinks, plods on" (243). The *Argo*
steers the middle course, and Jason's interpretation is no doubt
dictated by his philosophical orientation. Indifference is for Jason
the only logically defensible alternative for a man convinced of
life's essential absurdity. Hence Jason's hero is not Herakles,
defender of traditional values like "Honor, Loyalty...Fame," but
Theseus, who in his fearless way of dealing with the Queen of
Amazons proves to Jason "the beauty / of cool, tyrannical indifference" (104, 164).

Paradoxically, Jason's metaphysical indifference does not sti-
fle his personal ambitions in areas nonphilosophical. His philosophical leanings nevertheless influence his ethical behavior in the
sense that he is unable to believe in the existence of lasting values,
that is, Gardner's much-talked-about Faulknerian "eternal verities." To be able to accept "eternal verities" one would almost by
definition have to affirm at least some measure of order in human
affairs. Since Jason finds it impossible to be anything but tentative

in matters human or philosophical, his only guide is a situation ethics dictated by his own observations as they are registered and analyzed by his ever-sceptical mind. The result is a pragmatism which frequently is indistinguishable from sheer opportunism. This opportunism shows up in his religious views ("politeness to gods is best") as well as in his political actions, such as when he refuses to use his influence with Kreon to save the life of Amekhenos, the son of a former ally and helper; Jason is afraid that an intervention on his part might displease Kreon and thus ruin his own chances of succeeding Kreon on the throne of Corinth.

Most distasteful of all is of course the sacrifice of his own family in his play for political power. Jason's ambition is to resume the political experiment he had started at Iolkos before Medeia's revenge on Pelias and his family forced him to flee his native state. At Corinth he hopes to be able to realize his idea of a Philosopher's Kingdom based on the reasoned application of the principles of justice, equality, and moderation. Nice as this may sound, the sacrifices Jason is willing to make to achieve his goals show up the inherent weakness of his program, as well as his greatest crime as a human being: rationalistic Jason loves *ideas* more than he loves people. Hence he does not feel obliged to heed Medeia's lamentations at his leaving her for the Princess of Corinth:

> If you could show what I do
> in any way unjust or unlawful—if you could raise
> the shadow of a logical objection, I'd change my course
> for you. (94)

After the fact he can say without the smallest trace of remorse:

> And as for the marriage you hate,
> I say again what I've said before, with calm dispasssion
> I made that choice. (392).

Medeia's decision "to be one with the universe," that is, her impulse to live out the dire potential of her metaphysical convictions, brings about the disastrous results that have been described already. It is a part of the dialectical pattern of the epic that the many atrocities she commits are triggered, one by one, by some action or other on the part of Jason. As for Jason, we may see his search for political power as a way of compensating for lack of order in the metaphysical sphere: by creating a just state he would have created a modicum of *human* order where the gods have none to offer. However, events show his circle to be every bit as vicious as that of Medeia. His political philosophy is informed by his metaphysical orientation; since in his reading of the world no eternal verities are to be discovered, he asserts his own. His coolly intellectual conception of justice fails to observe a necessary respect for the feelings of the individual human being, and hence his political experiment explodes in his face when Medeia takes her revenge and Corinth goes up in flames.

This is the point at which Euripides concludes his play based on the Jason and Medeia legend. Gardner, however, adds an epilogue, a twenty-fourth chapter in which he spells out his synthesis. This postscript gives us Jason completely freed of his former rationalistic hubris. Mad Idas, now turned sane, must speak for Jason because the loss of his children also led to a loss of speech. Idas describes the change that has taken place in Jason:

> No man
> could guess such love, such rage at betrayal. She emptied
> herself.
> All the pale colonnades of reason she blew sky-high,
> like a new volcano hurled through the heart of the city. So he,
> reason's emblem, abandoned reason. (352)

Whereas Jason earlier had followed the dictates of reason only, he now acts on the basis of faith alone: he is back on the *Argo* in an attempt to find and become reunited with Medeia. He is thus trying to achieve synthesis on a number of levels.

First of all, his search for Medeia signals a desire, in John Trimbur's description, "for reunion with his inherent counterpart, a completion symbolized by the closing figure of serpents 'coupling with murderous intent'" (75). In neglecting Medeia, Elzbieta Foeller remarks, Jason has neglected "the dark irrational part of man." The clash between the two protagonists "can be seen as a clash within the human personality, for Jason and Medeia are most truly one. Their marriage is the sacred marriage and 'coniunctio oppositorum' of myth. The two complement each other to form a whole—Logos and Eros, yang and yin" (196). In trying to become reunited with Medeia, Jason is thus acting out what Gardner in a different context has described as one of man's fundamental impulses, "which is that all of us are really one thing—if you like, call it Shiva or Avitar—but one force, yet we're individuated. And there's this hunger to get at that other part of one's own self—which one can do by going inward, or by possessing another person totally" (Cuomo and Ponsat 61). Jason is thus clearly on his way to greater wisdom, a state approaching that of the seer Teiresias, about whom it is said that he "learned all the mystery of birth and death when he saw, with the eyes / of a visionary, the coupling of deadly snakes." The snakes were the rulers of Hades, Kadmos and Harmonia, and because he had seen things forbidden, Teiresias was turned into a woman for a time (23).

Just after Jason left Phineus's island he had a vision that keeps troubling him throughout the rest of the narrative. He dreamed that Death came to him with this enigmatic warning:

> Fool, you are caught in irrelevant forms:
> existence as comedy, tragedy, epic.
>   Trust not
> to seers who conceive no higher force than Zeus...
> Beware the interstices. (142–43)

Jason must go through the experience of nearly total destruction before he begins to appreciate the significance of the vision. In that last chapter he occasionally regains his voice to repeat the first part of the warning to the ghost ships following in the wake of the *Argo*. Apparently Jason has now come to see that *all* readings of the world are uncertain, including those that posit a universe which is meaningless at the core, a universe ruled by gods fighting their eternal battles. Truth is uncertain, hence he can now assert: "*Nothing is impossible! Nothing is definite! / Be calm! Be brave!*" (353). As for "the interstices," Jason appears now to have been awakened to the essential connectedness of the universe. His earlier diagnosis of the world had been almost clinical in its simplicity: "Things die. Alternatives kill" (181). He now seems to have discovered the difference between *contradictory* and *contrary* principles. If alternatives are viewed merely as contradictory principles, then disorder would be the most likely result; if, on the other hand, they are viewed as contrary principles (such as male/female), they can be yoked and order is possible.[6]

In the latest stage of his development Jason seems to have come by at last that one thing which is essential to survival in an apparently meaningless universe: negative capability, that is, the ability to live with uncertainty. He is now won over to that middle ground (read: synthesis) which he and Medeia formerly had found it so difficult to inhabit: the arena of unselfish human love. From being a man whose intellect had forbidden him to merely believe, he is now a man who has abandoned reason for faith.

Jason discovers the ordering possibility of faith through living, but also through *telling* about his experiences. Likewise the narrator discovers in the process of recording his dream vision yet another instrument for ordering a recalcitrant universe. Art, in Frost's well-known phrase, does have the potential of offering "a momentary stay against confusion," does have the potential for the creation of order, however fragile. On the penultimate page of the book the narrator/Gardner pays tribute to that possibility. Falling through the void, the narrator discovers with a shock that the tree he has been clinging to throughout the narrative falls with him. Then suddenly something happens:

> At once—creation *ex nihilo*, bold leap of Art,
> my childhood's hope—the base of the tree shot infinitely
>   downward
> and the top upward, and the central branches shot infinitely
>   left
> and right, to the ends of darkness, and everything was firm
>   again,
> everything still. (353)

3

In *Jason and Medeia* Gardner uses well-known Greek myths as source material for his exploration of the metaphysical categories of order and disorder. In *Grendel* he also makes sustained use of ancient myth, this time Anglo-Saxon. There is little direct translation of the source, but Gardner is true to the text of *Beowulf* in most matters of plot and setting. The author's ingenious invention is of course that the story is told through the eyes of the monster. In Grendel Gardner found a perfect vehicle for what he considers to be one of the most predominant phenomena on the contemporary intellectual scene: cheerful (and sometimes not so cheerful) nihilism. Gardner, like the Beowulf-poet, pits Grendel, a representative of disorder, against Hrothgar and his men, who in the book represent a nascent civilization, hence order. The cultural manifestations of Hrothgar's court again and again tease Grendel toward momentary belief in order, but each time the dragon's vision of absurdity and meaninglessness pulls him back into the ranks of disbelievers, until at the very end he undergoes his conversion as a result of his meeting with Beowulf.

Grendel is Gardner's most fervent metaphysical rebel. He insists with repetitive firmness on the lack of purpose in the universe: "The cold night air is reality at last: indifferent to me as a stone face carved on a high cliff wall to show that the world is abandoned" (9). "Stars, spattered out through lifeless night from end to end, like jewels scattered in a dead king's grave, tease, torment my wits toward meaningful patterns that do not exist" (11). Irony operates forcefully: an important aspect of the book's dramatic irony is the fact that Grendel can hardly open his mouth without spouting some simile or other. It should therefore come as no surprise to the reader when Grendel's conversion at the end consists in his recognizing that he is a poet, hence a creator of order. Grendel would no doubt have been greatly insulted, however, had he had this fact pointed out to him in the early stages of the novel when he was still under the spell of the dragon's vision. The dragon purports to have visionary powers, which he draws on to define his brand of cheerful nihilism. It is no wonder that some early reviewers took Grendel and the dragon to heart, believing them to be the author's true spokesmen in the novel; Gardner's portrayal of these two figures is characterized by an irresistible mirth. Who can withstand the humor of Grendel's first meeting with the dragon?

"Ah, Grendel!" he said. "You've come." The voice was startling. No rolling boom, as I would have expected, but a voice that might have come from an old, old man. Louder, of course, but not much louder.

"We've been expecting you," he said. He gave a nervous laugh, like a miser caught at his counting. His eyes were heavy-lidded, minutely veined, wrinkled like an elderly mead-drinker's. "Stand around the side, if you don't mind, boy," he said. "I get a cough sometimes, and it's terrible straight out front." The high dead eyelids wrinkled more, the corners of his mouth snaked up as he chuckled, sly, hardly hiding his malice. I quickly ducked around to the side.

"Good boy," he said. He tipped his head, lowering an eye toward me. "*Smart* boy! He he he!" He lifted a wrinkled paw with man-length talons for nails and held it over my head as if to crush me with it, but he merely brought it down lightly, once, twice, three times, patting my head.

"Well, speak, boy," he said. "Say 'Hello there, Mr. Dragon!'" He cackled. (58)

This passage reveals a familiarity with dragons and monsters
which can be traced back to Gardner's fondness for Walt Disney as
well as his studies of medieval literature. The humor also lends to
the dragon's message, no doubt intentionally, the kind of fashionable malaise which we find in the writings of the so-called black
humorists. The dragon sees the beginning and end of man's epoch,
and in that perspective he finds man's role to be meaningless:
"Pick an apocalypse, any apocalypse. A sea of black oil and dead
things. No wind. No light. Nothing stirring, not even an ant, a spi-
der...in Time's stream" (71).

Gardner tellingly prefaces *Grendel* with a quote from Blake's
"The Mental Traveller." This poem is described by E. D. Hirsch,
Jr., as "the fullest presentation in the lyric mode of [Blake's] pathway to despair" in that it describes a meaningless repetition of a
quest for spiritual fulfilment (121). But Blake, unlike Grendel
before his meeting with Beowulf, was able to work his way out of
despair, and he did so by affirming the contraries of existence. In
their seminal study of *Grendel*, Ellis and Ober show that, beyond
the obvious reference of the epigraph, Gardner had Blake very
much in mind when writing his version of the Old English epic.
Most importantly, Gardner borrows some of the key imagery in
The Marriage of Heaven and Hell as a means of pointing out the
extent to which Grendel's rejection of the world as meaning is
influenced by the dragon's vision: "The repetitive metaphor of the
hell of black and white spiders allows Gardner to emphasize one of
the main themes of *Grendel*, that Grendel has allowed himself to
be captured by the dragon's metaphysics" (54).[7] In *Marriage* that
imagery is only momentarily threatening. After the Angel, who
took the narrator to the edge of the "void boundless as a nether
sky," has disappeared, the narrator suddenly finds himself sitting
"on a pleasant bank beside a river by moonlight" (xxiii, xxiv).
When the Angel asks him how he escaped "the eternal lot" of contemplating the "infinite Abyss," the narrator counters: "All that
we saw was owing to your metaphysics" (xxv). Grendel, however,
is haunted by the dragon's metaphysics till the very end and has to
go into battle with Beowulf before he is able to renounce (at least
partly) the dragon's vision of meaninglessness.

The imagery of *The Marriage of Heaven and Hell* most likely
inspired Gardner's conception of one of the central tropes of *Jason*

and Medeia as well. At regular intervals we find the narrator clinging to an oak tree, presumably in an effort to brace himself against
the many expressions of the "dragon's metaphysics" which
migrate into that text as well. On one occasion we even find Jason
quoting the dragon outright. After telling Kreon's court about his
meeting with Phineus, Jason gives his own interpretation of the
old seer's story: "The essence of life is to be found in frustrations
of established order: the universe refuses the deadening influence
of complete conformity" (146). These are the very words that the
dragon uses in his efforts to convince Grendel of life's essential
meaninglessness (67).

For all the persuasiveness of the dragon's teachings, Grendel
is nevertheless continually drawn to his philosophical antipodes,
Hrothgar and his court. Like the dragon, he mocks them for their
insistence on the possibility of an orderly universe. The dragon, of
course, makes short shrift of man's many theories:

> They only think they think. No total vision, total system,
> merely schemes with a vague family resemblance, no more
> identity than bridges and, say, spiderwebs. But they rush
> across chasms on spider-webs, and sometimes they make it,
> and that, they think, settles that! I could tell you a thousand
> tiresome stories of their absurdity. They'd map out roads
> through Hell with their crackpot theories, their here-to-the-
> moon-and-back lists of paltry facts. Insanity—the simplest
> insanity ever devised! (64)

His never-ceasing mockery notwithstanding, Grendel cannot leave
man be. He is suffering from a severe case of philosophical
schizophrenia, a fact which, as we have seen, Grendel himself
acknowledges: "I hung balanced, a creature of two minds" (110).
The schizophrenia stems in part from one of his major afflictions
(explainable partly in terms of his mythical status as the eternal
outcast): he wants to be more man than man himself. Like many
of Gardner's other characters, Grendel is driven by what Nathan
A. Scott, Jr. (borrowing Jacques Maritain's phrase), in a different
context calls "that penchant for life in the angelic mode which is
fostered by the passion for the clear and distinct idea" (184). Grendel is manlike in that he has the capacity to think in abstracts.
When he meets man for the first time, it is only natural that he
should be intrigued by these creatures, at once both similar to and
unlike himself. One thing that distinguishes *homo sapiens* from

animals is, obviously, the fact that he has values, certain ideals that he tries to live by. But as certainly as there are ideals, there are also men who fail to live up to these ideals. Grendel will have none of this. He is an absolutist, and he is enraged by men's corruption of man's ideals; hence he decides to become Hrothgar's nemesis. Gardner's novel is a protracted study of what can happen when expectations of a life in the angelic mode (perfect order) clash with life in the human mode (imperfect order).

Grendel's early description of Hrothgar's society is actually a brief history of Anglo-Saxon settlement. At first the Scyldings are "ragged little bands that roam the forest...shivering in caves or little huts in the winter" (31), but they gradually develop an organized society. They clear hills, build small houses, and, symbolizing their unity, a meadhall. Roads are constructed and gradually tribes organize, to better protect themselves against enemies and to expand politically and territorially. They develop a legal system. Hrothgar is seen to establish himself as the most powerful king, signalled by his accumulation of wealth. He is thus fulfilling one of the ideals of his pagan society; as Gardner points out, "The amassing of wealth and fame (key ideas in *Beowulf*) are [sic] the adornment of the life of a good pagan" ("Fulgentius's *Expositio*" 231).

These are the facts Grendel gives us, but he fails to register their significance. Throughout his description of the settlement of the early Scyldings, his emphasis is not on their budding civilization, but on their violence and brutality: "no wolf was so vicious to other wolves" (32). He fails to understand, and therefore scorns, their attempts at ruling by law (32). He dismisses their heroism as verbal and mead inspired, and their wars make no sense to him because man kills not only to get food: "I was sickened, if only at the waste of it: all they killed—cows, horses, men—they left to rot or burn" (36). Because of his absolutist stance Grendel is unable to accept the fact that man is both good and evil; his reasoning is that since Hrothgar's men aren't all good, they are perforce all evil, and the only facts that interest him when he observes Hrothgar's society are those actions that prove man to be less than perfect. He registers the beauty of the meadhall only very fleetingly (31) and then speaks at great length about the seemingly pointless partying that goes on in the halls, ignoring the fact that the meadhalls also symbolize one of man's most powerful weapons in combatting chaos and darkness: togetherness and unity.

"One night," Grendel sighs, "inevitably, a blind man turned up at Hrothgar's temporary meadhall" (40). The Shaper, blind like

Homer, the archetypal poet, represents yet another way in which
man has traditionally fought off chaos: through art. In Grendel's
response to the Shaper the dilemma of his absolutist stance is
shown up in its starkest form: "Thus I fled, ridiculous hairy creature torn apart by poetry...and I...clutched the sides of my head as if
to heal the split, but I couldn't" (44). Grendel, his "mind aswim
with ringing phrases, magnificent, golden," is unable to reconcile
his deeply felt desire to believe the Shaper and his knowledge that
what the bard says is "not light for their darkness but flattery, illusion, a vortex pulling them from sunlight to heat, a kind of midsum-
mer burgeoning, waltz to the sickle" (48). The discrepancy between
imperfect man as Grendel knows him and the ideal man that the
Shaper celebrates is too great for the monster to deal with, and he
allows himself to be consumed by the dragon's vision of art as illusion. He is unable to sustain faith in the Shaper's power to improve
man or, in Grendel's own words, to turn "dry sticks to gold."

One of the functions of the Shaper is to inspire Hrothgar's
men to heroism. It is no wonder that Grendel, after having suc-
cumbed to the dragon's vision of art as illusion, is sceptical, to say
the least, of the heroic deeds inspired by that "illusion." Again
Grendel's absolutist inclinations get in the way of a fair assessment of human values, a point Gardner goes to some length to
make. The fact that Grendel is invulnerable to arms is not very
significant in *Beowulf*; in the Anglo-Saxon poem that motif is
introduced almost parenthetically, primarily, it seems, to characterize Beowulf's heroism (Beowulf's men try to help in his fight
with Grendel, but a protective spell guards the monster against
their swords). In his version, however, Gardner plays this up into a
major discovery for Grendel, no doubt in order to better characterize the monster's subsequent derisive rejection of heroism. The
author makes the *dragon* cast a protective spell over Grendel; in
Beowulf that is a trick that Grendel himself plays on Beowulf's
men (ll. 801–4). One effect of this modulation is to point out the
close connection between the dragon's rationalistic cynicism and
Grendel's rejection of heroism as an ideal. By thus emphasizing
Grendel's invulnerability (the motif is introduced at a far earlier
stage than in the Anglo-Saxon orginal), Gardner underlines something which Grendel chooses to ignore. The only act that could
have convinced Grendel of the viability of heroism as an ideal—
the killing of Grendel—has been rendered next to impossible, and
the fact that a lot of thanes get killed trying to achieve just that
does not reflect upon the tenability of the heroic code. The impor-

tant thing, then, is that people like Unferth still are willing, against overwhelming odds, to take on the formidable enemy. To Grendel the efforts of Unferth are nothing but an exercise in futility, given his own tremendous advantage, and he derives great pleasure from pelting the hapless Unferth with apples. Nevertheless, Unferth does go after Grendel, lending credibility to his own definition of heroism: "Except in the life of a hero, the whole world's meaningless. The hero sees values beyond what's possible. That's the *nature* of a hero. It kills him, of course, ultimately. But it makes the whole struggle of humanity worthwhile" (89). To modern antiheroic ears, Unferth's words obviously sound unfashionably pompous; within the framework of Anglo-Saxon ethics, valor of the kind that Unferth speaks of is one of the three foremost qualities of the soul (the other two are wisdom and the ability to amass wealth and fame; "Fulgentius's *Expositio*" 230, 231). The fact that true *heroism*, even in Grendel's meaning of the word, is possible, is made abundantly clear to him later on.

The lure of the dragon's vision of meaninglessness notwithstanding, man still has one or two more temptations to offer before Grendel's absolutism has taken him full course to a total rejection of man's insistence on meaning. Grendel himself gives the best of names to the new temptation: "Meaning as quality" (102). Wealtheow, "holy servant of common good" (100), at first exerts an influence on Grendel very similar to that of the Shaper: "She was beautiful, as innocent as dawn on winter hills. She tore me apart as once the Shaper's song had done" (100). Wealtheow's role in the narrative is twofold. She represents sacrifice, giving herself over to Hrothgar to save the lives of her own people—"she surrendered herself with the dignity of a sacrificial virgin" (100)—and her beauty has an ennobling effect on Hrothgar and his men, including Unferth and the Shaper, who now sings things "that had never crossed his mind before: comfort, beauty, a wisdom softer, more permanent, than Hrothgar's" (103). For a while even Grendel is "teased toward disbelief in the dragon's truths" (108), but only for a while. Even Wealtheow's beauty and gentleness fail to satisfy his hunger for an absolute and ultimate proof of meaning. His passion for the clear and distinct idea cannot bear a compromise of ideal beauty with the Queen's undeniable physicality, and in confusion he flees the hall of Hrothgar. Once again Grendel's absolutism makes it impossible for him to accept one of man's values, this time the beneficial value of beauty, because Wealtheow's beauty falls short of being absolutely pure and uncompromised.

One final example of a dialectical pattern is the one in which religion forms thesis and absolutist Grendel constitutes antithesis. At first the monster is attracted to the possibilities offered by religion: it was part of the Shaper's promise:

> It was a cold-blooded lie that a god had lovingly made the world and set out the sun and moon as lights to land-dwellers.... Yet he, the old Shaper, might make it true, by the sweetness of his harp, his cunning trickery. It came to me with a fierce jolt that I wanted it. As they did too, though vicious animals, cunning, cracked with theories. I wanted it, yes! (55)

However, the dragon intervenes with his gospel of meaninglessness, and with Grendel's rejection of the Shaper goes a contemptuous denunciation of religion. In his absolutist mind the fact that some of Hrothgar's people are unable to maintain faith becomes evidence that "religion is sick" (128). Also, one thing which certainly galls Grendel is the empty prattle of the first, second, and third priests: "It doesn't look right, beloved friend, wandering around in the middle of the night. A man should try to be more regular" (134). But in his disgust at these demonstrations of sham religion Grendel fails to make a distinction which Gardner points to in *On Moral Fiction*, the distinction between religion and theology (164–66). Gardner parodies theology—religion as law—in *Grendel*: "It is written that the old shall keep to the comfort of their beds!" "'Worship is the work of priests. What the gods do is the business of the gods.' You know the text" (133, 134). But he balances that parody with the "conversion" of Ork and the sincere faith of the fourth priest. Grendel, however, lumps them all together and therefore indiscriminately refuses to explore religion as a way of combatting the dragon's vision of meaninglessness.

A key idea in Blake's *Marriage of Heaven and Hell* appears in "The Argument": "Without Contraries is no progression. Attraction and Repulsion, Reason and Energy, Love and Hate, are necessary to Human existence" (xvi). These lines speak directly to Grendel's dilemma and point to the novel's ideational synthesis. Because of the absolutist state of his mind, he is unable to accept the contraries of existence; instead he consistently limits himself to only one of the contraries and thereby brings about his downfall. In observing the budding civilization of Hrothgar's society, he stares himself blind on the shortcomings of that society. He realizes that the Shaper's words are capable of changing reality; for instance, it was the Shaper who inspired Hrothgar to build Hart. But some of the things the Shaper sings are patently not true in the sense of being truthful descriptions of Hrothgar's men as Grendel knows them. That, however, is not a valid reason for rejecting the Shaper's art. On the contrary, it can be seen as a reason *for* embracing the scop's vision. The Shaper's role is not to keep staring into the abyss; rather than stating *how it is*, he is to conjure up visions of *how it ought to be* (see my Chapter 1). The Shaper's raw material is imperfect man; the antithesis he has to offer through his poetry is perfect man, and the synthesis he thereby hopes to bring about is improved man, the kind of man that would build Hart. "Without Contraries is no progression."

Inadvertently, Grendel plays a role not unlike that of the Shaper. Paradoxically, the one to make this clear to him is the dragon, the ultimate denier of meaning: "You improve them, my boy! Can't you see that yourself? You stimulate them! You make them think and scheme. You drive them to poetry, science, religion, all that makes them what they are for as long as they last" (72–73). Grendel thus becomes a symbol of what elsewhere in Gardner's fiction is called evil. In *The Resurrection*, James Chandler's wife complains that the unequal distribution of suffering in the world isn't fair, and Chandler answers her in terms which make us think of the dragon: "It's not meant to be fair. It's meant to be thoroughly perplexing, to drive you to Art and Scientific Progress and God" (243). Grendel is one of those destructive forces that men must reckon with; he is part of what Agathon calls (in describing Dorkis's acceptance of evil) "evil as a necessary principle of the world—time as a perpetual perishing, space as creation and wreckage" (198). As an epigraph for *The Sunlight Dialogues* Gardner chose this line from *The I Ching:* "The earth in its devotion carries all things, good and evil, without exception." This concept is of course informed by the kind of vision which dominates *The Marriage of Heaven and Hell;* one who *has* learnt to live with the contraries of existence, with life's goodness and its tragedy, is Hrothgar, and his principal teacher is Grendel. "Violence and shame have lined the old man's face with mysterious calm," Grendel notes, and he recognizes his own role in this: "This nobility of his, this dignity: are they not *my* work?" (121, 122–23). He plays a similar role vis à vis Unferth by making him devote himself to a life of heroism, and also for Ork, whom Grendel drives to faith and the distinctly Blakeian and Gardnerian realization that the ultimate wisdom "lies in the perception that the solemnity and grandeur of the universe rise through the slow

process of unification in which the diversities of existence are utilized, and nothing, *nothing* is lost" (133). One is reminded of
Dorkis, who said: "There's a sense in which nothing is evil.... To
certain people, everything that happens in the world is holy" (153).
Gardner, in sharing Blake's vision, reveals a spiritual kinship with
these people; the final line of *The Marriage of Heaven and Hell* is,
"For every thing that lives is Holy" (xxviii). The evil of "time as perpetual perishing, space as creation and wreckage" is in one sense
positive principle. Describing the ending of *The Resurrection*, Gardner has said,

> It's saying that *one* of the real sacral things about life is its
> tragedy, that out of death comes, in a *mysterious* way, a way
> you'd never expect, life going on, and improving, with wis-
> dom. (Christian 74)

These are insights that Hrothgar, Ork and the Shaper arrive
at, as does the Shaper's apprentice, about whom Grendel mocking-
ly says that after twelve years of watching the wreckage caused by
Grendel he "knows no art but tragedy—a moving singer. The credit is wholly mine" (47). Gardner works these themes out through
an elaborate set of dialectical patterns. He places Grendel in antithetical juxtaposition to a number of imperfect men; the evil that
Grendel represents brings about a thematically important synthesis: improved man. But it is one of the book's chief ironies that
Grendel, even though he is aware of the role he plays in this pattern, fails to apply these insights to his own situation; because of
his conception of the universe as meaningless, he decides to haunt
Hrothgar and his society, but he is unable to see that thereby he is
helping to *create meaning*, the kind of meaning which leads
Hrothgar, Unferth, Ork, the Shaper, and his apprentice to an affirmation of the contraries of existence and life's tragedy. Only after
the fiery Stranger has confronted him with arguments of the—literally speaking—most forceful kind does he begin to recognize
that perhaps there is some meaning and order after all.

The Stranger is never named, but he is of course Gardner's
version of Beowulf.[8] The Stranger appears in the form of a dragon
with wings, spitting fire, and Gardner has explained this seeming
deviation from the source:

> I didn't mean it to be a change [from the poem]. As a medieval-
> ist, one knows there are two great dragons in medieval art.

There's Christ the dragon, and there's Satan the dragon. There's always a war between those two great dragons. In modern Christian symbolism a sweeter image of Jesus with the sheep in his arms has evolved, but I like the old image of the warring dragon. That's not to say that Beowulf is Christ, but that he's Christ-like. (Ferguson et al. 44–45)

In a different context Gardner points out that in the original Beowulf was sent to Hrothgar as a reward because "he has never lost faith in the cosmic ruler's justice" ("Fulgentius's "*Expositio*" 240). That function of Beowulf is not prominent in *Grendel*, but Beowulf does prove that heroism (and, by extension, idealism) is not totally irrelevant as a means to fighting evil and disorder.

In terms of thematic structure, however, the most important function of Beowulf is as the summer-up, the one who ties it all together and gives words (sometimes cryptic) to that synthesis toward which the book has been striving. In his fiercely whispered brief speech to Grendel, he touches upon most of those things discussed so far, plus a few more. With flames slipping out of the corners of his mouth, he first confronts Grendel with his dragon-inspired vision of the universe: "*As you see it it is, while the seeing lasts, dark nightmare-history, time-as-coffin*" (170). As the dragon would have it: "It's all the same in the end, matter and motion, simple or complex. No difference, finally. Death, transfiguration. Ashes to ashes and slime to slime, amen" (73). But "time-as-coffin" or "universal wreckage" involves more than a movement from "ashes to ashes." Beowulf goes on: "*[B]ut where the water was rigid there will be fish, and men will survive on their flesh till spring.*" Gardner here brings in a motif which is central in *The Resurrection:* the sanctity of the cycles of life. Grendel sees seasonal change as yet another example of meaninglessness, meaningless repetition marked by "terrible sameness" (9). He speaks of himself as one more "dull victim, leering at seasons that were never meant to be observed." The sun is seen as spinning "mindlessly overhead," the shadows lengthening and shortening "*as if* by plan" (6, 7; my italics).

Gardner disagrees with Grendel; the pattern of cyclical change *is* a meaningful pattern. Describing the structure of *Grendel*, the author has said that the twelve chapters "are hooked to" astrological signs (Bellamy 174). Careful reading of the book shows that each chapter covers one of the twelve houses of the zodiac, beginning in the house of the Ram and then moving around the zodiac in chronological order.⁹ Grendel's many protestations to the contrary notwithstanding, Grendel *is* involved in patterns of the most basic kind, as Gardner's astrologically ordered narrative helps to bring out. Beowulf's reminder that men survive till spring on the flesh of fish awakens Grendel to a meaning he had known but had forgotten: the validity of the vegetation myth. For on the second page of his narrative Grendel gives voice to a perception which is reminiscent of Whitman's celebration of the life cycle in "Song of Myself": "The tender grasses peek up, innocent yellow, through the ground: the children of the dead." The next two sentences reinforce his own involvement in the cyclical pattern—which is also a dialectical pattern—of "creation and wreckage":

> It was just here, this shocking green, that once when the moon was tombed in clouds, I tore off sly old Athelgard's head. Here, where the startling tiny jaws of crocuses snap at the late-winter sun like the heads of baby watersnakes, here I killed the old woman with the irongray hair. (7)

The ultimate synthesis is therefore life itself, mutability, Blake's "progression," which is ensured through the never-ending dialectical opposition of the forces of "creation and wreckage."

The dragon would argue that man's role in this pattern is essentially a meaningless one because to him mutability is a negative principle ("ashes to ashes"). To Beowulf, and to Gardner, man's role *does* make a difference: "*Time is the mind, the hand that makes (fingers on harpstrings, hero-swords, the acts, the eyes of queens). By that I kill you*" (170). Art ("fingers on harpstrings") can, at least moderately, change reality, as the Shaper does by inspiring men to purposeful action. Beowulf shows that acts of heroism (which Grendel makes necessary) are possible and useful. And Wealtheow's acts of compassion and sacrifice, as well as her beauty, her "eyes," are also meaningful in that they help imperfect men to become better men. These are man's most powerful means of creating order and thus fighting chaos, and in their name Beowulf kills Grendel.

Gardner has said of Grendel that at the end of the novel he goes through a "conversion" (Christian 81). "In the last pages of the book," the author furthermore explains, "Grendel begins to apprehend the whole universe: life and death, his own death" (Bellamy 179–80). Beowulf forces Grendel to acknowledge the importance of man's limitations, the hardness of walls which makes his head hurt, but above all, Grendel's imminent death. And through his song about walls, Grendel finally allows for the meaning of death and therefore also of life:

"The wall will fall to the wind as the windy hill
will fall, and all things thought in former times:
Nothing made remains, nor man remembers.
And these towns shall be called the shining towns!" (172)

Grendel's song is, with minor changes, identical with the last stanza of Gardner's poem "Setting for an Old Welsh Line" (*Poems* 10–11). The old Welsh line is presumably lifted from the anonymous Welsh poem which appears as the epigraph of *The Resurrection*, underlining the thematic affinity between the two novels:

Eagle of Pengwern, it called far tonight,
it kept watch on men's blood;
Trenn shall be called a luckless town.

Eagle of Pengwern, it calls far tonight,
it feasts on men's blood;
Trenn shall be called a shining town.

The most significant line here is the last one, which appears, with slight modifications, in three different places. The poems speak of death and mutability. Grendel, through *his* poem, at long last not only apprehends the principle of mutability ("nothing made remains, nor man remembers") but also sees it, finally, as a positive principle: "And these towns shall be called," not "luckless," but "shining towns."

Grendel's conversion is a marginal one; the novel does not tell us whether he would have come around, had he had the time, to an affirmation of meaning beyond that of recognizing death and mutability as positive principles. His conversion is nevertheless significant in that it reinforces the general thematic thrust of the novel. The two single most important contraries of existence—life and death—are not any longer seen as cancelling each other out, suggesting meaninglessness; instead they are perceived as working in a dialectical process in which contraries lead to synthesis, to what Blake calls "progression," or what Gardner describes as "life going on, and improving with wisdom."

"Faith vs. rationality is what I always write about," Gardner has said (Christian 88). This summary description of the thematic direction of his art certainly has bearing on *Grendel*, and it ties in with the dialectical pattern explored in this chapter. Gardner defines existentialism as perverse rationality, because this school of philosophy refuses to look beyond the individual's own mental sphere in establishing its ethics (see Chapter 4). Grendel is the existentialist villain in the novel, joining ranks with Thaletes in *The Wreckage of Agathon* and Millie Hodge in *The Sunlight Dialogues*. According to Koprophoros, existentialism is part of Jason's crime also (296), which establishes the two mythical figures as spiritually next of kin, as it were. As is the case with Jason, the dominating impulse in Grendel's response to man and his values is intellectual. Even as he is most inspired by, and on the verge of believing in, the Shaper's vision, the voice of reason intervenes: "I knew what I knew, the mindless, mechanical bruteness of things, and when the harper's lure drew my mind away to hopeful dreams, the dark of what was and always was reached out and snatched my feet" (54). He is caught in the trap of "merely rational thought." As the fourth priest explains, "Merely rational thought...leaves the mind incurably crippled in a closed and ossified system, it can only extrapolate from the past" (135). By contrast, the business of faith is to make projections about the future.

Faith would appear to be an appropriate word for that synthesis constituted by a balanced acceptance of order and disorder that Gardner's books seek to dramatize. It is thus a term which may or may not denote religious faith. Gardner's steadfast concern with the different aspects of the role of faith in human lives may explain why *Beowulf* served so excellently in releasing the creative energy which produced one of Gardner's best works. Having both taught and written extensively on the Anglo-Saxon poem, Gardner knew it intimately and could draw on the ideational tensions of the source when reshaping the traditional myth to fit the context of the twentieth-century cultural scene. Gardner has provided the documentation we need for a study of the potential thematic interrelationship between the source and the text of *Grendel* in his long article on *Beowulf* ("Fulgentius's *Expositio*"). In this article he shows how the poem develops an involved heroic ethical code in which valor, wisdom, and generosity, or charity, are virtues that bring reward. The code is involved because the poet shows that at times the reward is not forthcoming. For instance, God, or the cosmic ruler, as Hrothgar would have called him, allows virtuous Hrothgar to suffer Grendel's ravaging for twelve years. But this does not affect the viability of the code. "It is the nature of the world that man must experience both the good and bad [cf. the contraries of existence]; but *ferhðes foreðanc* [the spirit's fore-thought]...can be trusted."[10] In the end, Gardner points out, Beowulf comes to help Hrothgar because he has "waited out his time of troubles and kept his faith that God would send payment" (253). However, there is one obstacle that even the most virtuous pre-Revelation man cannot overcome: mutability. On one level, therefore, Beowulf is a tragic figure; the powers he is fighting against will in the end conquer him. In this perspective, Beowulf is "a celebration of the best possible human being living by the best possible human—perhaps divinely inspired—code" (262). For Gard-ner, then, *Beowulf* is a poem about the validity of a heroic ethic, faith, and mutability. In its boldest form the poem's ethical code can be reduced to a very short phrase: faith pays.

Hrothgar's faith and heroic code hardly seem applicable today, at least not in their most direct form, but they were adequate to the needs of an eighth-century audience, and the poem testifies to the universality of the need to look for some source of spiritual guid-ance outside the individual. Most importantly, *Beowulf* warns its readers against the dangers of, among other things, perverted wis-dom, that is, the temptation to rely overly on man's power to rea-son, a temptation which easily can lead to misanthropic self-suffi-ciency (cf. Hrothgar's speech on pride, *Beowulf* ll. 1700–94). "Art," Gardner has said, "rediscovers, generation by generation, what is necessary to humanness" (*OMF* 6). To Gardner, faith, in his special sense of the word, *is* necessary to humanness, at it was to Hrothgar, Beowulf, and the Beowulf-poet. The epigraph reminds the reader that Grendel's despair is not unique; Blake, too, suffered the trau-mas of dejection. The integration of *The Marriage of Heaven and Hell* into the artistic web of *Grendel* underlines the fact, however, that there is also a way *out* of despair.

4

The very title of *The Sunlight Dialogues* prepares the reader for yet another Gardner novel in the dialectical mode. The com-batants are Clumly, Batavia's Chief of Police, believer in order human and divine, and Taggert Hodge, alias the Sunlight Man, a social and metaphysical rebel defending absolute freedom on the cosmic as well as the cultural level. This unusual novel of cop chasing robber involves some rather heavy philosophical sparring—the title refers to four dialogues staged by the Sunlight Man for the benefit of Clumly's education—at the end of which both protagonists are moved to modify their initial, rather rigid, social and metaphysical positions.

At the outset Clumly is portrayed as a staunch defender of a strict law-and-order stance. The images he employs to describe his role in society suggest the high seriousness with which he views his office. The police, he says, are "the Watchdogs of Society." He compares his job to that of a king, and his officers are his knights (378). Maintaining law and order is more than a matter of professional interest to Clumly: social order is for him closely linked to order on a metaphysical scale, as witnessed by a midnovel emendation of one of his convictions. In the context of his "watchdog" speech to officer Kozlovski, he says, "A man can't run a police force if he doesn't trust his men" (22). As things start to get tangled and he begins to sense that "his knights all fail him" (378), Clumly expands on the earlier notion: "*I'll tell you something. A man can't run a universe if he doesn't trust his men*" (370). Presumably it is this need for a continual reconfirmation of evidence of order on a grander scale that makes him a regular follower at Batavia's many funerals. They fill him, he says, with a sense of pleasure: "At last, whatever tensions, uncertainties, joys and sorrows warred in the heart, law and order were restored, and there was peace" (380).

In an interview Gardner has remarked that Clumly "once read Dante on a ship, though he no longer remembers it. It sank deep into the swamp of his mind and now throws strange light on his modern-seeming problems." The author further points out that the narrator "has obviously read and pondered hard on Malory's [*Le Morte Darthur*] which presents a medieval worldview totally opposed to Dante's" (Ferguson et al. 62).

This background information lends support to Judy Smith Murr's observation, cited earlier, that in addition to the war that Clumly and the Sunlight Man conduct against each other, they are both of them fighting internal battles as well, a fact which adds to the dialectical intensity of the book. Dante, as David Cowart points out, "is present in Clumly's conviction that the ideal of order has some absolute validity and perhaps in his unconscious tendency to classify men as lost, redeemable, or saved according to their ability and willingness to abide by the law." Clumly comes closest to remembering his Dante, Cowart says, "when he dreams of pursuing the Sunlight Man into the Sea of Metaphysics with a crew of 'unbelievers, heretics, usurers, perverts, suicides'" (*Arches & Light* 61).

The message of *Le Morte Darthur* is exactly the opposite, pointing to a *lack* of order as witnessed by the social upheavals that it describes. Clumly senses that there is something rotten going on in the state of New York, not to say the Western hemisphere, what with a rising crime rate, race riots, and the Vietnam War. Deep down he himself harbors anarchic dreams of freedom, which he fears, however, because of their potential for further adding to the general confusion.

> [H]e thought...how it had felt to be totally free, standing looking down at the prow of a ship dimly lighted at night, with the ocean stretching away on all sides ambiguous as an oracle.... Though he'd firmly put it behind him, he had not in all his years forgotten that vision, that temptation. One's struggle with the devil never ends. (13)

Malory's influence on the conception of the narrative is to be found most obtrusively in the many references to a medieval social order. There is Clumly's projection of himself as a king surrounded by his knights. We also learn that when the Chief of Police courted his wife, she used to read to him from a book about Sir Lancelot, "some story of adventure and romance so touching and foreign to them both that it made them blush and stop the reading for a while from embarrassment and fear" (13). The police station is a "high brownstone and concrete imitation castle set back among dying elms and maple trees" (148); here and there in Batavia one finds houses built in the style of the ancestral home of the Hodge family, "solid, unspeakably dignified with its great blunt planes of chalky orange brick, its Victorian porches, its cupola: the most beautiful architecture in the world, symbolic of virtues no longer to be found" (43–44).

The Maloryan echoes serve several purposes in the novel. For one thing, they lend a touch of Camelot to the Police Chief's law-and-order efforts, revealing an inability on Clumly's part to bend and adjust old-fashioned value judgments to new times. A good medieval knight was inherently loyal to the established codes of chivalry; Clumly likewise blindly accepts for a long time the rightness of law books: "My job is Law and Order.... I'm aware...there are differences of opinion about some of the laws we're paid to enforce, but a cop hasn't got opinions" (23).

More important still, Malory's influence on the narrator is catalytic, as is the setting, in releasing a highly important part of the book's thematic energy. The setting, Gardner explains, was chosen very carefully:

If you're going to talk about the decline of Western civilization or at least the possibility of that decline, you take an old place that's sort of worn out and run-down. For instance, Batavia, New York, where the Holland Land Office was...the beginning of a civilization...selling the land in this country. It was, in the beginning, a wonderful, beautiful place with the smartest indians in America around. Now it's this old, run-down town which has been urban-renewalized just about out of existence. The factories have stopped and the people are poor and sometimes crabby; the elm trees are all dead, and so are the oaks and maples. So it's a good symbol. If you're writing the kind of book I was writing in *Sunlight Dialogues* or *The Resurrection* both of them books about death, both spiritual death and the death of civilization, you choose a place like that. (Ferguson et al. 54)

Le Morte Darthur matches the mood of this setting perfectly. In this "carefully constructed myth of the rise and fall of a powerful kingdom," Gardner explains, Malory explores "the forces which bring kingdoms into being and the forces, internal and external, which destroy them.... Malory's grim vision has relevance for any kingdom or civilization: the very forces which make civilization necessary must in the end, if Malory is right, bring it to ruin." Gardner points out that Malory was fascinated "with deadly paradox—events which simultaneously support and undermine the kingdom" (*Le Morte Darthur: Notes* 5). Clumly's apotheosis of the Police Officer as Watchdog of Society is the most important instance of such a paradox in *The Sunlight Dialogues*. Democratic law has been a central concern for political thinkers in the West since the time of Greek antiquity; Clumly's experiences with the Sunlight Man reveal that a traditional and narrow concept of law and order is inadequate in dealing with the forces of cultural and cosmic entropy.

At the beginning of this chapter Chaucer's method of counterpoise was cited as a possible model for Gardner's dialectical narrative strategy. The use of ironic counterpoise in, for instance, the *Canterbury Tales*, Gardner points out, makes the tales rather unmedieval in that it allows for a "profluence" which is "dialecti-cal"; the ensuing synthesis did not always confirm the tenets of medieval orthodoxy. Gardner finds a similar openmindedness in *Le Morte Darthur:* "Malory untangles traditional plots and cuts traditional details in such a way that what remains forces the read-er into an uneasy—and finally unmedieval—ambivalence" (*The Poetry of Chaucer* 222). Gardner calls *Le Morte Darthur* "the first major work of prose fiction in English," and to him it "remains today one of the greatest" (*Notes* 5). By using Malory as a reso-nance box, as it were, for *The Sunlight Dialogues,* Gardner lends a special kind of authority to his own dialectical method. Through the use of an echoic method he draws the reader's attention to a larger dialectical pattern, the dialectics of the literary tradition. Malory also provides an aesthetic justification for the comprehen-sive scope of Gardner's novel. *The Sunlight Dialogues* comes very close to matching Malory's Arthurian romance in terms of intrica-cy and subtlety of plot and character. Malory needed a complex form to reflect the composite nature of English society toward the end of the medieval period; similarly, Gardner needed a broad can-vas to paint a picture which would do justice to the no less com-plex social fabric of contemporary Western society.

The Sunlight Man as a fictional character fits nicely into the context of medieval romance, a magician of hardly less formidable powers than Malory's Merlin. He is the "sum total of all Clumly had been fighting all his life" (226), a vehicle of disorder, social and metaphysical. In Gardner's description he is a man capable of imagining "all the possibilities of the world...but he finds no order, no coherence in it" (Bellamy 188). Taggert Hodge is another Gardnerian character hungering for a life in the angelic mode. He was given a taste of that life when he grew up at Stony Hill under the protective wings of his father, Congressman Hodge. The Con-gressman had been able to provide Tag with that wholeness of vision that he had since lost and lamented so bitterly. While his father was alive, the "Good became, in his presence, an aquastor, an ethereal form made as visible and tangible as an angel standing on a stone. It was impossible to say afterwards, 'There are no angels.' At worst one must say...*Dear God, where are the angels?*" (241) After the death of the Congressman, the Hodge children experienced a "kind of power failure, a sickly decline into vision" (576), a vision which was fractured and lacked focus. Tag Hodge, David Cowart observes, tries to compensate for his sense of loss by fastening on that "quintessential American ideal," an intense celebration of individual freedom which can only be described as anarchic: he assumes the identity of the Sunlight Man (*Arches & Light* 70). Events prove that the Sunlight Man's true identity is confusion, but the theories that he hides his confusion behind provoke Clumly into greater insight. The Sunlight Man's ideas also provide a *cultural* context for the order/disorder dichotomy, a context which is lacking in *Jason and Medeia* and *Grendel*.

In the four dialogues, the Sunlight Man addresses differences between ancient Hebrew culture, from which the West derives many of its key ideas concerning justice and the regulation of social order, and Babylonian culture.[11] With a basis in different conceptions of the true reality of the world, these cultures came to develop antithetical religions, as well as social codes along lines which are familiar to us from *Jason and Medeia*. The Babylonians, the Sunlight Man claims, "asserted a fundamental co-existence, without conflict, of body and spirit, both of which were of ultimate worth. And as for the connection between body and spirit, they ignored it. It was by its very essence mysterious" (318). The Hebrews, however, affirmed superiority of the spiritual over the physical, and they believed that man's relation with the spirit world could be codified. The Babylonians thus came to treasure man's intuition and his powers of divination as means of living harmoniously with an inscrutable universe; the Hebrew culture, on the other hand, came to rely on man's reason as an instrument in figuring out civil and religious law. Jason would by this account be a "Hebrew," and so is Clumly, who at one point is characterized as "*heavy-minded, ponderously reasonable*" (283). Medeia and the Sunlight Man are "Babylonians."

In terms of human consequences the Babylonian worldview is strangely similar to the predominant view in *Jason and Medeia*; character upon character in that book complains that the ways of the gods are unknowable to man, the gods thus serving as emblem for what a modern sensibility would call an absurd universe ruled strictly by chance. The Babylonians spoke in terms of personal destiny (*simtu*) and the greater destiny of the universe, of which man can know nothing (*istaru*). The Sunlight Man postulates the existence of a cosmic order, but since it can only be known to man after (or simultaneously with) the fact, it amounts to little more than a euphemism for Chance, that is, disorder. Whereas the Hebrews willingly surrendered their freedom to comply with divine will, the Sunlight Man, as a good Babylonian, commits himself to a principle of anarchic freedom so that, as he says, he can be ready to act with the gods once their intentions manifest themselves.

According to the Sunlight Man, the modern age, with its high valuation of science and distrust of intuition, has inherited the Hebrews's rational hubris. Clumly is a natural target for his anarchistic manipulations since the legal system, of which the Chief of Police is an extension, is based on a perception of the world with which he so strongly disagrees. Through parable he confronts Clumly with the possibility that maybe he has misread reality; maybe the underlying premises of the Western legal system, which in many and intricate ways delimit individual freedom, are wrong. Because its laws are tied to rule and logical system, Western civilization is based on a principle of "averaging." To a Judeo-Christian all "crimes are equal," the Sunlight Man tells Clumly, "because you define the crime, not the criminal" (327). No set of rules can adequately deal with the special circumstances of every individual case, he claims. Rather than covering "*all* the cases...blurring all human distinctions," the Sunlight Man commits himself to a program of viewing each case separately: "I love justice, you love law" (328).

The problem which confronts both cop and robber in this philosophical agon is sharply delineated by the Sunlight Man: "Beyond a certain point, intuition can no more deal with the world than intellect can" (321). Clumly recognizes the limitations of his own earlier strict and rational conception of the law when toward the end of the book he lets the Sunlight Man go; Tag Hodge's apotheosis of rule by intuition and individual freedom produces in him monstrous indifference toward other people, something which leads to disasters nearly as cataclysmic as those caused by Medeia.

In his last sermon the Sunlight Man tells Clumly a vision which, except for the social detail, might have been spoken by Malory and resembles strongly the one addressed to Jason by Paidoboron. The topic is the inherent decline of civilizations:

> The age that is coming will be the last age of man, the destruction of everything. I see coming an age of sexual catastrophe—a violent increase of bondage, increased violence and guilt, increased disgust and ennui. In society, shame and hatred and boredom. In the political sphere, total chaos. The capitalistic basis of the great values of Western culture will preclude solution of the world's problems. Vietnam is the beginning. No matter how long it takes, the end is upon us, not only in the East but in Africa too, and South America.

Civilizations fall because of the errors inherent in them, and our error will kill us.

Clumly wants to know what *is* the error, and the answer is the one Oidipus gave to the Sphinx: "It's man, Clumly! Man!" (631; cf. *JM*, 291).

When Gardner described *The Sunlight Dialogues* as a book about the decline of Western civilization, he added an important modifying clause: "or at least the possibility of that decline." Man *is* the problem. Relating the present context to the discussion of rational morality above, one is reminded, once again, of how closely related are Gardner's basic philosophical orientation, his view of man's potential and possibilities, and his own artistic practices. In his upstairs room, getting ready to meet the Sunlight Man one last time, Clumly thinks to himself, "Here, above where the trees intercepted the sunlight, there were certainties, including certainties of doubt" (606). Throughout Gardner's books we see dramatized again and again the idea that the only certainty a man possesses is the certainty of uncertainty. Is the universe ordered or not? In *On Moral Fiction* Gardner offers his own very curt verdict: "The truth is certainly that the universe is partly structured, partly unstructured, otherwise entropy would be total" (11). There is for man the hope of achieving at least some order, if not metaphysical, then social. If the problem is man, man is also the solution. By exercising his imagination, man has the potential for widening the pockets of order. Gardner exercises *his* imagination through his art (which is what his concept of moral fiction is all about); Clumly, who in the beginning of the book is Law and Order incarnate, does likewise by seriously engaging in debate with an advocate of disorder. The synthesis of the two positions, his moment of insight, comes in his speech to the Dairyman's League. Grieved by the death of the Sunlight Man and his victims, the Chief of Police addresses his audience on the nature of laws. His present stance is an amalgamation of his earlier position and modifications which are easily traceable to the Sunlight Man's lectures, including a warning against indifference and righteousness. Clumly can never match the Sunlight Man's oratory, and luckily the author does not attempt to pull any such trick on the reader. The speech is a hopelessly rambling mix of sentimentality and confused statistics. The important thing is clearly not so much *what* Clumly says as the fact that he makes the gesture. The speech signals his capacity for empathizing with the other and his willingness to accept responsibility for necessary change. The Chief of Police has taken a giant step from commitment to one kind of order, which was narrow and constricted, to another, which is open and inclusive, offering hope for the future. This movement is dramatized poetically when the author has the audience's applause carry Clumly a number of steps up Dante's orderly Platonic ladder. It was bearing him up, the narrator says, "like music or like a storm of pigeons, lifting him up like some powerful, terrible wave of sound and things in their motions hurtling him up to where the light was brighter than sun-filled clouds, disanimated and holy" (673).

5

Gardner begins his book on Chaucer's poetry with a long introduction in which he discusses the prevailing medieval attitudes concerning the role of spiritual and physical love in the lives of men. His purpose in dealing with this topic already in his introduction is to single out from the start one of the most persistent thematic concerns in Chaucer's poetry. The discussion focuses on whether or not physical love (and by extension care for things physical—in short, "the World") is acceptable as an end in itself. The orthodox view was that carnal love "is finally justified by its spiritual value" and that its only justification "is that it brings people closer to God" (*The Poetry of Chaucer* xx, xxi). This theological position, when adhered to very strictly, easily led to a distrust, indeed distaste, for everything physical, as in the case of the monkish ideal of *contemptus mundi*.

Throughout Gardner's works there are characters who are caught up in a dialectic of *body versus soul*. Before turning to the important question of why a twentieth-century writer shackles his characters with a medieval problem, a problem which in many ways was "solved" already in the Renaissance,[12] let us look at some of the manifestations of this dichotomy in Gardner's texts.

Feverishly preparing the magical tricks which he will be using in his séance with Clumly, the Sunlight Man recites a poem he claims to have written once. The poem is a long one, but needs to be quoted in toto here for the light that it sheds on Taggert Hodge's predicament, as well as that of a host of other Gardner characters.

Burning nights and days in his sullen grove,
Funereal as onyx, hind legs splayed,

Sick and omnivorous, the ruptured goat
Participates in the antics of the brain.

His monstrous groin cries out to mount the wind
As the mind cries out for subtleties worth thought
And the heart for a sacrifice as thick as time:
Hunger and surfeit gathered in one red heat.

His eyes are blank as stones. He has no name,
No physics for his rage. Collects his force,
Attacks and painfully couples; then, alone,
Broods once more on anger; finally dies.

I am unhinged by that fierce unholy image:
Fed up with gentleness, and sick with thought,
I will tear down my kingdom hedge by hedge,
Make war on the scree-gashed mountains, lord the night!

I turn to life! In every glittering maid
I'll plant my burning wrath till the last flame
That cracks my chest is spent away to head
And the parched ribcage cools to easy dying.

I'll learn to mock responsibilities,
These cold whereases capping the living well
That churns, beneath the ground, by fiercer laws.
I'll have no truck with words. Discretion. Guilt.

I'll put on joy, or something brother to joy;
Butt down the delicate gates I've helped to firm.
I'll turn blind eyes on tears, stone ears on sighs,
No more the pale good friend. A mindless storm.

For I have cause! I've proved what reason is—
Paid with contempt, indifference. Honored laws
I do not need; made peace with foolishness
That steals my hurtling-downhill time and laughs.

I too have blood to burn. I know the case
Of those I am of use to. A human voice
Making the time pass, keeping the night outdoors.
No more! Go hire pale virgins in my place!

Virgins. Who smile, who weep, who ask to be loved.
I am no raging goat (nor meant to be):
A kindly ass in glasses, lightly moved,
Sniffing back tears at the movies tenderly.

Or worse. A ruptured goat with a thinking head,
Aware that maidens fall betrayed not by
My pagan code but of their own dumb need
As I fall headwards, raging thoughtfully.

Where is the man, while body and head make war!
Holy Abstraction, catch us up as we fall!
Turn us to saints. Distract us out of earth
To love of things celestial and unreal!

Make me the singer of lovers' agonies,
No victim now, pale comforter to victims,
Some kindly grandmother with inward eyes
Forgiving harmless fools for slight destructions.

Make me the mindless brute in Plato's cell,
Walled from sense, bereft of the flesh's curse:
Teach me the trick of granite, burning yet still,
A seeming rest in a tumbling universe. (310–11).

This poem brings to mind Grendel, who begins his narrative
with a scornful description of a ram in heat:

Flanks atremble, eyes like stones, he stares at as much of the
world as he can see and feels it surging in him, filling his
chest as the melting snow fills dried-out creekbeds, tickling
his gross, lopsided balls and charging his brains with the
same unrest that made him suffer last year at this time, and
the year before, and the year before that. (He's forgotten them
all.) His hindparts shiver with the usual joyful, mindless ache
to mount whatever happens near—the storm piling up black
towers to the west, some rotting docile stump, some sprad-
dle-legged ewe.

"Why can't these creatures discover a little dignity?" Grendel complains (6). His basic problem is his unquenchable thirst for a life in
the angelic mode; the facts of reproduction are repulsive to him
because they are emblematic of life at its most physical, most
nonangelic level. But as Ellis and Ober point out, he is himself
caught up in a similar pattern: "The first grim stirrings of springtime
come.... I go up—as mechanical as anything else—fists clenched
against my lack of will, my belly growling, mindless as wind, for
blood" (8–9). In denying the beneficial effects of Wealtheow's beau-

ty, Grendel is thus making a quixotic gesture, striking out at the indignity of man's being tied to the physical. The terms in which he rejects the Queen betray his anger and show how strong his commitment to the angelic mode is: "I would begin by holding her over the fire and cooking the ugly hole between her legs.... I would squeeze out her feces between my fists. So much for meaning as quality of life!" (109–10). Grendel's own bloodlust is paralleled by what he takes to be men's lust for blood because it is in the spring that they go out ravaging and murdering. Ellis and Ober convincingly argue that "Grendel's rejection of, and horror at, the Queen's sexuality is thus part of his total rejection of the animal side of man—man's bloodlust, killing, gross lack of dignity" (59).

The Sunlight Man also longs for a life in the angelic mode, and in his poem he gives man's close kinship with "Brother Ass" as one of the reasons why such an existence is so hard to attain. The poetic persona—one assumes, a projection of Taggert Hodge, reviewing his earlier life—begins by conjuring up an image of "the ruptured goat." Like Prufrock, he is fed up "with gentleness, and sick with thought," and he vows to emulate the goat's much simpler existence of mindless reproduction. But his rebellion does not last very long. Again like Prufrock, he has to recognize that the anguished position he is in is not changed that easily: "I am no raging goat (nor meant to be)," or at least he is not only that, but "worse. A ruptured goat with a thinking head." Since the mind does not permit him to be like Prufrock's "pair of ragged claws," the only escape is into "Holy Abstraction" and a "love of things celestial and unreal!"

The speaker's desire for an existence like that of "the mindless brute in Plato's cell / Walled from sense, bereft of the flesh's curse," reflects ironically on Taggert Hodge's situation. Not long after the recitation of the poem, the Sunlight Man uses his own artistic elaboration on Plato's story of the cave to suggest to Clumly that his concept of law and order was based on a misjudgment of reality (327). In postulating the possibility of anarchic freedom, the Sunlight Man is himself a gross misjudger of reality. In a crucial scene with Millie, a scene which John Napper chose for one of the book illustrations, thereby highlighting its thematic importance, the Sunlight Man undresses her in an effort to humiliate her. Afterwards the scene haunts him: "The thought of Millie's naked breasts...filled him with an obscene and bestial hunger that mocked his grief and disgusted him. In the gas chambers, no doubt, they copulated" (306). For all his talk of freedom, the Sunlight Man, too, turns out to be shackled by the chains of carnality, no matter how hard he tries to work for a "distraction out of earth" in order to achieve love of some abstract ideal of cosmic indifference.

The predicament of Grendel and the Sunlight Man is a well-known problem for a number of other Gardner characters. Puritanical James Page is shaken to the very foundation of his being when he is reminded of his carnality in a meeting with Estelle Park:

> But the thing that had mainly gotten into James Page was Estelle's smile. Old fool that he was—so he put it to himself—for an instant James had felt powerfully attracted to her, emotion rising in his chest as sharp and disturbing as it would in any schoolboy. Even now he was upset and surprised by it. Metaphysically upset, in point of fact, though the word was not one James Page would have used. They were old and ugly, both of them, and the body's harboring of such emotions so long past their time was a cruel affront, a kind of mockery from heaven. (217)

Henry Soames is at one point troubled by dreams of abusing Callie sexually (37), and George Loomis is likewise angered by thoughts of the temptations of the flesh. Lying restless in his bed at night, he thinks of two girls he had recently met:

> They were pretty, poised between child and woman, so pretty his heartbeat had quickened a little, and he'd imagined how they would look in those pictures you could buy in Japan, coarse rope cutting their wrists and breasts and thighs. The instant he thought it, his stomach went sour. They were young, pure: beautiful with innocence, yet corruptible. The one who smiled invited it. She was hungry for it. *Serpentis dente.* (256)

Wilkins in "The King's Indian," we remember, tries to combat the lure of the flesh by gorging himself on it, raping Miranda; when that "remedy" fails to satisfy him, he tries to become one with the universe by committing suicide.

Jason, too, for a while gives free rein to his most basic physical desires. Even though his uncle Pelias is the nominal king of Iolkos, Jason, upon returning with the Golden Fleece, becomes de facto head of state. He uses his newly won power to carry out a political experiment, creating a kind of Philosopher's Kingdom

based on a reasoned implementation of ideals of equality and justice. His commitment to a just and reasonable government
notwithstanding, he finds it difficult to "famish the animal" in
himself; he decides to "let passions in, the divinity of flesh," and
begins to pursue his lust by sleeping with slave women on the side
(268). However, his flirtations with debauchery only serve to
incense Medeia, bringing about the fall of Pelias and hence the end
of Jason's rule at Iolkos. To Jason, Medeia is "agent of my worst
passions"; he sees in her lunatic plotting against Pelias an expression of the kind of madness that would result if he persisted in celebrating "the divinity of the flesh." Hence he vows to relinquish
the body's hold on his mind, advising the court of Corinth, "Let
man take his reasoning place, expecting nothing" (269). He wants
to start anew at Corinth, trying to create there the kind of just and
reasonable kingdom which the forces of passion had brought to a
close at Iolkos. But this means cutting off Medeia, an act which
produces a madness of eschatological consequence. Koprophoros,
who is always a reliable interpreter of the true import of Jason's
adventures, sums up the meaning of Jason's resolve this way:
"Lord Jason's theory...is that mind and body are by nature, and in
principle ought to be, totally divorced" (296).

Why, then, these frequent dramatizations of the pain, and
sometimes disasters, which accompany an inability to heal the
split between body and mind, a thematic concern which on the
face of things would seem to have greater bearing on the social and
intellectual climate of a medieval rather than a twentieth-century
writer? The answer to this question is to be found in the pervasive
metaphorical function of this particular motif.

Our best clue here is a statement by Gardner cited in the discussion of *Jason and Medeia* earlier in this chapter; the statement
concerned Gardner's semimystical belief that "all of us are really
one thing...one force, yet we're individuated. And there's this
hunger to get at that other part of one's own self—which one can
do by going inward, or by possessing another person totally"
(Cuomo and Ponsat 61). Gardner makes this statement in connection with observations on the basic difference which he perceives
between Henry Soames and George Loomis in *Nickel Mountain.*
Both Henry and George have accidentally killed a person and are
troubled by a heavy sense of guilt. Henry is able to work his way
out from under that guilt when he discovers George Loomis's mistake, that is, his inability to confess and share his guilt with the
community. George, we remember, is one of those persons suffer-

ing from the unresolved dialectic of body and mind. He makes his angry observation about the corruptibility of innocence only seconds after he has decided that it was too late to tell the community about his accidentally killing the Goat Lady, "no doubt too late from the beginning" (255). Gardner has accounted for the presence of the Goat Lady in *Nickel Mountain* by saying that he needed her "for certain symbolical purposes, a real animal person, the very special qualities of George Loomis's guilt in relationship to her, and so on" (Winther 518). By killing the Goat Lady, George obviously also symbolically kills, that is, denies or represses, the animal side of his nature; he thus makes himself less than a whole being and shuts himself out from the community. Henry, on the other hand, is able to forgive himself for being less than perfect, less than angel; once he makes the recognition, he finds the room filled with ghosts, which, according to Gardner, is meant to suggest that he is "not only back in communion with the community, but with all time and space" (Cuomo and Ponsat 62).

A more or less identical ghost scene is repeated in Gardner's last novel, *Mickelsson's Ghosts*, with, one assumes, much the same symbolical significance. In this book, too, sex and physical desire operate symbolically. Mickelsson's spiritual degeneration is given emblematic expression through graphic descriptions of his frequent visits to the local prostitute in the small Pennsylvania town where he has retreated to try to sort out his troubled existence. During these visits Mickelsson suffers from various kinds of physical distress (nausea, heart seizures, splitting headaches), which no doubt are intended as implicit commentary on the protagonist's attempt to run away from his obligations as a rational and moral being by nurturing the instinctual and animalistic aspects of his being only. Mickelsson works his way back to sanity and the community, and the beginning of his regeneration is marked by the author's description of a love scene which is almost iconic in its form, totally free of the anxiety which accompanied his visits to the prostitute. An important part of his cure is thus a redressing of the balance between mind and body, making him a whole human being. The room being filled up with ghosts, "not just people but also animals—minks, lynxes, foxes" (590), underscores the metaphorical dimension of the body versus mind motif, symbolizing the importance of unification of self for all of creation.

The synthesis toward which Mickelsson, Soames, and others are moving is a recognition of the fact that man is neither beast nor angel, but something in between. Koprophoros would seem to

speak with the full authority of the author when he takes Jason to
task for his one-sidedness:

> What I claim, with respect to Jason's idea...is that man is
> whole, his passions as priceless as his crafty mind, and mys-
> teriously connected, if not, indeed, identical—so that rejec-
> tion of the body is a giant step toward madness.... I celebrate
> the flesh unashamedly: I watch and guide it with mind as a
> doting mother does her child. I celebrate dancing and the cre-
> ation of images and uplifting fictions. (297)

Koprophoros's jubilant celebration of the flesh should then be read
with both a literal and metaphorical meaning in mind. From the
point of view of psychological well-being there is certainly every
reason why man should strive to maintain a proper balance
between the physical and mental aspects of his being. But the
dialectic of body versus mind in Gardner's books also serves an
emblematic purpose; those characters who manage to blend the
two into a proper synthesis achieve a wholeness of being which
moves well beyond a prosaic adjustment of one's physiological and
mental needs. Among other things, achieving such a synthesis also
means finding one's place in the community, keeping guilt down
to manageable proportions, and accepting man's inherent fallibility—in short, carving out a sensible and balanced existence, not in
the angelic but in the human mode.

Gardner's resolution of the body versus mind dichotomy is
strongly paradigmatic. His commitment to a dialectical approach
to artistic exploration repeatedly leads him to a denunciation of
any absolute position. Gardner's dialectical persuasion thus
accounts for the philosophical and psychological motivation
behind his protracted battle with certain aspects of contemporary
culture. One of the greatest cultural heroes of our epoch, Jean Paul
Sartre, is also Gardner's intellectual villain par excellence for
asserting "a universe of whim, confusion, and nausea" (*OMF* 25).
Such a view of the world, to Gardner, is perversely rational in its
one-sidedness. Like Grendel and the Sunlight Man and a number
of other Gardner characters, Sartre, in the eyes of our novelist, had
a "habit of viewing all events from in front of the firing squad"
(48). Gardner's artistic efforts represent an extended effort to bring
about the lowering of those Sartrian guns. His strategy is dialectical, and the synthesis he strives to achieve in his art is a "secular
wisdom"[13] which persistently seeks to take into account the

inherent duality of the human condition. Man *is* "man of mind" and must assume full responsibility for his role in history. But man is *also* man of heart and body; his rational faculties alone, Gardner continuously reminds us, do not suffice if he wishes to take full and wise measure of the adjustments and actions which are necessary to human survival and, ultimately, the continuance of civilizations.

NOTES

Introduction

1. For a full bibliography of Gardner's writings, see John M. Howell's *John Gardner: A Bibliographical Profile* and Robert Morace's *John Gardner: An Annotated Secondary Bibliography*.

2. Prior to this publication, Gardner had been the subject of three doctoral dissertations, but these were all multiple-author studies, allotting one or two chapters only to Gardner's fiction. Craig John Stromme, "Barth, Gardner, Coover, and Myth," Diss. State University of New York at Albany, 1978; Leonard Culver Butts, "Nature in the Selected Works of Four Contemporary American Novelists," Diss. University of Tennessee, Knoxville, 1979; and Stephanie Fish Price, "Expanding Horizons: Character in the Contemporary Novel," Diss. University of Utah, 1980.

3. Two more books have appeared (too late for consideration in my study) since Butts's work: Jeff Henderson, *John Gardner: A Study of the Short Fiction* (Twayne Publishers, 1990) and Dean McWilliams, *John Gardner* (G. K. Hall, 1990).

Chapter 1. Life Follows Fiction

1. I base this discussion on biographical information obtained from Howell's "Chronology" in *John Gardner: A Bibliographical Profile* (xv–xxi) and his essay "The Wound and the Albatross," as well as Stephen Singular's *New York Times Magazine* profile and interview with Gardner.

2. Subsequent references to Gardner's fiction, poetry, and often-cited critical works will be abbreviated.

3. In his essay "The Wound and the Albatross: John Gardner's Apprenticeship," John M. Howell discusses how the accident is put to artistic use in *The Resurrection* and *Nickel Mountain*, as well as in "Redemption" and "Stillness" in *Stillness and Shadows*. He convincingly argues that the accident helped make "Gardner's consciousness...a battleground for the classic duel between determinism and free will, and he would spend the rest of his life trying to reconcile these competing forces" (2).

4. In his discussion of Joseph Heller's *Something Happened*, Gardner reveals that he has rather flagrantly misread the text in question. Heller, says Gardner, reflects a prevalent feeling in the late sixties and early seventies: "Even for many noble, life-affirming people there seemed no way out but miracle, some such terrible miracle as happens in Heller's novel, releasing Bob Slocum from his own weakness and at least one of his painful psychological burdens, the existence of his loving, pitiful idiot son" (89). But it is Slocum's *normal* son who dies in the accident at the end of the book, and the misreading is a serious one because it misses one of the chief ironies in Heller's novel: throughout the book Slocum has been hoping for the death or removal in one way or another of Derek, his idiot son. But Derek lives on, while Slocum's normal child, the only person in the book toward whom he shows any real affection, dies when Slocum, in a clumsy attempt to comfort the boy after he has been run down by a car, inadvertently smothers him.

5. Gardner cites the same example in several interviews, and he thought well enough of it to use it in describing the young author Buddy Martin in the autobiographical short story called "Stillness" (printed in *The Art of Living*; not to be confused with the "Stillness" section of *Stillness and Shadows*).

6. Gardner has identified "Vlemk" as an attempt to work out in fictional form the key ideas of *On Moral Fiction*; see Winther 519–20.

7. See, for instance, his essay "Art, Will, and Necessity," in *The Last Decade* (140).

8. In *The Great Tradition: George Eliot, Henry James, Joseph Conrad*, Leavis argues that literature should provide visions of possibility, and that in the works of great artists "certain human possibilities are nobly celebrated" (2, 12).

9. *Buddy* is the name of the story's boy narrator, but also, no doubt significantly, Gardner's nickname as a boy; see Howell's *Bibliography* xv.

10. For Gardner's own approval of this reading of the Shaper's function in *Grendel*, see Winther 513–14.

11. In the posthumously published confessional essay "Learning from Disney and Dickens," Gardner speaks at length about the cartoonist element in his own writings; looking back on his fiction written during the last twenty years, he here seems mildly impatient with himself at his proclivity for coming up with "short-legged, overweight, twitching cartoon creations" (22).

12. This is not the place to develop the argument that these are indeed Gardner's "heroes." For now, let me just point out that the author has identified Peeker and the Clumlys as the heroes of their respective novels; see Christian 76 and Bellamy 188–89.

13. This form of moral fiction would seem to correspond rather closely to Northrop Frye's concept of fiction in the "ironic mode," the typical mode, he argued in 1957, of most serious fiction during the last hundred years (34–35).

14. The rulings of the First and Second Soviet Writers' Congress are cited in Fokkema and Kunne-Ibsch 97, 99.

Chapter 2. Rational Morality

1. In "Life Follows Fiction—Never Doubt It," Gardner cites *Process and Reality* in defense of the view that all life is connected (3); in *On Moral Fiction* he paraphrases a passage from the same book in support of the idea that great art is "emotionally metaphysical" (171).

2. In his brief speech Ork quotes no less than four passages from *Process and Reality*; the passages, only slightly modified, appear on pages 248, 522, 525, and 517 in Whitehead's book. I discuss the thematic significance of these quotations in my Chapter 6.

3. In this discussion of Collingwood's theory of consciousness I quote from the following pages of *The New Leviathan*: 48, 51, 74; but all of Part 1 is relevant to this discussion, especially Chapters 1, 7, 8, and 11–17.

4. In the following discussion I quote from these pages in Blanshard's book: 294, 315, 343, 397.

5. 148. The following summary is made on the basis of Chapters 21, 24, and 34–37. Specific references are made to pages 148, 139, and 62.

6. 308. This part of my discussion of Collingwood's ideas is based on Chapters 34–37 of *The New Leviathan*.

7. Winther 520. My summary of Gardner's comments on *Freddy's Book* is based on pages 520–24 of this interview.

Chapter 3. The Aesthetics of Exploration: Theoretical Considerations

1. *The Principles of Art* 111; Collingwood discusses "the technical theory of art" on pages 17–20, "art as magic" on pages 57–77, and "art as amusement" on pages 78–104.

2. Angus Fletcher, *Allegory: The Theory of a Symbolic Mode* (Ithaca, N.Y.: Cornell University Press, 1964).

Chapter 4. Tradition and the Artist's Moment

1. The concept of genre adopted here is one that is akin to Wellek and Warren's definition of the term in *Theory of Literature:* "Genre should be conceived, we think, as a grouping of literary works based, theoretically, upon both outer form (specific metre or structure) and also upon inner form (attitude, tone, purpose—more crudely, subject and audience). The ostensible basis may be one or the other (e.g. 'pastoral' and 'satire' for the inner form; dipodic verse and Pindaric ode for outer); but the critical problem will then be to find the *other* dimension, to complete the diagram" (231).

2. For an interesting discussion of the ending of *Mickelsson's Ghosts* as well as the occurrence of ghosts and other supernatural phenomena in the novel, see Henderson's article "The Avenues of Mundane Salvation."

3. I base this whole discussion of the yarn and the tale on pages 27–31 of *The Forms of Fiction.*

4. In the following discussion of *Grendel* I am much indebted to Carl Just, who in *Darstellung and Appell in der "Blechtrommel" von Günter Grass* conducts an analysis of Günter Grass's novel in terms that I here adopt for my comments on Gardner's book. Just bases his reading of Grass on the projection of the German petite bourgeoisie as an intended audience. Just claims that in order for the book to have the intended effect (what Just calls "die korrektive Wirkung," that is, reflection and reorientation on the part of petit bourgeois readers), Grass describes those characters in the novel that represent the petite bourgeoisie in such a way that the intended audience can identify and initially sympathize with them.

5. See my Chapter 6.

Chapter 5. Collage Technique I

1. Gardner uses the terms *collage technique* and *echoic method* in a letter to the editor, *Chicago Tribune* 13 Apr. 1980, sec. 7: 10.

2. Gardner has publicly identified Joyce as an early influence on his writing (Winther 512).

3. Terence Hawkes points out that in *On the Theory of Prose* (Moscow, 1925 and 1929) Sklovskij calls for "the suppression of naturalistic 'motivation' in the novel (because it reinforces habitual perception in the reader) and a consequent emphasis on literary self-consciousness and self-reference (which 'defamiliarizes' our perception): in short, to a demand for an art form pre-eminently aware of and sensitive to its own communicative conventions" (66). Defamiliarization to Sklovskij, there-

fore, was a metafictional device in the sense that it serves to draw attention to the text's status as artifice; the book of books for Sklovskij was *Tristram Shandy*, a novel much applauded by metafictionists.

4. "A Writer's View," especially 20–26; all unidentified references in the following are to these pages of Gardner's article.

5. I base the following summary of Gardner's understanding of nominalism on these pages of *The Life and Times of Chaucer:* 82, 145–56, 215, and 292–93.

6. *The Didascalion of Hugh St. Victor,* as cited by Gardner in *The Poetry of Chaucer* xxxii.

7. See *The Poetry of Chaucer* xviii and *The Life and Times of Chaucer* 293.

Chapter 6. Collage Technique II: A Case Study

1. In shaping the *Jolly Independent* episode in "The King's Indian" Gardner reproduces parts of "Pym" ad verbum, or with only minor changes of style; see *The King's Indian* 224–27 and "Narrative of A. Gordon Pym" 5–12.

2. See *The King's Indian* 237–38 and "Pym" 229–30.

3. See *The King's Indian* Chapter 23 and "Pym" Chapter 4.

4. See *The King's Indian* Chapter 29 and "Pym" Chapter 25.

5. See *The King's Indian* 212 and *Moby-Dick* 107.

6. See *The King's Indian* 237 and *Moby-Dick* 159.

7. Cf. *Paradise Lost,* Book II, l. 267.

8. Cf. "The Rime of the Ancient Mariner," IV, ll. 284–85: "A spring of love gushed from my heart / And I blessed them unaware."

9. In addition to *Moby-Dick* and "Narrative of A. Gordon Pym," Tanner uses *The Scarlet Letter* as an example.

10. Edward H. Davidson provides a very comprehensive study of the influence of English Romanticism on Poe; I base my discussion of Coleridge and Poe on his book, especially Chapters 2, 7, and 9. Those passages I quote appear on pages 61 and 67.

11. Cited by Kaplan 153.

12. This is Roppen's apt phrase; see page 142 of his article.

13. See Abrams 170 and Davidson 266, n. 16.

14. *The Letters of Edgar Allan Poe* 1: 257; I am indebted to my colleague Chester P. Sadowy for putting me on the track of this particular allusion.

15. Cf. "Eureka" 217, 218.

16. In his *Dismisura* article ("A Writer's View") Gardner aligns Poe (and Melville) with the new fictionists, saying that the so-called "new fiction has opened a door that has been closed too long. In America, no real masters have stepped through it since Poe and Melville" (28).

17. Cited by Kaplan 163; further references to Kaplan's article are to pages 156, 157.

18. The Daniel-Belshazzar story is one that the Gawain-poet retells in "Purity"; see Gardner's edition of *The Complete Works of the Gawain-Poet* 181–200.

19. *The Complete Works of the Gawain-Poet* 59, 134; Gardner's *Jerusalem* is also in a sense "moated."

20. Gardner, *Sir Gawain and the Green Knight: Notes* 58; see also *The Poetry of Chaucer* 8.

21. This is Georg Roppen's felicitous phrase; see page 138 of his article on *Moby-Dick.*

22. The Gawain-poet says, "And Jonah gave up his great pride, and he cried out to God" (*The Complete Works of the Gawain-Poet* 212).

23. Cf. *The Complete Works of the Gawain-Poet* 67–70.

Chapter 7. Dialectics

1. For a spirited defense of the epic poem as an active genre also in the twentieth century, see Henderson, "John Gardner's *Jason and Medeia:* The Resurrection of a Genre" (77–78).

2. In his preface to *Jason and Medeia* Gardner claims to "freely translate" these classical texts. It appears that he has received more than a little help from E. V. Rieu's 1959 translation of *Argonautica*, since long sections of the Jason and Medeia story, as translated by Rieu, reappear with sometimes only very minor changes in Gardner's epic. Similarly, Gardner appears to be particularly indebted to R. C. Trevelyan's 1939 translation of *Medeia*, even though there are more cases of phraseological divergence here than in his use of the former text. In my text I have adopted Gardner's spelling of Greek names and titles.

3. A dialectics of order and disorder (with its many thematic ramifications) is certainly not the only structural principle at work in *Jason and*

Medeia. In two articles Jeff Henderson has shown how psychic and physical moblity in time gives shape to the structure of this epic ("The Avenues of Mundane Salvation" [618–24] and "John Gardner's *Jason and Medeia*").

4. In Euripides' *Medea* Jason appears on the scene only *after* messengers and the chorus have informed the audience about the impending wedding of Jason and Kreon's daughter.

5. Appolonios Rhodios tells the Jason story in a straight-forward linear manner, beginning with the building of the *Argo* and ending with Jason and Medeia's return to Akhaia after the successful securing of the Golden Fleece.

6. I am indebted to Elzbieta Foeller's article in making this distinction between "contradictions" and "contraries"; cf. Foeller 197. I will have more to say about the question of contraries when discussing dialectical patterns in *Grendel.*

7. This imagery is first introduced during Grendel's "interview" with the dragon (61) and is reintroduced in thematically significant places: after Grendel has rejected Ork and his religion (137), during Beowulf's verbal exchange with Unferth (164), and two times during Grendel's fight with Beowulf (169 and 173).

8. In an excerpt from *Grendel* published in *Esquire* prior to the publication of the novel (October 1971, 139, 180–86, 189–90, 194, 196), Beowulf *is* named (196).

9. For a close study of how Gardner has worked astrology into *Grendel,* see Stromme, "The Twelve Chapters of *Grendel.*"

10. "Fulgentius's *Expositio*" 253; cf. *Beowulf* 109, l. 1060.

11. I base the following presentation of the Sunlight Man's indebtedness to a Babylonian worldview on two sources: Greg Morris's article in the Morace and Van Spanckeren collection (where Morris accounts in great detail for Gardner's dependence on Leo Oppenheimer's book *Ancient Mesopotamia: Portrait of a Dead Civilization*) and David Cowart's chapter on *The Sunlight Dialogues* in *Arches & Light.*

12. As Gardner points out, Shakespeare, for instance, "settled" the question in *Antony and Cleopatra:* "[I]n the Platonic ascent, it is this world's beauty which defines the beauty of the next, not the other way around" (*The Poetry of Chaucer* xxiv).

13. I have borrowed this felicitous phrase from Nathan A. Scott, Jr.'s characterization of Lionel Trilling's intellectual program; see Scott 170.

WORKS CITED

Primary Sources

Fiction and Poetry

The Resurrection. 1966. New York: Ballantine Books, 1974.

The Wreckage of Agathon. New York: Harper and Row, 1970.

Grendel. New York: Knopf, 1971.

The Sunlight Dialogues. New York: Knopf, 1972.

Jason and Medeia. New York: Knopf, 1973.

Nickel Mountain: A Pastoral Novel. New York: Knopf, 1973.

The King's Indian: Stories and Tales. New York: Knopf, 1974.

October Light. New York: Knopf, 1976.

Poems. Northridge, Calif.: Lord John Press, 1978.

Freddy's Book. New York: Knopf, 1980.

The Art of Living and Other Stories. New York: Knopf, 1981.

Mickelsson's Ghosts. New York: Knopf, 1982.

Stillness and Shadows. Ed. Nicholas Delbanco. New York: Knopf, 1986.

Children's Books

Gudgekin the Thistle Girl and Other Tales. 1976. New York: Bantam, 1978.

In the Suicide Mountains. New York: Knopf, 1977.

The King of the Hummingbirds and Other Tales. 1977. New York: Bantam, 1979.

Opera Libretto

Frankenstein. Dallas, Tex.: New London Press, 1979.

Criticism, Scholarly Works, Essays, and Articles

The Forms of Fiction. New York: Random House, 1962. The other editor of this book is Lennis Dunlap.

The Complete Works of the Gawain-Poet in a Modern English Version with a Critical Introduction. Chicago: University of Chicago Press, 1965.

Le Morte Darthur: Notes. Lincoln, Neb.: Cliff's Notes, 1967.

Sir Gawain and the Green Knight: Notes. Lincoln, Neb.: Cliff's Notes, 1967.

"Fulgentius's *Expositio Vergiliana Continentia* and the Plan of *Beowulf*: Another Approach to the Poem's Style and Structure." *Papers on Language and Literature* 6 (Summer 1970): 227–62.

"Life Follows Fiction—Never Doubt It." *Currents* (University of Rochester, N.Y.) 9 Nov. 1973: 1+.

The Construction of Christian Poetry in Old English. Carbondale: Southern Illinois University Press, 1975.

The Poetry of Chaucer. Carbondale: Southern Illinois University Press, 1977.

The Life and Times of Chaucer. 1977. New York: Vintage Books, 1978.

On Moral Fiction. New York: Basic Books, 1978.

"A Writer's View of Contemporary American Fiction." *Dismisura* (Alatri, It.) 39–50 (1980): 11–31.

Letter. *Chicago Tribune* 13 Apr. 1980, sec. 7: 10.

"Learning from Disney and Dickens." *New York Times Book Review*, 30 Jan. 1983: 3+.

(For a complete bibliography of Gardner's writings the reader is referred to the bibliographical studies by Howell and Morace listed below.)

Secondary Sources

Abrams, M. H. *The Mirror and the Lamp: Romantic Theory and the Critical Tradition*. 1953. London: Oxford University Press, 1974.

Appolonius of Rhodes. *The Voyage of Argo: The Argonautica.* Trans. and introd. E. V. Rieu. Harmondsworth: Penguin Books, 1959.

Bellamy, Joe David. *The New Fiction: Interviews with Innovative American Writers.* Urbana: University of Illinois Press, 1974.

Beowulf: A Dual Language Edition. Trans. Howell D. Chickering, Jr. New York: Anchor Books, 1977.

Blake, William. *The Marriage of Heaven and Hell.* Ed. Sir Geoffrey Keynes, with an Introduction and Commentary. London: Oxford University Press, 1975.

Blanshard, Brand. *Reason and Goodness.* London: George Allen and Unwin, 1961.

Booth, Wayne C. *The Rhetoric of Fiction.* Chicago: University of Chicago Press, 1961.

———. *The Company We Keep: An Ethics of Fiction.* Berkeley: University of California Press, 1988.

Boulger, James D., ed. *Twentieth Century Interpretations of "The Rime of the Ancient Mariner."* Englewood Cliffs, N.J.: Prentice-Hall, 1969.

Butts, Leonard Culver. "Nature in the Selected Works of Four Contemporary American Novelists." Diss. University of Tennessee, Knoxville, 1979.

———. *The Novels of John Gardner: Making Life Art as a Moral Process.* Baton Rouge: Louisiana State University Press, 1988.

Chatman, Seymour. *Story and Discourse: Narrative Structure in Fiction and Film.* Ithaca, N.Y.: Cornell University Press, 1978.

Christian, Ed. "An Interview with John Gardner." *Prairie Schooner* 54 (Winter 1980/81): 70–93.

Coale, Samuel. "'Into the Farther Darkness': The Manichaean Pastoralism of John Gardner." Morace and VanSpanckeren 15–27.

Coleridge, Samuel T. *Biographia Literaria.* Ed. J. Shawcross. Oxford: Oxford University Press, 1907. Vol. 1.

———. "The Rime of the Ancient Mariner." *The Complete Poetical Works of Samuel Taylor Coleridge.* Ed. Ernest Hartley Coleridge. Oxford: The Clarendon Press, 1912. Vol. 1: 186–209.

Collingwood, R. G. *The New Leviathan, or Man, Society, Civilization and Barbarism.* Oxford: The Clarendon Press, 1942.

——. *The Principles of Art*. London: Oxford University Press, 1938.

Cowart, David. *Arches & Light: The Fiction of John Gardner*. Carbondale and Edwardsville: Southern Illinois University Press, 1983.

——. "*Et in Arcadia Ego*: Gardner's Early Pastoral Novels." Morace and VanSpanckeren 1–14.

Croce, Benedetto. *Esthetic as Science of Expression and General Linguistic*. Trans. Douglas Ainslie. London: Vision Press: Peter Owen, 1953.

Culler, Jonathan. *Structuralist Poetics*. London: Routledge and Kegan Paul, 1975.

Cuomo, Joseph, and Marie Ponsat. "An Interview with John Gardner." *A Shout in the Streets* 1,2 (1977): 45–63.

Darwin, Charles. *The Descent of Man and Selection in Relation to Sex*. 2 vols. New York: D. Appleton, 1871.

Davidson, Edward H. *Poe: A Critical Study*. Cambridge, Mass.: The Belknap Press of Harvard University Press, 1964.

DeLuca, Geraldine, and Roni Natov. "Modern Moralities for Children: John Gardner's Children's Books." Morace and VanSpanckeren 89–96.

Edwards, Don, and Carol Polsgrove. "A Conversation with John Gardner." *Atlantic* 239 (May 1977): 43–47.

Eliot, T. S. "The Three Voices of Poetry." *On Poetry and Poets*. By T. S. Eliot. London: Faber, 1957. 89–102.

Ellis, Helen B., and Warren U. Ober. "*Grendel* and Blake: The Contraries of Existence." Morace and VanSpanckeren 46–61.

Euripides. *Medea*. Trans. and introd. R. C. Trevelyan. Cambridge University Press, 1939.

Feidelson, Charles, Jr. *Symbolism and American Literature*. Chicago: University of Chicago Press, 1953.

Ferguson, Paul F., et al. "John Gardner: The Art of Fiction 73." *Paris Review* 21 (Spring 1979): 37–74.

Fletcher, Angus. *Allegory: The Theory of a Symbolic Mode*. Ithaca, N.Y.: Cornell University Press, 1964.

Foeller, Elzbieta. "The Mythical Heroes of John Barth and John Gardner." *Kwartalnik Neofilologiczny* 27,2 (1980): 183–97.

Fokkema, D. W., and Elrud Kunne-Ibsch. *Theories of Literature in the Twentieth Century: Structuralism, Marxism, Aesthetics of Reception, Semiotics*. 1978. London: C. Hurst, 1979.

Frye, Northrop. *Anatomy of Criticism: Four Essays.* 1957. Princeton, N.J.: Princeton University Press, 1971.

Geist, Stanley. *The Tragic Vision and the Heroic Ideal.* N.p.: n.p.: 1939.

Greiner, Donald J. "Sailing Through *The King's Indian* with John Gardner and His Friends." Morace and VanSpanckeren 76–88.

Halliburton, David. *Edgar Allan Poe: A Phenomenological View.* Princeton, N.J.: Princeton University Press, 1973.

Harvey, Marshall L. "Where Philosophy and Fiction Meet: An Interview with John Gardner." *Chicago Review* 29 (Spring 1978): 73–87.

Hawkes, Terence. *Structuralism and Semiotics.* London: Methuen, 1977.

Henderson, Jeff. "The Avenues of Mundane Salvation: Time and Change in the Fiction of John Gardner." *American Literature* 55 (December 1983): 611–33.

———. "John Gardner's *Jason and Medeia*: The Resurrection of a Genre." *PLL* 22 (Winter 1986): 76–95.

———, ed. *Thor's Hammer: Essays on John Gardner.* Conway: University of Central Arkansas Press, 1985.

Hirsch, E. D., Jr. *Innocence and Experience: An Introduction to Blake.* New Haven, Conn.: Yale University Press, 1964.

Hoffman, Daniel. *Poe Poe Poe Poe Poe Poe Poe.* New York: Doubleday, 1972.

Howell, John M. *John Gardner: A Bibliographical Profile.* Carbondale: Southern Illinois University Press, 1980.

———. "The Wound and the Albatross: John Gardner's Apprenticeship." Henderson, ed., *Thor's Hammer: Essays on John Gardner* 1–16.

Iser, Wolfgang. *The Implied Reader.* Baltimore: Johns Hopkins University Press, 1974.

Janssens, Uta. "The Artist's Vision: John Gardner." *Dutch Quarterly Review of Anglo-American Letters* 9, 4 (1979): 284–91.

Jauss, Hans Robert. *Literaturgeschichte als Provokation.* Frankfurt am Main: Suhrkamp Verlag, 1970.

Johnson, Samuel. "Preface to Shakespeare." *Literary Criticism: Pope to Croce.* Ed. Gay Wilson Allen. New York: American Book Company, 1941.

Just, Carl. *Darstellung und Appell in der "Blechtrommel" von Günter Grass.* Frankfurt am Main: Athenäum Verlag, 1972.

Kaplan, Sidney. "An Introduction to Pym." *Poe: A Collection of Critical Essays.* Ed. Robert Regan. Englewood Cliffs, N.J.: Prentice-Hall, 1967. 145–63.

Kazin, Alfred. "Moral John Gardner." *Esquire* 9 May 1978: 35–36.

Kristeva, Julia. *Séméiôtiké: Recherches pour une Semanalyse.* Paris: Editions du Seuil, 1969.

Leavis, F. R. *The Great Tradition: George Eliot, Henry James, Joseph Conrad.* London: Chatto and Windus, 1948.

Lodge, David, ed. *20th Century Literary Criticism: A Reader.* London: Longman, 1972.

Logan, William. "Gardner's Book: Myth with Lapses of Imagination." Rev. of *Freddy's Book. Chicago Tribune* 16 Mar. 1980, sec. 7: 1.

Melville, Herman. *Moby-Dick.* Evanston and Chicago: Northwestern University Press and the Newberry Library, 1988. Vol. 6 of *The Writings of Herman Melville.*

———. "To Nathaniel Hawthorne." 16 Apr. 1851. Letter 83 in *The Letters of Herman Melville.* Eds. Merrel R. Davis and William H. Gilman. New Haven: Yale University Press, 1960. 123–25.

Mendez-Egle, Beatrice, ed. *John Gardner: True Art, Moral Art.* Living Author Series No. 5. Edinburg, Texas, 1983.

Milton, John. *Paradise Lost.* Ed. Alastair Fowler. London: Longman, 1971.

Morace, Robert A. *John Gardner: An Annotated Secondary Bibliography.* New York: Garland, 1984.

———, and Kathryn VanSpanckeren, eds. *John Gardner: Critical Perspectives.* Carbondale: Southern Illinois University Press, 1982.

Morris, Greg. "A Babylonian in Batavia: Mesopotamian Literature and Lore in *The Sunlight Dialogues.*" Morace and VanSpanckeren 28–45.

———. *A World of Order and Light: The Fiction of John Gardner.* Athens: University of Georgia Press, 1984.

Murr, Judy Smith. "John Gardner's Order and Disorder: *Grendel* and *The Sunlight Dialogues.*" *Critique: Studies in Modern Fiction* 18 (1977): 97–108.

Natov, Roni, and Geraldine DeLuca. "An Interview with John Gardner." *The Lion and the Unicorn* 2 (1978): 114–36.

O'Donnel, Charles. "From Earth to Ether: Poe's Flight into Space." *Twentieth Century Interpretations of Poe's Tales: A Collection of Critical*

Essays. Ed. William L. Howarth. Englewood Cliffs, N.J.: Prentice-Hall, 1971. 39–46.

Poe, Edgar Allan. *The Complete Works of Edgar Allan Poe.* Ed. James A. Harrison. New York: Thomas Y. Crowell, 1902. 17 vols.

———. "Eureka." *The Complete Works of Edgar Allan Poe.* Vol. 16. 179–315.

———. *The Letters of Edgar Allan Poe.* Ed. John Ward Ostrom. Cambridge, Mass.: Harvard University Press, 1948. Vol. 1.

———. "Ligeia." *The Complete Works of Edgar Allan Poe.* Vol. 2. 248–68.

———. "Narrative of A. Gordon Pym." *The Complete Works of Edgar Allan Poe.* Vol. 1. 5–245.

———. "The Philosophy of Composition." *The Complete Works of Edgar Allan Poe.* Vol. 14. 193–208.

———. "The Poetic Principle." *The Complete Works of Edgar Allan Poe.* Vol. 14. 266–92.

Price, Stephanie Fish. "Expanding Horizons: Character in the Contemporary Novel." Diss. University of Utah, 1980.

Rad, Gerhard von. *The Message of the Prophets.* Trans. D. G. M. Stalker. 1967. New York: Harper and Row, 1972.

Roppen, Georg. "Melville's Sea: Shoreless, Indefinite as God." *Americana Norvegica.* Ed. Brita Seyersted. Vol 4. Oslo: Universitetsforlaget, 1973. 137–81.

Ruud, Jay. "Gardner's Grendel and *Beowulf*: Humanizing the Monster." *Thoth* 14 (Spring/Fall 1974): 3–17.

Sartre, Jean Paul. *Being and Nothingness.* Trans. and introd. Hazel E. Brown. New York: Philosophical Library, 1956.

Scott, Nathan A., Jr. *Three American Novelists: Mailer, Bellow, Trilling.* Notre Dame, Ind.: University of Notre Dame Press, 1973.

Sedgwick, William Ellery. *Herman Melville: The Tragedy of Mind.* Cambridge, Mass.: Harvard University Press, 1944.

Shorris, Earl. "In Defense of the Children of Cain." *Harper's* 247 (August 1973): 90–92.

Sidney, Sir Philip. *The Defense of Poesie. Literary Criticism: Plato to Dryden.* Ed. Alan H. Gilbert. New York: American Book Company, 1940. 406–61.

Singular, Stephen. "The Sound and Fury over Fiction." *New York Times Magazine* 8 July 1979, Sec. 6: 13+.

Skagestad, Peter. *Making Sense of History: The Philosophies of Popper and Collingwood.* Oslo: Universitetsforlaget, 1975.

Stolnitz, Jerome. "Beauty." *The Encyclopedia of Philosophy.* Ed. Paul Edwards. New York: MacMillan and The Free Press, 1972. Vol. 1. 263–66.

Stromme, Craig John. "Barth, Gardner, Coover, and Myth." Diss. State University of New York at Albany, 1978.

———. "The Twelve Chapters of *Grendel.*" *Critique: Studies in Modern Fiction* 20, 1 (1978): 83–92.

Tanner, Tony. *City of Words: American Fiction 1950–1970.* New York: Harper and Row, 1971.

Towers, Robert. "So Big." Rev. of *Mickelsson's Ghosts. New York Review of Books* 24 June 1982: 17–18.

Trilling, Lionel. "Art, Will, and Necessity." In Lionel Trilling, *The Last Decade: Essays and Reviews, 1965–1975.* 129–47.

———. *The Last Decade: Essays and Reviews, 1965–1975.* Ed. Diana Trilling. New York: Harcourt Brace Jovanovich, 1979.

———. "Mind in the Modern World." *The Last Decade: Essays and Reviews, 1965–1975.* 100–128.

———. "What Is Criticism?" *The Last Decade: Essays and Reviews 1965–1975.* 57–99.

Trimbur, John. "Survival and Redemptive Vision in *Jason and Medeia.*" Morace and VanSpanckeren 68–75.

VanSpanckeren, Kathryn. "Magical Prisons: Embedded Structures in the Work of John Gardner." Morace and VanSpanckeren 114–29.

Waugh, Auberon. "Getting to Grips with Unreality." Rev. of *Grendel. The Spectator* 229 (1 July 1972): 14.

Wellek, René, and Austin Warren. *Theory of Literature.* 3rd ed. 1962. New York: Harvest-Harcourt, 1977.

Whitehead, Alfred North. *Process and Reality: An Essay in Cosmology.* New York: MacMillan, 1929.

Wilson, Edmund. *Axel's Castle.* New York: Charles Scribner's Sons, 1936.

Winther, Per. "An Interview with John Gardner." *English Studies* 62 (December 1981): 509–24.

INDEX